£10.95

NEW LESBIAN CRITICISM

NEW LESBIAN CRITICISM
Literary and Cultural Readings

Edited and Introduced by
/Sally/Munt/

HARVESTER
WHEATSHEAF

New York   London   Toronto   Sydney   Tokyo   Singapore

First published 1992 by
Harvester Wheatsheaf,
Campus 400, Maylands Avenue,
Hemel Hempstead,
Hertfordshire, HP2 7EZ
A division of
Simon & Schuster International Group

Typeset in 10/12 pt Janson by
Keyboard Services, Luton.

Printed and bound in Great Britain by
BPCC Wheatons Ltd, Exeter

British Library Cataloguing in Publication Data

New lesbian criticism: literary and cultural
readings.
  I. Munt, Sally
  820.9
  ISBN 0–7450–1166–7
  ISBN 0–7450–1167–5 pbk

---

1 2 3 4 5   96 95 94 93 92

Dedicated to the memory of
Helena Thomson
(1958–90)

CONTENTS

ACKNOWLEDGEMENTS

Sexuality and the Swiss Children's Novel used by permission. Copyright ©
1991 Martha Baer of the V-girls.

Excerpts from *Lesbian Texts and Contexts: Radical revisions*, edited by Karla
Jay and Joanne Glasgow, reprinted by permission. Copyright © 1990
Karla Jay and Joanne Glasgow.

Katie King, 'Audre Lorde's lacquered layerings: The lesbian bar as a site
of literary production', *Cultural Studies*, **2**, 3, Routledge: October 1988,
pp. 321–42, reprinted by permission.

INTRODUCTION

/Sally/Munt/

The specific anxiety inhibiting the production of this introduction became clearer to me after a week's procrastination during which I wrote a list of everything I felt I needed to read first – two hundred entries long. I'm a bit anally fixated, I'll admit, but Lesbian Theory is also rife with its own insecurities: its practitioners are acting under a compulsion to tell the truth, to record, to evangelise, and to be politically correct. Its balancing act of celebration and self-criticism, of construction and deconstruction, requires of its practitioners, always already working under censure, a dexterity exhausting in its exactitude. Academic isolation is common, and the cost of this is that the written word becomes extremely – perhaps overly – important. Books have functioned as rites of passage, and signs of kinship for lesbians. Our literary tradition is a history of the linguistic traces of a common identity. So, after several more days of displacement activity, (picking cat hairs off the sofa one at a time, bleaching the laces in my trainers, ironing my underwear and flossing my teeth three times a day), I decided to take myself aside in a pertinently (and supra-clean) postmodernist fashion, in order to tell my unreconstructed self that the internalised tyranny of political correctness, combined with the compulsion to represent the entirety of Lesbian Criticism for all time and throughout all cultures, was a recipe for a universal ulcer. So sticking to my own thoughts on the state of Lesbian Criticism, I want to say a few things I've personally observed, which are, inevitably, biased towards my British perspective.

First, to think about the positioning of Lesbian Studies: if we were to draw one of those ubiquitous but rather handy Venn diagrams of two circles interlocking in the middle, and label one 'Women's Studies' and the other '(Lesbian and) Gay Studies' (already we are using metaphors of space, but I'll come back to that later), the dinky crossover segment in the middle is of course Lesbian Studies, marginalised by and defined in relation to both (see Figure 1). This may explain some of the defensiveness of lesbian theory – on the one hand seeing off the more dominant discourse of heterosexual feminism, and on the other hand Gay Studies, into which work on lesbianism is sometimes subsumed. (Note that Gay Studies and Women's Studies *don't* intersect, historically having shown an antipathy towards each other.) To complicate matters further I'm going to add a third circle, which intersects with both Women's Studies and (Lesbian and) Gay Studies, and I'll call this one Critical Theory (see Figure 2).

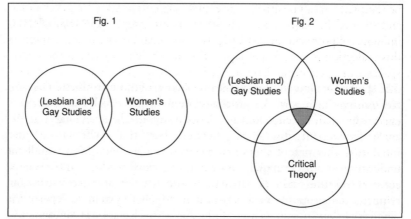

Now, Critical Theory intersects with Women's Studies in the area of Feminist Theory, and with (Lesbian and) Gay Studies in the area of Sexuality (which has tended to privilege studies on heterosexuality or male homosexuality, heavily influenced by Foucaldian theory, and using gay male models of sexual transgression). Nevertheless, this small triangle of Lesbian Studies tends to appear a bit beleaguered, framed on all sides by spheres of intellectual exploration more acceptable to the academy. This positioning may also explain some of the difficulties inherent in identifying its discrete intellectual trajectory.

I don't want to be romantic about this marginality as a space 'where the oppressed live apart from their oppressors as "pure".[1] The arguments, conflicts and recriminations between lesbian theorists refute any attempt by us to inhabit a sanitised, superior isolation. Lesbians have got to get their hands dirty – both those appointed to do the job of 'difference' and those disappointed that their difference gets them nowhere. We still need our jobs, and we need to be making theoretical and personal alliances for our own and, indeed, everybody else's intellectual health. The empirical conditions which have constrained the development of a coherent and nuanced field of study are familiar to all those lesbian lecturers marginal-ised within their departments in low-status, untenured or insecure posts. Even – and perhaps only – in the USA, where Lesbian Studies has a greater degree of intellectual credibility, in the minority of universities which have seized upon a new trend, the few 'names' have the burden of signify-ing thousands of others. Meanwhile lesbian-baiting and homophobia, insidiously internalised, leave levels of conceptualising untheorised and unspoken.

The interrelatedness of these academic subjects can be read as a trans-position of the individual lesbian subject writ large, a state I would also be tempted to read positively: discourses are entwined within each other, and defined in relation to each other, as are people. For example, the influence of poststructuralist and postmodernist theories upon chapters in this collection is strong, perhaps reflecting the way in which theoretical spaces can open up and be utilised by others. This volume's working title 'Dykonstruction' comprised a neologistic gesture towards Derrida, recognising the importance of deconstructing and reconstructing our own narratives of difference. Indeed, lesbians are particularly adept at de-construction, patiently reading between the lines, from the margins, inhabiting the text of dominant heterosexuality even as we undo it, undermine it, and construct our own destabilising readings. This type of cultural analysis, which poststructuralist theory has offered to the lesbian critic, is not proposed as a coherent new belief system to replace the wholistic humanist self, but rather locates her as a dissident, drawn into a process of critical interaction with the dominant. But 'dykonstruction', whilst signalling the volume's indebtedness to poststructuralism, did not convey its, or indeed Lesbian Criticism's, multi-discursive character. With both Women's Studies and (Lesbian and) Gay Studies, work in areas such as discourse theory, historiography, ethnography and literary criticism has been usefully appropriated by Lesbian Studies. When we relate this structure to the personal level we enter into debates concerning the limits of identity politics, and the emergence of models of space/location and voice which originally developed out of Black feminist critiques of the Women's Liberation Movement.[2] With a doubling movement in mind – to substantiate and individuate Lesbian Studies from within as a discrete discipline, and to strengthen links and develop mutual interests from without – I want to take two complementary passages from bell hooks's *Yearning: Race, gender and cultural politics* (1991), which characterise our need to be both intro- and extrovert:

> I have been working to change the way I speak and write to incorporate in the manner of telling a sense of place, of not just who I am in the present but

where I am coming from, the multiple voices within me. I have confronted
silence, inarticulateness. When I say, then, that these words emerge from
suffering, I refer to that personal struggle to name that location from which I
came to voice – that space of my theorizing. (p. 146)

Radical postmodernism calls attention to those shared sensibilities which
cross the boundaries of class, gender, race, etc., that could be fertile ground
for the construction of empathy – ties that would promote recognition of
common commitments, and serve as a basis for solidarity and coalition. (p. 27)

Because the internal struggle to speak emanates from the polyvocal expression of discursive *Is*, the 'space of my theorizing' is thus one of 'shared
sensibilities' – that is, a space which is not categorised by antagonistic
notions of difference, which seeks to split, divide and hierarchise one kind
of oppression over another. An 'I' which does not deny experience and
suffering but seeks to locate these in other people displays a profoundly
social context to theory, advocating alliance, not antipathy.

It seems to me that this sort of vigilance could avoid two of the dangerous tendencies which have afflicted feminism: first, as Katie King[3] has
observed, the desire to taxonomise the women's movement to make one's
own political position appear to be the telos of the whole; and secondly,
the separation between the academic, institutionalised theory of feminism
and its political praxis. Lesbian theory needs to endorse its own polyvocality, encourage dialectical exchange, and reject the defensive postur-
ing of truth-games. In addition, the intellectual excitement gained from
theorising the lesbian subject should not exclude the consciousness of her
material existence in a manifestly homophobic environment. The kind of
split between academic and grass-roots feminism evident in the 1980s is
partly a result of the way the establishment can assimilate in order to
de-radicalise. The way in which (Lesbian and) Gay Studies is being seen
in some North American and British universities as now occupying the
radical space which was once feminism, displacing feminism as something
more academically conventional, is disturbing (although in many respects
I find a similar move difficult to imagine with Lesbian Studies).

We are back to theorising spaces again, a topic which Bonnie Zimmerman treats cogently in her own chapter, 'Lesbians Like This and That'.
For lesbian academics these metaphors of space relate intrinsically to their
personal location, in particular their fetishistic role within departments
and schools. The pressures of being out and teaching lesbian material
include dealing with students and staff to whom you always seem to
be representing sexual difference in its entirety; who collapse personal
identity with theoretical integrity in a totalising motion which can only
work against you, whether you are patronised, idealised or stigmatised.

The problem of the personalising of lesbian discourse within the academy
('. . . is she or isn't she?') is that it leaves women vulnerable, caught
between being reified and colluding with their own invisibility. At the
Feminist Theory conference in Glasgow in July 1991, a performance of
the V-girls' 'Academia in the Alps: in search of the Swiss Mis(s)' cameoed
this dilemma of speaking the unsayable:

> *Sexuality and the Swiss Children's Novel*
> I intended to speak today about underlying sexual themes in various Euro-
> pean children's classics, but what I really want to talk about is my own
> sexuality. I don't know – I feel the time has come. I don't want to go on like
> this . . . passing . . . passing as straight. I'm tired of letting all those friendly
> students and colleagues of mine make their remarks, laugh at fags and
> conspire with me against myself because they think my high heels and my
> femme face make me one of them. I mean, how long should I leave out this
> fundamental fact of myself? Long enough, I guess, to demonstrate my value
> on committees and my excellent scholarship. Or maybe I won't leave it out.
> Maybe I'll include it – here – that I'm a lesbian – gently, openly, with that
> same femme hairstyle that misled you all those flirty times in the mailroom.
> I'll say it warmly, lovingly, as if I were saying it to her, offering it in trust,
> thinking of her even as I tell you, her quick eye, her intelligent hands, her
> heart so complex and enormous. I'll say it quietly but surely, because I'll
> know you'll take it in fully, seeing the quality of our partnership. You'll be
> hoping we continue to seek out our pleasure, pursue our shared lives. . . .
> Then, that said, we'll continue with the lecture or the meeting, turn to page
> 73, for example, the end of a chapter, the repressed contents of a dream.[4]

The performance identified the crucial conflict between personal and
political voices: the desire to speak about the personal, but also to with-
hold it.

The personal is the one discourse we now love to hate: Minnie Bruce
Pratt called it 'the narrow circle of the self';[5] Parveen Adams 'the absence
behind identity'.[6] The 'I' of experience is now intellectually discredited as
a voice, 'site-specific criticism', the 'claiming of a territory' counts as the
privatisation of experience, a shared enterprise we shouldn't profit from at
the expense of others. In part, this reaction rises out of the dogma of 1980s
feminism which insisted that all articulations attended to the 'correct'
perspective on race, class, gender, age, sexual orientation, physical ability
and geographical/cultural positioning, etc.; as Susan Bordo has asked,
with some frustration, 'just how many axes *can* one include and still
preserve analytical focus or argument?'[7] There is always someone more
different than you, and it seems to me that the anxiety about speaking
personally comes both from the sprinkling of liberal guilt which whispers
'privilege', and from the fear of the intellectual indiscretion of essentialism.

My own ambivalence about this is reflected in the book: initially, when commissioning pieces, I asked contributors to locate themselves in their own chapters. The primary motivation for this request was one of accessibility, the autobiographical discourse providing for many readers a point of identification which enables them to 'key-in' to the more elusive theory. A humanising strategy, which was to be inflected (I'd hoped) by the traces of a positive images approach, was the more latent agenda. Some complied, and some didn't (I learned a lot about editorial limitations in compiling this project): Reina Lewis picked it up explicitly in her own piece, drawing attention to the positioning of lesbian literary criticism at the intersection of literary criticism and identity politics; as she says, 'I am therefore invited to place myself in the very line of self-determining lesbian writing subjects that I seek to undercut.' When I came to write my own piece, somehow the notion that I was a white working-class dyke from Yorkshire just didn't fit. Itemising identities in order to authenticate knowledge is a practice I've always rather suspected – as Edward Said observed:

> . . . inside the circle stand the blameless, the just, the omnicompetent, those who know the truth about themselves as well as the others: outside the circle stand a miscellaneous bunch of querulous whining complainers.[8]

As one of my students (white, middle-class, heterosexual, able-bodied, young . . .), said to me recently, 'I'm a snob . . . it's about the only identity there is left for me.'

Prohibiting the personal voice, though, denies its historical importance in the production of politicised subjects – the early Women's Liberation Movement was effectively galvanised by the process of consciousness – raising the personal as political. A less essentialising version of experience would recognise its construction in ideological practices, allowing for the expression, perhaps, of essentialist moments as an expedient political trajectory. The protests in Britain over Section 28[9] in the late 1980s would be an example of this: many men and women identified as gay or lesbian for the first time, *self-consciously* moving out of one political location into another, recognising the contextual imperative. The current climate of homophobia also emphasises the need for a distinct entity of Lesbian Criticism as a legitimate discourse, independently resourced. On a personal level we also need to retain empathy for others' struggles. Instead of reifying ourselves into a hardened diamond, we need to remain rough-hewn and set in relation to others. This makes it sound sentimental, but in fact it is more difficult to support dialogic polyvocality than to promote monologic absolutism.

Two years ago, when I started this collection as a result of the frustration

I experienced teaching lesbian literature in Brighton, there wasn't a single critical volume I could recommend to students; tracking down articles and copious photocopying was tedious, and underlined our marginality. Even Jane Rule's *Lesbian Images* (1975) was out of print. Since then a few pioneering texts have appeared – the ones I know are Karla Jay and Joanne Glasgow's *Lesbian Texts and Contexts: Radical revisions* (1990); Bonnie Zimmerman's *The Safe Sea of Women: Lesbian fiction 1969–1989* (1990); Mark Lilly's *Lesbian and Gay Writing* (1990); and Elaine Hobby and Chris White's *What Lesbians Do In Books* (1991). It's not enough to construct a tradition, let alone a canon. The production of even these texts is a testimony to the social movements of the Thatcher/Reagan years, and their inscription within a consumerist aesthetic. A postmodern culture has seen the development of reading communities with purchasing power, which publishers have rightly perceived as potential micro-markets.

There are a number of cultural factors which have permitted a discourse of lesbian criticism to materialise into book form. It would be pre-emptive to predict its direction, given its dependence not just on the political and economic spheres but also on the larger trends in theory I gestured towards above. For example, French feminists influenced by poststructuralism working in the area of sexual difference have grasped the figure of the lesbian as a way of theorising *out* of gender binarism. One of the key protagonists is, of course, the materialist Monique Wittig, a writer who has travelled over from lesbian theory into mainstream critical thought. It's encouraging to visualise the traffic as two-way and, despite the pressures of individuation, conceptualising lesbian theory as innovative rather than purely reactive, tempers the excesses of the siege mentality. Whether or not Wittig's transcendental lesbian is read as an intentionally parodic construction or an essentialist slippage,[10] the debates about the identity of this *figurative* lesbian crystallise the terms of current attempts to theorise cultural origins. Diana Fuss has cogently summarised some parameters:

> The lack of consensus and the continued disputes amongst feminists over the definition of 'lesbian' pivot centrally around the question of essentialism. Exactly, who is a lesbian? Is there such a thing as a lesbian essence? Does 'woman' include 'lesbian'? Can we speak of a 'lesbian mind' as distinct from what Wittig calls 'the straight mind'? The definitions of lesbian in feminist discourse are various and inventive. As a counterweight to Rich's overly general 'lesbian continuum', Catharine Stimpson provides us with an admittedly 'conservative and severely literal' definition of lesbianism as 'a commitment to skin, blood, breast, and bone' (1982, 244). Audre Lorde offers a more metaphysical definition of lesbians as 'strongly women-identified women where love between women is open and possible, beyond physical in every

way' (Hammond 1980, 18). To Judy Grahn, 'the subject of lesbianism is very ordinary; it's the question of male domination that makes everybody angry' (1978, 55). Bonnie Zimmerman attempts to pull together the metaphysical with the severely literal by positing a lesbian essence which must nonetheless be consistently and continuously historicized: 'I do believe that there is a common structure – a lesbian "essence"', she confesses, but 'careful attention to history teaches us that differences are as significant as similarities' (1985, 215–216).[11]

Myself, in the main I agree with Fuss that ' "lesbian" is a historical construction of comparatively recent date, and that there is no eternal lesbian essence outside the frame of cultural change and historical determination'.[12] However, this strictly intellectual definition wouldn't stop me *feeling*, and sometimes behaving, as though the total opposite were true. We need our dream of a lesbian nation, even as we recognise its fictionality – rather as we need our Madonna myth: an image of lesbian sexuality which we have projected as authentic, as the 'real' Madonna. The pleasure derived from this reading, that of an apparently knowing reinscription, is of her belonging to us, and as readers/consumers our oppositional sexual desire is affirmed, ironically, by an apparently paradigmatic heterosexuality. It is a fantasy which effectively cements a common identity (but trivialises contradiction).

A more poetic construction of the lesbian is offered up by Nicole Brossard in *The Aerial Letter*, which Bonnie Zimmerman has chosen to preface and frame her own chapter. It tries to pluralise lesbian identity, in a way which has parallels with feminism(s)'s refractions during the 1980s, but still retains the desire to name that *something* which is distinctive:

> There are lesbians like this, lesbians like that, lesbians here, and there, but a lesbian is above all else the centre of a captivating *image* which any woman can claim for herself. The lesbian is a mental energy which gives breath and meaning to the most positive of images a woman can have of herself. Lesbians are the *poets* of the humanity of women and this humanity is the only one which can give to our collectivity a sense of what's real.

The unfixing of the construction lesbian from taxonomised bodies into the realm of the figurative releases the idea of a lesbian critical aesthetic. Perhaps this is how we can read Madonna as one of us.

Part of the conventional role of an editor is to write an introduction which, by a magical sleight of pen, transforms several disjointed essays into a seamless whole. I have to admit I usually skip the obligatory exegesis of contents myself, prefering to make up my own mind as to a collection's linkages and patterns (or cracks). So I don't want to manufacture a definitive master narrative of *New Lesbian Criticism* which would give you the impression of one comprehensive theory. The work being done in Lesbian Criticism is still in progress – an infant, evolving aesthetic which is strongly explorative. I will say, though, that this volume's engagement with contemporary critical theories and texts is one of its distinctive strengths.

Bonnie Zimmerman's piece discusses the directions taken by lesbian theorists of late, and the resultant potential and pitfalls possible for the 1990s, taking up the essentialist/social-constructionist debate and its implications. By asking whether the privileging of the lesbian subject then defers/demotes the categories of race or class to 'another other', as it were, Zimmerman sets up a dialectic which weaves through the volume. She concludes by asking how we can make our theories useful – this too identifies a common concern of lesbian theory: that it should be situated in a material practice. Reina Lewis's chapter identifies the way in which structuralist theories of the death of the author run into conflict with the desire to have positive images of lesbian writers. The tension between a more self-critical theory on the one hand, and the politics of scarcity on the other, is representative of the way dominant literary aesthetics cannot be laid smoothly over any receptive group and be used to speak for/of them. My own piece has a similar concern, although it is focused on postmodernism. I have tried to show how Sarah Schulman's successful appropriation of parody and play as a way of problematising identity is foregrounded in earlier works, which later novels find somehow insufficient to represent more imminently painful issues such as grief (*After Delores*) and the political imperative of AIDS (*People in Trouble*). I interpret this narrative development not as rejecting postmodernism but as soberly assessing its potential to represent the harder contingencies of lesbian life.

Katie King and Anna Wilson both focus their contributions on *Zami*. As Wilson points out, '*Zami* is on the verge of canonisation within white feminist academia as the token Black lesbian voice.' The fact that all five Black contributors commissioned to write articles for this collection did not deliver reflects the pressure on the few to represent the many. I see this omission as a weakness of the collection, but on the other hand I also want to resist the structure which I perceive as reverse racism – that is, when race becomes *the* signifier of difference. These authors do diverge in their ethnicity and class, but if Reina Lewis is right, authorial identities must come second to privileging textual difference, instead of dominance. Like Angela Weir and Elizabeth Wilson, Katie King takes the 1950s as a literary moment in the construction of lesbian identity, and sites her reading within a contemporary reinscription. She takes on Lorde's problematisation of 'the

D word' as an illustration of the fields of power operating within 'the very house of difference', locating this political concern with the publication of *Zami* in the early 1980s feminist movement. Lorde's use of the term biomythography, King argues, reminds us that we can't escape our textual histories, and the lacquered layerings of the past. Anna Wilson's chapter explicitly intersects work in two new areas of literary theory, lesbian with African-American criticism. Her synthesis indicates new directions for both, and questions the way in which the familial and generational metaphors of African-American literature inevitably exclude lesbian writers such as Lorde, legitimating only certain forms of textual relations, and concomitantly, how lesbian literary history is almost exclusively white. Wilson too traces textual historicity, connecting its theoretical limitations with political manifestations of identity.

This volume's presentation of a selection of literary readings identifies its particular interest in contemporary fiction and popular culture, drawing on and intersecting with the kind of work which cultural studies has pioneered in the last decade. Angela Weir and Eliabeth Wilson's piece on the evolution of lesbian popular culture during the 1950s depends on the reappropriation of 'libidinised trash' as proper objects of literary inquiry, recalling all the work feminists have done recently on reclaiming popular readings for women. But Weir and Wilson, along with Hilary Hinds, also gesture towards the insufficiency of the dualistic opposition low/high culture to locate these texts. Weir and Wilson use some of these novels to identify moments of liberation which contradict the conventional view of th 1950s as rigidly reactionary, charting the journey of suburban women to a radical urban bohemia. By identifying the prevalence of Freudian myths of sexuality during the period, they preface some of the work Gillian Spraggs explores in her own chapter; she interweaves this with a carefully wrought critique of traditional Christianity, two discourses which, in Western culture, have circumscribed possible utterances of female sexuality throughout the twentieth century. Jane Rule's *Desert of the Heart* is in the expressive realist tradition, which Spraggs takes as a vehicle to explore Rule's moralism manifested in the two discourses' central images: Hell, and the mirror.

Another of this volume's particular characteristics is its focus on the few canonical texts which are central to the fledgling lesbian literary tradition, taking each of these as representative and, indeed, constitutive of moments in lesbian history: *Zami*, *We Too Are Drifting*, *The Price of Salt*, Ann Bannon's *Beebo Brinker* series, *Desert of the Heart*, *The Wanderground*, *The Female Man*, *Oranges Are Not the Only Fruit*, and even – at least through notoriety – *Macho Sluts*. Sonya Andermahr links her analysis of *The Wanderground* and *The Female Man* specifically to the articulation of lesbian feminist separatism during the early 1980s, identifying two distinct models which she labels the 'political' and the 'utopian'; these models relate to two distinct trajectories – one she sees as opening up political change, and one closing it down. Hilary Hinds's essay explores the ambiguous cultural status of *Oranges Are Not the Only Fruit* by a close analysis of its reception as a quality drama, particularly in the mainstream press. This piece is a cogent analysis of how a text can 'cross over' into dominant culture; of the mechanisms that permit its positive reception as serious television, and the historical conditions which have defused and decentred its radical lesbian content. The Rushdie Affair redirected the audience's moral outrage towards religious fundamentalism, relocating race as the hated Other in the hierarchy of differences rather than the lesbianism, which was defused and desexualised as naive and romantic. Finally Lisa Henderson, perhaps, redresses the balance. She, like most others in this volume, develops a reader-response analysis of her text, this time of lesbian pornography. Her theoretical base is also poststructuralist, as articulated through the disciplines of cultural and communication studies. She draws attention to what she calls the 'salvation motive' of anti-pornography politics as reminiscent of the mass-culture critiques of the 1940s and 1950s. This ideology of protection actually polices lesbian desire, whereas the stories she has chosen from *On Our Backs* and *Macho Sluts*, she argues, contain a dialectic of transgression and demystification of desire. Henderson also outlines the problem of fantasy, however, in its thorny relation to the real, which is the cornerstone of the pornography/censorship debate. She argues that the two, like sex and capitalism, cannot be collapsed together in a totalising moment.

New Lesbian Criticism's intervention into literary critical debates is to explore the possibility of what might constitute a specifically lesbian critique of these methodologies. Partly, this is enabled by lesbian culture's ability to be so *writerly*: we are particularly adept at extracting our own meanings, at highlighting a text's latent content, at reading 'dialectically', at filling the gaps, at interpreting the narrative according to our introjected fictional fantasies, and at foregrounding the intertextuality of our identities. If we accept that language is unstable, then within its heterosexuality we must also be able to find its homosexual other. A lesbian reader's literary competence brings to the text a set of interpretative conventions for decoding and encoding which is rich in its own historical, cultural and linguistic specificity. This volume does not define what a lesbian critical aesthetic might be, but I'd like to hope that it is part of a growing project which asks the right kinds of questions.

I would like to thank Pam Turner and Betty Geeves for their secretarial support, and Jackie Jones and Lois McNay for their helpful comments.

Notes

1. bell hooks, 'Choosing the margin as a space of radical openness', pp. 145–53 in *Yearning: Race, gender and cultural politics*, London: Turnaround, 1991, p. 151.
2. For a cogent problematisation of the origins of these arguments, see Eva Mackey's (unpublished) paper 'Revisioning "home" work: Feminism and the politics of voice and location' for the MA in Social Anthropology, University of Sussex, spring 1991. She identifies three primary sources in the 'revised politics of location' debate as: Lata Mani, 'Multiple mediations: Feminist scholarship in the age of multinational reception', *Feminist Review*, **35**, 1990; Chandra Talpade Mohanty, 'Feminist encounters: Locating the politics of experience', *Copyright* **1**, 1, 1987; 'Under Western eyes: Feminist scholarship and colonial discourses', *Feminist Review*, **30**, 1988, pp. 61–8; On race and voice: 'Challenges for liberal education in the 1990s', *Cultural Critique*, **14**, 1990; and Gayatri Chakravorty Spivak, 'French feminism in international frame', *Yale French Studies*, **62**, 1981; Sarah Harasym, ed., *The Post-Colonial Critic*, London: Routledge, 1990.
3. Katie King, 'The situation of lesbianism as feminism's magical sign: Contests for meaning in the U.S. women's movement, 1968–72', *Communication*, **9**, 1, 1988, pp. 65–91.
4. Martha Baer of the V-girls, from their panel performance entitled 'Academia in the Alps: In search of the Swiss Mis(s)', performed at Glasgow Feminist Theory Conference, 13 July 1991.
5. Minnie Bruce Pratt, in Elly Bulkin, Minne Bruce Pratt, and Barbara Smith, *Yours in Struggle: Three feminist perspectives on anti-Semitism and racism*, New York: Long Haul Press, 1984, quoted in Susan Bordo, 'Feminism, postmodernism, and gender-scepticism', in Linda Nicholson, ed., *Feminism/Postmodernism*, London: Routledge, 1990, pp. 133–56 (p. 138).
6. Parveen Adams, in a paper given to the Feminist Theory Conference, 'The art of analysis – Mary Kelly's *Interim*', University of Glasgow, 13 July 1991.
7. Susan Bordo, 'Feminism, postmodernism, and gender-scepticism', p. 139.
8. Edward Said, 'Intellectual in the post-colonial world', *Salmagundi*, **70–71**, 1986, pp. 44–81 (50), quoted in Diana Fuss, *Essentially Speaking: Feminism, nature and difference*, London: Routledge, 1989, p. 115.
9. Section 28 of the Local Government Act, which came into force in Britain during 1988, forbade local authorites to promote homosexuality or 'pretended family relationships'. It had the effect of producing a great deal of institutional nervousness extending to many areas of British life in supporting lesbian or gay individuals or projects, which greatly extended the specific legal sphere of the Act. On the other hand, the political mobilisation of thousands of lesbians and gay men was a testimony to the resistance and spirit of a previously largely dormant subculture.
10. See for example, Namascar Shaktini 'A revolutionary signifier: The lesbian body', in Karla Jay and Joanne Glasgow, eds, *Lesbian Texts and Contexts: Radical revisions*, New York: New York University Press, 1990 London: Onlywomen Press, 1991, pp. 291–303; Diana Fuss, *Essentially Speaking*, pp. 39–53; Judith Butler, *Gender Trouble: Feminism and the subversion of identity*, London: Routledge, 1990, pp. 111–28.
11. Diana Fuss, *Essentially Speaking*, pp. 44–5.
12. *Ibid.*, pp. 44–5.

LESBIANS LIKE THIS AND THAT
Some Notes on Lesbian Criticism for the Nineties

/Bonnie/Zimmerman/

> There are lesbians like this, lesbians like that, lesbians here, and there, but a lesbian is above all else the centre of a captivating *image* which any woman can claim for herself. The lesbian is a mental energy which gives breath and meaning to the most positive of images a woman can have of herself. Lesbians are the *poets* of the humanity of women and this humanity is the only one which can give to our collectivity a sense of what's real. (Nicole Brossard, *The Aerial Letter*)

In 1981, I wrote an article called 'What has never been: An overview of lesbian feminist criticism', which has become an often-used introduction to the concerns of lesbian-focused critics in the 1970s and early 1980s. My purpose in this present essay is not to provide the same kind of exhaustive survey of published articles and books and unpublished papers presented at national conventions in the mid to late 1980s; such a project is no longer feasible – happily, one might say. Lesbian theory is much more evident throughout current literary criticism than it was in 1981. Instead, I intend to introduce a few considerations about the directions taken by lesbian theory over the past decade and the possibilities and, perhaps, pitfalls that lie ahead.

In 'What has never been', I surveyed and analysed the work of literary critics who consciously chose to read as lesbians. I suggested that these critics had developed a perspective on cultural creativity that grew out of the particularity of lesbian experience. Contested as definitions of that particularity might be – what lesbianism means and who can be claimed for it was, and continues to be, an arena for intense debate – this notion of lesbian *perspective* unified much lesbian criticism in the 1970s. The recurring tropes of lesbian theory (and not just literary criticism, as philosopher Marilyn Frye's essay 'To see and be seen' demonstrates) were taken from a Western tradition that privileges sight as a metaphor for knowledge: perspective, point of view, vision, re-vision, and – my essay's own gesture towards the tradition – overview. One might say that the basic 'insight' of lesbian critical theory was that the particularity of lesbian experience leads the writer to produce texts with a unique lesbian perspective on reality, and the reader/critic to see and therefore decipher encodings of lesbian experience in those texts. Lesbian critics attempted to establish a tradition of overt and coded lesbian texts that would extend the metaphors of vision further: to render lesbians visible in a society that has hitherto refused to notice us. These metaphors based on sight were joined by another set of sensory tropes – that of overcoming the long silencing of lesbian voices by recovering and hearing an authentic version of the lesbian story.[1]

'Classic' lesbian theory, then, proceeded from a set of assumptions: that one could (with difficulty, perhaps) define a category called lesbian, that lesbians shared certain experiences and concepts, and that discursive practices – literary texts, critical analyses, political theories – proceed from lived experience. Anyone moderately well versed in the critical debates of the 1980s can see (I find the use of this metaphor inescapable) that many of these terms have been called into question. Experience, authenticity, voice, writer, even lesbian itself – all have been scrutinised, qualified, and sometimes abandoned by theorists trained in deconstructive and poststructuralist modes of analysis. When I now reread my somewhat naive call, in 'What has never been', for more interaction between lesbian theorists and those of other critical schools, I am struck by how thoroughly lesbian critics have, enthusiastically or otherwise, entered into the current great debates.

The influence of poststructuralist theories is but one of the factors changing lesbian criticism. Social-constructionist theory has also questioned the validity of positing any kind of essentialist, universal or transhistorical identity, such as 'woman' or 'lesbian'. This has been accompanied – in the United States at least – by a decline in the hegemony of feminism over lesbian theory and a new interest in gay and lesbian theory as a category of analysis. In gay and lesbian studies, lesbians function as female homosexuals linked to male homosexuals on the basis of a socially constructed gay-and-lesbian position. This is obviously quite different from the 1970s notion of lesbianism as a variation – perhaps a privileged variation – of female experience or identity. The culminating and perhaps paradigmatic text of that era, for all the controversy over it, was Adrienne Rich's 'Compulsory heterosexuality and lesbian existence'.

As the 1980s progressed, however, the sharpest attack on the idea of a unified lesbian identity and theory came not from deconstruction or from gay-and-lesbian studies, but from lesbians of colour. The first faultline identified in lesbian feminist theory was that of racism, the unexamined assumption that all female or lesbian experience is the same, and that this experience can be reduced to that of white middle-class Western women or lesbians. This critique has caused white lesbian and feminist theorists, like myself, to follow the lead of women of colour and begin the hard and often unsettling reconceptualisation of the nature of identity and the subject. The paradigmatic text of the 1980s may well be Gloria Anzaldúa's *Borderlands/La Frontera*, with its celebrated figure of 'the new mestiza', the subject standing on the borders between multiple cultures and identities.[2] The paradigmatic text for the 1990s, of course, has yet to be written.

The primary strategies of the recent past, therefore, have involved the deconstruction of the lesbian as a unified, essentialist, ontological being and the reconstruction of the lesbian as metaphor and/or subject position. This shift in emphasis is reflected in the tropes we now use; they refer less to the act of seeing than to the place from which one sees. Metaphors of position and space now dominate in the way those of sight did a decade ago. Lesbian critics seem less interested in what we see than in the act of seeing itself; less concerned with the product (the text) than with the process (critical reading). Another way of putting this is that we are less focused on essential, 'deep' *knowledge* than on historically situated *knowing*. Despite this shift in emphasis, I have used the word 'reconstruct' above rather than 'construct' because, as I will be arguing, current theory manifests substantial continuities as well as discontinuities with theories put forth by writers in the 1970s such as Bertha Harris, Barbara Smith, Monique Wittig and Marilyn Frye, among others. Indeed, I would go so far as to say that current criticism stands at an intersection between lesbian separatism and deconstruction. This suggests tantalising possibilities, as well as obvious problems.

At this point, I would like to turn to specific examples of what lesbian critics are writing and publishing in the early 1990s. I will begin with the first anthology of lesbian criticism, *Lesbian Texts and Contexts: Radical revisions*, edited by Karla Jay and Joanne Glasgow, which contains twenty-two original essays by writers and critics, many of whom (including myself) have long been involved in the production of lesbian texts and theories. Reading through these essays, I noticed a cluster of words and images that appeared in widely differing contexts (all quotations from Jay and Glasgow):

In the gaps, the 'holes,' or the 'spaces,' by a willful (though erratic/erotic) trajectory, comes desire, excess. (Meese, p. 77)

. . . lesbian narrative space [is] a disruptive space of sameness as opposed to difference which has structured most Western narratives. (Farwell, p. 93)

. . . her sexuality is neither conventionally female nor conventionally male but rather identifies an erotic potential possible only outside the patriarchal, heterosexual territory of rigid definitions and polar oppositions. (Fetterley, pp. 158–9)

. . . [the ellipse] serves to figure woman-in-culture, where she denotes absence (of the phallic signifier), silence, and nonpresence. . . . I believe that this form of grammatical-rhetorical 'deviation' figures not merely the experimental or avant-garde, but the Sapphic. (Benstock, p. 192)

Monique Wittig . . . has struggled with this problem by rupturing with the phallocentric subject, and, as I hope to show, has produced a lesbian signifer . . . (Shaktini, p. 291

. . . lesbian love is a discourse that disrupts or radically interrogates all of the authorizing codes of our culture. (Parker, p. 319)

I began to see in these excerpts – admittedly quoted out of context – a singular figure taking shape. She is a disruptor of heterosexuality, a presence standing outside the conventions of patriarchy, a hole in the fabric of gender dualism. She cannot be contained within these institutions; she exposes their gaps and contradictions; she signifies a radical absence. Her desire functions as excess within the heterosexual economy. Hence she positions herself outside these institutions, or creates space within them. She also creates a narrative or textual space in which she interrogates accepted norms of textuality and sexuality, and constitutes herself as subject. Within that space she also creates a lesbian relationship between self and other. She is the metaphorical lesbian, the lesbian-as-sign.

This is heady and romantic stuff. There is a long tradition – stemming at least from the early-twentieth-century Natalie Barney/Renée Vivien circle – in which lesbians portray them/ourselves as radicals, outlaws, and transgressors against Man's law. In the early 1970s, when I came of age as a lesbian feminist, we drew upon the language and ambience of the counterculture and radical movements to argue that the lesbian was 'the rage of all women', a 'monster' within patriarchy, a 'threat' to male supremacist institutions.[3] The metaphorical lesbian of contemporary criticism may be but the latest version of this powerful myth. I find myself enamoured of this creature, or deconstructive strategy, but knowing that love can be 'blind' (old metaphors never die, especially when they are embedded in clichés), I would like to discuss some questions raised by this theoretical discourse, drawing upon the work of the critics themselves (those included in the Jay and Glasgow text and several others) as well as my own ideas.

Can any figure or textuality exist outside patriarchal discourse? Does this not flirt dangerously with 'essentialism'?

Because many of these theorists locate themselves within deconstructive and poststructuralist schools of thought, it is helpful to keep in mind how poststructuralists talk about culture and reality. Much of this theory draws upon the ideas of Lacan, specifically that signification – the realm of the symbolic, or of language – is organised under the sign of the phallus, which represents the Law of the Father. (In my old-fashioned way, I think of these concepts as a different way of representing what feminists have always called 'patriarchy'.) The Symbolic Order dominates 'all human culture and all life in society' (Moi, p. 100). Phallocentrism is coextensive with the world as we know it, or at least with discursive practices.

In what way, then, can the lesbian, lesbian desire, or lesbian textuality exist outside this system? The writer who has attacked this question most forcefully is Monique Wittig who, according to Namascar Shaktini, simply displaces the phallus by establishing the lesbian body as her 'central point of reference' (Jay and Glasgow, p. 291). The lesbian functions as the 'Archimedes point' from which to wield the fulcrum that unsettles hetero-sexuality. But does the lesbian, metaphorical or otherwise, exist 'outside' anything? Elizabeth Meese confronts this dilemma bluntly:

> I would like to think that lesbianism, like feminism, could position itself 'outside.' There's a comfort in the tidiness offered by the absence of complicity and the certainty of an absolute difference. But lesbianism, as an attack on hetero-relations, takes (its) place within the structure of the institution of heterosexuality. The lesbian is born of/in it. (Jay and Glasgow, p. 82)

Diana Fuss, in her investigation of essentialism in contemporary theory, also questions whether there can be 'such a thing as "free space," in a strictly anti-essentialist view', and criticises Wittig for suggesting that 'a lesbian is innocent and whole, outside history, outside ideology, and outside change' (Fuss, pp. 43–4). She agrees with Shaktini that Wittig exchanges one 'transcendental signifer' – the Lacanian phallus – for another – the lesbian body. Fuss, however, rejects the exchange.

There are some provocative ideas here worth pursuing. Meese, like lesbian feminists in the 1970s (particularly Charlotte Bunch, Marilyn Frye and Adrienne Rich), presents lesbianism as an attack on hetero-relations, or heterosexuality. To that extent it must exist in some kind of relation to the institution it purports to deconstruct. But existing in relation to an institution is not quite the same thing as existing in, as Meese claims. Couldn't we say that lesbianism exists both inside and outside heterosexuality, much as people of colour function both inside and outside the dominant white structure? I think of Sally Gearhart's utopian fantasy *The Wanderground*, in which the hill women establish a separate society outside the locus of patriarchal power, but also maintain a subversive presence inside. Might this not be a model for conceptualising the lesbian difference? To be sure, in order to disrupt heterosexuality (or patriarchy or gender dualism) one must engage with/in it. But one must also maintain a separateness, a difference, an 'outsideness', or simply be devoured by the dominant term, or culture. Meese suggests this dialectic when she quotes Claudie Lesselier's description of 'the tension inhabiting the lesbian subject as both included in and standing against the social discourse which produces it' (Jay and Glasgow, p. 76).

A second point we might consider is the double movement of much contemporary lesbian criticism and literature. Alice Parker describes the 'multifaceted project' of Quebecoise writer Nicole Brossard as both de-constructive – 'to evacuate the space occupied by Woman' (to which we might add the space occupied by Lesbian) – and reconstructive – 'the creation of a space for the woman/lesbian subject of writing to articulate her desire, to refigure/revalue her self-apprehension' (Jay and Glasgow, p. 304). The first moment is strictly anti-essentialist, but the second is utopian and surely requires taking 'the risk of essentialism' (a popular phrase these days), since it assumes – indeed, insists upon – the existence of a category called 'lesbian' or 'woman'.

Finally, we might ask what it means for a lesbian to claim the authority to set up a 'transcendental signifier' in competition with the phallus. Perhaps Wittig's strategy can be read as a defiance – indeed, a mockery – of masculine arrogance (much like the rhetorical strategies of Luce Irigaray). I like to think that she is creating a lesbian voice that audaciously asks: just *who* claims that reality is coextensive with patriarchy, or that signification requires the phallus? In this way, Wittig's 'lesbian body' actually undermines the solemnity of poststructuralist theorising by exposing it as a mere story, much like any other.

Why is 'lesbian' a privileged signifier?

One question I would raise about some contemporary criticism is its tendency to set up 'lesbian' as a special – or 'magical' – sign, perhaps to the elimination or displacement of other radical signifiers (King, 1986). It is not only recent critics who give lesbians pride of place in feminist theory, of course. This political or rhetorical strategy began with 'The woman-identified woman' manifesto, written in 1970, was raised to the level of theory by lesbian separatists such as The Furies collective, and has continued through the 1980s. My cohort of lesbian feminists had a strong tendency to position ourselves as the vanguard of the revolution, both political and cultural. French-flavoured theories merely provide the terms and conceptual framework for the latest manifestation of this phenomenon. The lesbian is posited as being in a unique position to deconstruct heterosexuality, patriarchy, gender – indeed, just about anything. However, many signifiers stand in opposition to dominant structures: 'feminist', for example, may be just as effective in deconstructing patriarchy; 'gay man', as Fuss points out, also stands in opposition to heterosexuality; and politically controversial terms such as 'bisexual' or 'sadomasochist' have been advanced as deconstructing other essentialisms within lesbian or gay theory itself.

But for me the most serious question raised by this strategy is the place of other figures on the margin, such as people of colour or the working class. Why not posit the woman of colour, such as Anzaldúa's new mestiza, as privileged signifier, if such a signifier is desirable at all? Indeed, Teresa de Lauretis suggests that we stop setting up a competition for position as privileged subject or sign, and instead think in terms of the 'eccentric subject', the subject who exists across boundaries and in a marginal or tangential relation to the white, Western, middle-class, male centre (de Lauretis, 1990, p. 145). The lesbian is one, but only one, embodiment of this ec-centric subject, with her own particularities, her own histories, her own textual strategies, and her own specific disruptive practices. One future direction for lesbian criticism, then, lies in investigating the specificity of the lesbian subject, or subjects.

Who is this lesbian? What is her subject position, her subjectivity?

For some critics, moreover, lesbian theory has been too quick to generalise a lesbian subject, too content in its postulation of a free-floating sign. Fuss, for example, criticises Wittig for her 'tendency to homogenize lesbians into a single harmonious group and to erase the real material and ideological differences between lesbians' (Fuss, p. 43). And Biddy Martin points out that narrators of lesbian autobiographies often fail to examine 'the systemic institutional relationships between those differences, relationships that exceed the boundaries of the lesbian community, the women's movement, or particular individuals, and in which apparently bounded communities and individuals are deeply implicated' (Martin, p. 78). In other words, by positing the lesbian as 'excess' in the patriarchal system, we may fail to note the identities that function as 'excess' within our own newly created lesbian community.

At this point, I will take the risk of acting as critic of my own work. In writing my recent study of lesbian fiction from 1969 to 1989, I found myself constantly falling into that trap of generalising a lesbian subject, even when I situated that lesbian subject in a specific historical context and even as I attempted to show the failures of such generalisation. Pulled between the desire to affirm a historical lesbian collective identity and to 'de-stabilise' (another popular term today) that identity by introducing the discourses of differences within, I did not entirely satisfy either goal. Hence I am personally interested in ways of theorising how lesbians in different historical and cultural contexts develop a sense of themselves as lesbians, or whatever terms and categories are present in each specific situation.

How do we create a historically specific lesbian subject?
Can we still claim a lesbian history, culture and tradition?

In my introduction, I noted that an initial project of lesbian critics had been to establish a lesbian history and tradition, much as feminist critics had done for 'the women's tradition'. In the anti-essentialist nineties, such tradition-building is a much more troublesome task. It is not simply a matter of uncovering and interpreting sources, contending with homophobia and heterosexual bias, or even debating over who can and cannot be called lesbian – the kinds of issues I raised in 'What has never been'. Now, I would need to defend the claim that any continuity, category or identity can even exist. Given a strict anti-essentialist or social-constructionist perspective, we cannot use 'lesbian' to refer to any identity or behaviour pre-dating the late nineteenth century, and may need to restrict our inquiries to Western capitalist societies. Hence, Sappho was a Lesbian but not a lesbian, 'romantic friendship' is a phenomenon quite unlike contemporary lesbianism, and twentieth-century lesbian 'heras' like Virginia Woolf cannot reliably be placed in that category (see, for example, Rosenman). In contrast, essentialist writers – most notably Judy Grahn in *Another Mother Tongue* and *The Highest Apple* – offer 'evidence' of a universal, underground gay and lesbian history that has been maintained uninterrupted through myth, folklore and custom.

I have overstated my case, to be sure, but I wish to illustrate what is at stake for lesbians in both essentialist and anti-essentialist theories. In fact, I would agree again with de Lauretis that these terms needlessly polarise and distort lesbian history and culture (de Lauretis, 1989). All notions of lesbian – whether essentialist or anti-essentialist, universal or socially constructed, 'lesbians like this' or 'lesbians like that' – are themselves products of particular historical discourses and serve specific political and theoretical purposes. For example, as I have learned in my years of teaching and lecturing, the notion of a lesbian existence that can be located (albeit in different forms) in all cultures and historical eras can be empowering, especially for women just coming out as lesbians. Since heterosexist societies render lesbians invisible and unspeakable, to show and name large numbers and varieties of women as 'lesbians' can be a political act. Not surprisingly, such notions – often labelled essentialist – were important to the pioneering generation of the 1970s, and may still be of considerable consciousness-raising value today. On the other hand, lesbians in the 1980s found anti-essentialist concepts, emphasising fragmentation, difference and mutability, useful in undermining the monolithic notion of the Lesbian Self (with all its rules and boundaries) that often resulted from that earlier theorising.

Consequently, I would suggest that we approach lesbian history and literary tradition as a shifting matrix of behaviours, choices, subjectivities, textualities and self-representations that is always situated in a specific historical context. The notion of 'history', 'tradition' or 'culture' rests not so much with the actors in the past as with the readers in the present. Lesbian readers, of literature or historical events, proceed by a double movement: to research how women in the past may have understood themselves in relation to and against heterosexuality, and to analyse the continuities and discontinuities between different historical manifestations of something that we in the twentieth century call 'lesbianism'.

Harriette Andreadis, for example, identifies the poetry of Katherine Philips as lesbian, in part because it is 'amenable to lesbian reading in the twentieth century' (Andreadis, p. 59). But further, Andreadis argues that Philips adapted conventional heterosexual love poetry to her own fervent feelings for women, and thus 'her manipulations of the conventions of male poetic discourse constitute a form of lesbian writing' (Andreadis, p. 60). Rather than being silenced by 'male' language, Philips was empowered as a 'lesbian' poet. Andreadis further suggests a way of looking at a lesbian literary tradition that takes fully into account female–female eroticism, homophobia, heterosexual bias and literary conventions.

Many essays in *Lesbian Texts and Contexts* (as well as in scholarly journals) continue to work on the historical figures that sparked lesbian imagination in the 1970s: Cather, Dickinson, Woolf, H. D., Barnes and Hall among them. Many of these critics themselves employ the 'metaphor-seeking imagination' that Gillian Whitlock identifies as a key to understanding Radclyffe Hall as a lesbian writer (Whitlock, p. 569). This is yet another suggestion that we need not accept a cleavage between essentialism and anti-essentialism, or between lesbian as sign and lesbian as historically constituted subject. The lesbian, or any of her earlier avatars, may always have been constructed in metaphorical terms. Perhaps that is one of the particular contributions of lesbians: to disrupt what we accept as reality and suggest new connections between signs. To quote Nicole Brossard once more: 'A lesbian who does not reinvent the word/world is a lesbian in the process of disappearing' (Brossard, pp. 134/136).

What goes on in the narrative space that we name
'lesbian'? Who does the lesbian meet? The heterosexual
couple? The patriarch? The other woman? Who is this
'other woman'?

Lesbian and feminist movements have often emphasised the notions of space and separation: whether the autonomy of the women's liberation movement, the radical politics of lesbian separatism, or the practical desire for women-only spaces to hold meetings and events. The function of separate space within feminist and lesbian theory and daily life demands further attention, especially at a time when, in the United States, the desire for separate space for women is being questioned both ideologically and concretely. But what interests me here is the equivalent notion in criticism that lesbian textual practices create (or lesbian readers perceive) a *narrative* space in which writer and reader, or writer and assumed audience, or female characters, come together in a relationship defined as lesbian. Several critics assert that this action undercuts the difference between self and other, subject and object, upon which Western thought is based. As Marilyn Farwell explains: 'Confusing the boundaries between subject/object and lover/beloved undercuts the heterosexuality which is based on this dualism. The point in the narrative where this deconstruction begins is what I would call lesbian narrative space' (Jay and

Glasgow, p. 98). In another essay on lesbian as metaphor, Farwell suggests that this deconstruction leads to 'a network of relationships among author, reader, text, and even literary foremothers' (Farwell, p. 112). Several essays in *Lesbian Texts and Contexts* pursue this strategy. Judith Fetterley suggests that a 'woman's voice making love to a feminine landscape' is the key to understanding Willa Cather's art and her place as a lesbian writer (Jay and Glasgow, p. 161). Jane Marcus suggests that the 'rhetorical strategies of *A Room of One's Own* construct an erotic relationship among the woman writer, her audience present in the text, and the woman reader' (p. 173). My own essay proposes the 'scene of sisterhood' in George Eliot's novels as a momentary rupture in the otherwise heterosexual narrative (p. 137). In general, lesbian critical reading proposes the blurring of boundaries between self and other, subject and object, lover and beloved, as the lesbian moment in any text.

We need to acknowledge, however, that the lesbian reader, writer or protagonist does take up a position as self in relation to an/other woman, or women. We may blur the boundaries between self and other, subject and object, but there are boundaries there to be blurred. Who, then, is the other woman? To Penelope Engelbrecht, she is not an other in the sense of object, but an 'Other/self'. This designation underscores a crucial sameness between lesbians: '[It] simultaneously refers to ontological separateness and typological sameness: two women, two lesbians, Subject and Other/self. . . . [Both] have a single referent, "lesbian"' (Engelbrecht, p. 92). Similarly, Farwell refers to lesbian narrative space as 'a disruptive space of sameness' (Jay and Glasgow, p. 93).

It is this idea that exposes the most obvious contradiction between lesbian theory, with its controlling metaphors of space and sameness, and classic deconstruction. Heather Findlay, for example, demonstrates how deconstruction 'erase[s] the possibility of a specifically female homosexual practice' precisely because it privileges heterogeneity and contains homogeneity (Findlay, p. 59). The very act of carving out a separate lesbian space of sameness is stigmatised in some deconstructive texts (she singles out Derrida and Elizabeth Berg) in favour of a 'bisexual', 'androgynous' mode of operations – 'the most disruptive *feminist* position' (p. 60). Findlay boldly names this argument for what it is, homophobia, and then, agreeing with Shaktini but disagreeing with Fuss, goes on to offer Wittig's *The Lesbian Body* as a specifically *lesbian* deconstruction of heterosexuality. Findlay's analysis certainly raises questions about the usefulness of deconstruction for lesbian theory.

Jane Gallop questions the metaphor of lesbian sameness in a manner different from that of classic deconstruction. In an essay based on French feminist writer Annie Leclerc, she re-emphasises 'the otherness of the other woman' as opposed to 'an essentialist affirmation of the universal, anatomically based identity of all women' (Gallop, p. 144). In Leclerc's 'love letter', based upon paintings by Vermeer that place a middle-class woman in relation to her maid, the salient difference is that of class. Gallop argues further that Leclerc's understanding of difference extends beyond the material to an ontology of otherness missing in much lesbian theory: '[Vermeer's painting] gives her an image of what, in her writing, she is striving for: an acceptance of the distance as well as the proximity between women' (p. 153).

Gallop raises a point that cannot be overemphasised by lesbian critics. While sexual difference may not exist between or among lesbians, all other forms of difference do. These include differences of identity – race, class origins, employment status, age, religion, physical abilities – and while we may struggle against these differences within our individual 'spaces', they have a material and institutional reality that cannot be denied or wished away. There are other differences as well: desire, for example, is often painfully unequal. Nor can we turn aside from those erotic and symbolic differences suggested by butch–femme role-playing or lesbian sadomasochism; or, if we do postulate a 'community' among lesbian writers, readers, audiences and characters, who is in charge? Surely we are not all processing to consensus over the production and meanings of texts? In short, it may be that lesbian space is defined as much by difference as by sameness. It is the differences within our difference that carry such exciting potential.

What is the relationship between the metaphorical lesbian and 'real' lesbians? How do we reconcile the differences between our theories and the beliefs lesbians hold in everyday life? In other words, how do we make our theories useful?

I want to end with a final thought about the relationship between lesbian theory and lesbian existence. As I have argued throughout, there exists a continuity within lesbian theory from 'The woman-identified woman' in 1970 to the deconstructive critics of 1990, one that suggests the strength of the identities we have been constructing since the inception of the women's liberation movement and the gay liberation movement in the late 1960s. Within that continuity, 'lesbian' is positioned as a metaphor for the radical disruption of dominant systems and discourses. It is equally clear to me that most lesbians – all those 'lesbians here, and there' – do not perceive themselves and their lives in those terms. Frankly, I can do so only on my very best days. Most theorists today are anti-essentialist, suspicious of 'experience' and 'truth' as categories, and enamoured of disruption and fragmentation; most lesbians in everyday life believe they always have been lesbians, rely on their experience and sense of what's real to make literary judgements, and seek the condition of wholeness and normality. The discourses of 'common sense' and contemporary theory seem to be moving further and further apart.

This distinction was brought home to me when I read Barbara Smith's call for a fiction that manifests the traditional literary qualities of 'verisimilitude and authenticity' – by which she means 'how true to life and realistic a work of literature is' and how accurately it portrays 'a characterization which reflects a relationship to self that is genuine, integrated, and whole' (Smith, p. 222). Smith does not use the prevailing language and concepts of contemporary literary criticism, but those of common sense or 'ordinary life'. I believe she does so because she is proposing an ethical or political approach to literature – that is, a theory of writing based on its usefulness to specific communities of readers. We certainly might debate over what is and is not useful, or what is or is not within the realm of literature. Like many contemporary critics, I am sceptical about applying the standards of 'verisimilitude' and 'authenticity' to literary texts, but I also recognise that this is exactly what my students and friends do expect from literature. I am uneasy about setting the critic up as a superior, expert reader, wielding highly specialised language, whose role is to educate the masses. So what is the responsibility of the critic to the writer, to the text, and to the community of readers? Perhaps the most interesting work in the 1990s will be found in the answers we write to that question.

Notes

1. A point that has been raised recently, and had previously been ignored, is that these sensory metaphors are 'abelist' – that is, they assume an access to sensory experience that does not, in fact, exist for all women. Such criticisms remind us that language inscribes power relations in multiple and interlinking ways.
2. There are, of course, many other important and influential texts by women or lesbians of colour, including perhaps the best-known of these, *This Bridge Called My Back: Writings by radical women of color*.
3. See, for example, Radicalesbians, 'The woman-identified Woman'; Bertha Harris, '*What we mean to say*: Notes toward defining the nature of lesbian literature'; Charlotte Bunch, 'Lesbians in revolt'.

Works Cited

Andreadis, Harriette (1989) 'The Sapphic-Platonics of Katherine Philips, 1632–1664.' *Signs*, **15**, 1, pp. 34–60.
Anzaldúa, Gloria (1989) *Borderlands/La Frontera: The New Mestiza*. San Francisco: Spinsters/Aunt Lute.
Brossard, Nicole (1988) *The Aerial Letter*, transl. Marlene Wildeman. Toronto: The Women's Press.
Bunch, Charlotte (1975) 'Lesbians in revolt', in Nancy Myron and Charlotte Bunch, eds, *Lesbianism and the Women's Movement*. Baltimore, MD: Diana Press.
de Lauretis, Teresa (1989) 'The essence of the triangle or, taking the risk of essentialism seriously: Feminist theory in Italy, the U.S., and Britain.' *differences*, **1**, 2, pp. 3–37.
de Lauretis, Teresa (1990) 'Eccentric subjects: Feminist theory and historical consciousness.' *Feminist Studies*, **16**, 1, pp. 115–50.
Engelbrecht, Penelope J. (1990) '"Lifting belly is a language": The postmodern lesbian subject.' *Feminist Studies*, **16**, 1, pp. 85–114.
Farwell, Marilyn R. (1988) 'Toward a definition of the lesbian literary imagination.' *Signs*, **14**, 1, pp. 100–18.
Findlay, Heather (1989) 'Is there a lesbian in this text? Derrida, Wittig, and the politics of the three women', in Elizabeth Weed, ed., *Coming to Terms*. New York: Routledge.
Frye, Marilyn (1983) *The Politics of Reality: Essays in feminist theory*. Trumansburg, NY: Crossing Press.
Fuss, Diana (1989) *Essentially Speaking: Feminism, nature and difference*. New York: Routledge.
Gallop, Jane (1986) 'Annie Leclerc writing a letter, with Vermeer', in Nancy K. Miller, ed., *The Poetics of Gender*. New York: Columbia University Press.
Gearhart, Sally (1978) *The Wanderground*. Watertown, MA: Persephone.
Grahn, Judy (1984) *Another Mother Tongue: Gay words, gay worlds*. Boston, MA: Beacon Press.
Grahn, Judy (1985) *The Highest Apple: Sappho and the lesbian poetic tradition*. San Francisco: Spinsters Aunt Lute.
Harris, Bertha (1977) '*What we mean to say*: Notes toward defining the nature of lesbian literature.' *Heresies*, **3**, 5–8.
Jay, Karla and Joanne Glasgow (1990) *Lesbian Texts and Contexts: Radical revisions*. New York: New York University Press.
King, Katie (1986) 'The situation of lesbianism as feminism's magical sign: Contests for meaning and the U.S. women's movement, 1968–72.' *Communication*, **9**, pp. 65–91.
Martin, Biddy (1988) 'Lesbian identity and autobiographical difference[s]', in Bella Brodzki and Celeste Schenck, eds, *Life/Lines: Theorizing women's autobiography*. Ithaca, NY and London: Cornell University Press, pp. 77–103.
Moi, Toril (1985) *Sexual/Textual Politics: Feminist literary theory*. London: Methuen.

Moraga, Cherríe and Gloria Anzaldúa, eds (1981) *This Bridge Called My Back: Writings by radical women of color*. Watertown, MA: Persephone.

Radicalesbians (1973) 'The woman-identified woman', in Anne Koedt, Ellen Revine and Anita Rapone, eds, *Radical Feminism*. New York: Quadrangle/New York Times Book Co.

Rich, Adrienne (1980) 'Compulsory heterosexuality and lesbian existence.' *Signs*, **5**, 4, pp. 631–60.

Rosenman, Ellen Bayuk (1989) 'Sexual identity and *A Room of One's Own*.' *Signs*, **14**, 3, pp. 634–50.

Smith, Barbara (1990) 'The truth that never hurts: Black lesbians in fiction in the 1980s', in Joanne M. Braxton and Andrée Nicola McLaughlin, eds, *Wild Women in the Whirlwind: Afra-American culture and the contemporary literary renaissance*. New Brunswick: Rutgers University Press, pp. 213–45.

Whitlock, Gillian (1987) '"Everything is out of place": Radclyffe Hall and the lesbian literary tradition.' *Feminist Studies*, **13**, 3, pp. 555–82.

Zimmerman, Bonnie (1981) 'What has never been: An overview of lesbian feminist criticism.' *Feminist Studies*, **7**, 3, pp. 451–75.

Zimmerman, Bonnie (1990) *The Safe Sea of Women: Lesbian fiction 1969–1989*. Boston, MA: Beacon Press.

THE DEATH OF THE AUTHOR
AND THE RESURRECTION OF THE DYKE

/Reina/Lewis/

Introduction

Lesbian literary criticism, like lesbian and gay studies generally, has been as much a project of (re)discovery as of literary criticism. Its retelling and reinterpretation of stories is an exercise in history-making that, like all history, reflects the concerns of the present. Our critical practice says as much about us as it does about the past or the texts themselves. Research follows the trends of the moment as we try to find precedents and positive images for the way we live our lives today.[1]

This essay is concerned with the tendency among some lesbian literary criticism to reread texts exclusively in the light of their authors' (newly discovered) homosexuality. I shall assess the theoretical implications of this resurrected author in relation to other critical theories which minimise the role of the author as the determinant of the text and locate meaning in the text itself or in the process of reading. This involves reconsidering subjectivity and identity.

Lesbian literary criticism questions not only the (sexual) identity of authors and texts, but also that of the critical writer. Although many cultural critics are moving towards an inscription of themselves into the critical text (recognising that the social and subjective position from which they write will impact on the text), there is simply no possibility of avoiding this for writers engaged in lesbian critical activities. It is invariably assumed that anyone who writes on lesbian subjects is herself lesbian. It is thus an area of critical study beset by nascent and contradictory definitions, one that defines its critical practitioners.

/17/

As someone who was invited to be part of this volume because the editor knows that I am lesbian, I am constituted as both subject and object of the study. The editorial brief encouraged contributors to adopt an experiential tone and to write themselves into the study as an anchor point with which the reader could identify in their quest for meaning. This, considering that my project is a critique of precisely that prioritisation of identification in reading, is something of a paradox. This conundrum is typical of lesbian literary criticism because of its position at the intersection of literary criticism and identity politics. A postmodernist approach would welcome the insertion of the writer's subjectivity but use it to undercut the fantasy of a unified and controlling authorial voice, whereas in identity politics, subjective experience is often offered as the validation of the authorial voice. I am therefore invited to place myself in the very line of self-determining lesbian writing subjects that I seek to undercut. None the less, I do write . . . and I do want to be part of the club. . . . Hence the 'we' that occurs in my essay is not so much a reference to a universal, undifferentiated lesbian reading subject (although there are points where the 'we' is clearly lesbian) as an appeal to the imagined community[2] of shared opinion (lesbian or otherwise) who may visualise a similarly reconceptualised 'lesbian nation' and reading practice.

I shall be using essays from the Lesbian History Group's book *Not a Passing Phase* as a case study. The group take literary women or literary material as the basis for five out of nine essays, and the book crosses the boundaries between history and literary criticism. Its treatment of the issues of authorship and identity has implications for the necessarily interdisciplinary field of lesbian studies.

Authors, writers and dykes

Traditionally, liberal criticism has seen the author and her/his intent as the main origin of meaning in the text. Anyone who has dutifully read their way through Austen, Eliot and Henry James with attention to tone, feeling and structure has experienced the impact of F. R. Leavis's influential 'Great Tradition' that established the canon of English literature in the 1940s.[3] Although Leavisite analysis emphasised the active process of reading, the reader's interpretation is always seen as subordinate to the sovereign meaning inscribed in the text by the author. Criticism, after the semiotic structuralism of Roland Barthes, stressed that meaning in the text can extend beyond the author's intentions and operate autonomously through the working of sign and signifier.[4] In addition, the concept of the author has been dissected to produce a divide between two entities: the author and the writer.[5] This divide posits the author as the point of origin constructed for the text by critic and readers, and the writer as the 'real' historical personage who manipulates physical materials to create the text. This allows us to move away from intentionalistic accounts and separate the writer from the meaning in the text.

These two terms, author and writer, coupled with the postmodernist view of identity as fragmented and contradictory, let us see the contradictions of the texts, their authors and the social spaces experienced by the individuals who wrote them. It does not mean that we think books write themselves; it means instead that we allow the gaps, suppressions and silences of texts to speak to the stresses and discontinuities of the writers' experiences and the authorial positions from which they are held to enunciate.[6] This is an appropriate critical response for lesbian and gay readers and writers whose relationship to representation has traditionally been one of coding and subversion.

Lesbian literary criticism, in keeping with other projects of rediscovery (for example, Black and women writers and artists), tends to return to liberal humanist ideas of the subject. It is all very well being told that the sovereign controlling subject is dead, but for groups who were denied access to the authoritative reading and writing position the first time round, there is a very real need to occupy it now. As lesbians we want role models, we want to feel part of a cultural tradition, to know that we have a history of creativity, one that speaks to our experience and concerns. But – and it is a big but – can we construct this history without reneging on the theoretical developments to which we too have contributed?

In the face of a homophobic society we need creative and critical processes that draw out the complexity of lesbian lives and same-sex choices, not a retreat into the comforting myths of heroines and unfractured/unimpeachable identities. Creatively, this means a literary practice that moves beyond the limitations of positive images; critically, it means engaging with debates about subjectivity and authorship that move beyond the desire for a centred controlling authorial subject. We deserve a complex and nuanced critical framework, and to see ourselves as part of a diverse group – not just as the unified 'other' of heterosexuality locked into heroic combat with patriarchal straightdom. Martha Vicinus, in her call for a more sophisticated lesbian history, demands that we move beyond the early stages in which some lesbian historians have seemed:

> more concerned with finding heroines than with uncovering the often fragmentary and contradictory evidence which must make up the lesbian past.[7]

The same could be said for lesbian literary critics. Rather than categorise lesbians and lesbian texts as innately 'other' to the heterosexual structure of literature and society, I am interested in the tendency of lesbian literary criticism to visualise *itself* as other or oppositional to the literary canon. Lesbian literary criticism displays what I would characterise as a 'necessary heroicisation' that pertains to the lesbian canon, lesbian authors, lesbian literary critics and criticism alike – a tendency to construct new heroines in order to insert great lesbians into the traditional history of great men. This strategy, while difficult to avoid, is limited in the long term, since it produces an alternative version of the authorised view of history when what we really need is a history that sees the diversity of personal experience and recognises that the determining factors of race, nationality, class, gender and sexuality are locked together in a shifting relationship in which different terms, or combinations of terms, will have precedence at different times (i.e. sexuality is not always the key factor). This is difficult, but not impossible, to incorporate into a history that is premissed on sexual identity. The problematic desire for a unified and heroic self-image is one of the central dilemmas of contemporary lesbian cultural politics.

For activists engaged in a struggle against heterosexism and homophobia it is difficult to mobilise, analyse and agitate without falling back on the sense of a shared and uncontradictory identity. In addition to the need for a unified image I am concerned about the conflation of civil-rights rhetoric, identity politics and authorship in lesbian critical practice.[8] Its reliance on the concept of a self-determining subject with innate (i.e. pre-social) rights implies the pre-social existence of the subject. For those writers committed to the refusal of essentialism, who wish to maintain that subjectivity is socially produced, it is problematic to premiss the struggle for a better existence on the demand that those in power recognise lesbians' innate human rights.[9] The emergence of 'diversity' as a buzz-word in identity politics signals that we are beginning to reconceptualise as fragmented and socially contingent the various commonalities to which we appeal.[10]

Critically, this raises questions for the way we consider authors and readers.[11] The anti-humanist slant of poststructuralism does not mean that we are all such tragically split subjects that we cannot even clean our teeth, let alone write novels, but that we can recognise ourselves as contradictory and complex beings. Thus we can read from more than one position (what other explanation is there for lesbian enjoyment of mainstream novels?) and write multifaceted texts. This non-voluntaristic position stresses the diversity of our desires and experiences, and also allows for the impact of the unconscious and unknown in our lives and work.[12]

We do need to find a lesbian cultural tradition, but I would prefer one that opens up possibilities for us to one that closes them down. It is not enough to write lesbian subjects back into history and literature unless we also question the nature of that subjecthood.

What is lesbian literary criticism?

I see four main concerns in relation to the project of lesbian literary criticism:

1. What is lesbian literary criticism, and how does it constitute its field of study? Do all the critics have to be lesbian, do all the texts have to be lesbian, and what definitions of lesbian are we using?
2. How do we, as literary or cultural theorists, deal with the emphasis on author which often results from the reclamation or identification of lesbian texts as the product of a lesbian author?
3. How do we negotiate the effects of scarcity regarding the rarity of material and the inflated expectations of readers?
4. How do we answer the questions of readership and reader-response raised by lesbian literary criticsm? These range from ivory-tower ponderings on the generation of meaning to grass-roots demands for positive images.

Constituting the field

Before the lesbian literary critic can begin she has to rehearse the debates about just what counts as lesbian, for unlike women's studies, where it is reasonably clear who counts as a gendered subject, lesbian studies have to make their subjects afresh. The field does not seem to have reached the point of solidification and legitimation where such a display is rendered redundant. So, to put it briefly – lesbian and gay studies tend to regard sexuality as either innate or socially constructed.[13] There are further divisions of opinion in each camp, but basically, the essentialists argue for a transhistorical and transcultural constant of homosexuality that has always and will always be present in variously similar manifestations. The constructionists see sexuality as socially produced, not innate. They stress the discontinuities of homosexual experience and social role, arguing that the very concept of a lesbian or gay identity with which the West is familiar today is socially contingent, produced by the emergence of an ideology of individualism and a socio-medical discourse of sexuality.[14]

The early sexologists' classification of homosexual and lesbian types, in the late nineteenth century, has had great impact in Europe and its spheres of influence.[15] It is still being debated whether they described and re-classified existing same-sex behaviour or invented it from unrepresentative and dubious research.[16]

I would argue that there have always been women who love other women in relationships of primary significance, whether or not they were sexual. We cannot assume that a lesbian identity is coterminous with the existence of same-sex female object choice, and in many cases we simply cannot know if sexual contact occurred. If we recognise the historical and cultural specificity of our current notion of sexual identity, then we must be prepared to find that same-sex relationships are differently defined and represented in texts from a different period or culture.[17] Foucauldian ideas of the construction of sexuality have been widely used in lesbian and gay studies, but we need to extend the terms of debate when we are trying to locate lesbian and gay history and culture that is not white Euro-American. The dynamics of imperialism have rewritten and reclassified many peoples' histories, and lesbian and gay material is one of the casualties,[18] compounded by the marginalisation of lesbians who are not white, aristocratic or intellectual in the tendency to concentrate on great individuals. The writing of a history of lesbian communities that moves beyond the individual to an analysis of how the forces operating on and around individuals determine their experience and enunciation of same-sex relationships will go – and is going – a long way to avoid those exclusions.[19]

The Lesbian History Group expand the definition of lesbian history to include histories of homophobia and heterosexism. This reverses the onus of proof in relation to the literary project by pointing to the assumed heterosexuality read on to everyone, in – or despite – the absence of evidence to the contrary. Thus they insist that we can safely claim a lesbian identity for any woman who gave:

> her primary energies to women, who [put] on record that she lived with or loved another woman with rather more validity than many of the heterosexual ones [identities] that biographers have scattered about.[20]

The group vary on how to demarcate a lesbian identity. They discuss whether to count women as lesbian only if genital sexual contact is proven, or to take Adrienne Rich's idea of the lesbian continuum: all women are potential lesbians by virtue of the primacy of their emotional bonds with other women.[21]

Sheila Jeffreys, in 'Does it matter if they did it?' makes it very clear that whilst it does matter (being best friends with a woman does not equal 'sharing lesbian oppression nor lesbian experience'), it is also important to question why we are so hung up on knowing.[22] She claims that it is not just blatant homophobia that makes it hard to identify writers as lesbian – it is also a problem for us, as cultural theorists, to imagine 'lesbian' as a title that can incorporate and suggest a whole intellectual, social and emotional world. For as long as the word summons up a predominantly sexual image, we are stuck with the narrowest form of identity.

Rich's theory of the lesbian continuum rests on an essentialism that has implications for language and critical theory. Her call for a new poetry to express the totality of women's experience relies on a transparent notion of language as representation which Catharine Stimpson characterises as 'an emblazoned naïveté'. I recognised myself in her characterisation of Rich's worried opponents:

> *Surely*, they whisper nervously, she must know about our post-structural awareness of the nature of the sign. *Surely*, she must realize that language is a fiction, not a transparent vehicle of truth. . . . *Surely*, she must now admit that this system creates the human subject, not the other way around.[23]

The angst which emerges from trying to validate both the field and oneself in academia whilst retaining grass-roots support and involvement under-cuts lesbian studies, just as it has undercut other politically motivated fields. The sometimes contradictory requirements of politics and criticism explain some lesbian literary criticism's overly exclusive reliance on an author-centred approach. Lesbian literary criticism sets up its line of pedestals for lesbian writers, just as feminism constructed a literary canon to rival traditionally male-centred literature teaching. The politics of the margin that once determined feminist action (and still does to a lesser extent) is present today in lesbian scholarship and politics. The hardships of Britain after Section 28 (and, as we go to press, further threatened by clause 25 and paragraph 16) bring a greater emotional charge to the study of lesbian texts and foreground our sanctification of experience, identity and opposition.

Re-creating the lesbian author

Research which reveals the lesbian sexuality of authors often leads to a critical approach that reads texts as the inscription of their lesbian identity. An osmosis is set up in which writers known/suspected to be lesbian are found to have included lesbian scenes or characters in their work (the interpretation of which can now be validated on the grounds of the author's own sexual orientation); in return, incidents which are interpreted (or clearly marked) as lesbian are seen to throw a new light on authors previously secured as heterosexual.[24] This desire to reinterpret on the grounds of a newly 'discovered' identity holds true for politicians and pop stars alike – do we now read Madonna's lyrics as lesbian anthems, since (as rumour has it) she came out as a dyke? I am as interested as the next dyke in whom we get to claim as our own, whether it is Madonna or Florence Nightingale, but I am wary of good gossip turning into literary criticism.

Not a Passing Phase struggles with the contradictions inherent in a reconstructionist history: the group both disbelieve the facts of hetero-patriarchal history (which has hidden lesbian women from history) and are engaged in the project of writing an alternative history that implicitly offers itself as the truer account. The writers struggle dykefully with this problem. The relationship between novels, autobiography and private letters is restimulated to produce new meanings which are exciting and provocative.

I have my own stake in the reclassification of past lesbian luminaries. Imagine the scene . . . there I am, like a good researcher working away on nineteenth-century women's writing and imperialism, in which I am quite clearly and conscientiously taking texts as the products of subjects discursively inscribed into certain gendered, classed and nationed enunciative positions, and most certainly not reading the texts as the direct inscription of authorial experience and intent, when I read in *Not A Passing Phase* that Charlotte Brontë and George Eliot were lesbians. 'My God,' I panic, 'they're claiming "my women" and dealing with them in just the sort of anecdotal way that I'm determined to avoid!' But what the Lesbian History Group have to say is very interesting, and I am unwilling to add to our marginalisation by consigning the whole issue to a footnote, especially when lesbianism is an important part of other sections of my project (like my analysis of how it crops up and is repressed in the critical reception of images of convents and harems). So: how do we deal with these new authorial identities and their relation to the texts?

Pam Johnson's article '"The best friend whom life has given me": Does Winifred Holtby have a place in lesbian history?' is an excellent example of a history that deconstructs texts and conjectures about other possible meanings without positing them as definite.[25] She reads Vera Brittain's account of her friendship with Holtby against the grain of the text and explains how *Testament of Friendship* says more about the impossibility of Brittain identifying herself or Holtby as lesbian than it does about their actual sexuality. Johnson uses other historical material to read the gaps and stresses of Brittain's account in order to deduce Holtby's lesbianism despite Brittain's careful avoidance, or denial, of it. However, she does veer into constructing the letters as unproblematically more truthful than the novel.

This sets up a meritocracy between 'hard' historical facts and 'soft' fictional accounts, as if fiction can be explicated only by the presentation of 'objective' and 'real' external evidence. I would be the last to suggest that we see fiction as existing in a vacuum, but I would shift the inquiry equally on to the 'factual' historical sources. The repressions and re-constructions of life experience that are seen to occur in the transition from letters and diaries to novel are similarly inscribed into the production of the letters themselves. We can regard non-fiction historical texts as equally fictive in that they, like all cultural products, are not an objective representation of truth but are mediated by the subjective interior and anterior conditions of their production. We do not have to take any text at its face value. Both fiction *and* 'history' can be read against themselves.

But reading against the grain of the text means reading against the author, against the idea of her as the mistressful unified sovereign creator of the text. The author becomes a fragmented subjectivity inscribed within the contradictions of the text. Johnson provides a fine exegesis of Brittain's denial of Holtby's lesbianism, pointing to the homophobia of Brittain, the literary establishment and the contemporary Women's Movement. We should take from this example not that Holtby and Brittain were lesbians (even if they didn't know it themselves) but that the assumption of a sexual identity of any sort is always and necessarily riddled with contradictions and denials, some of which will emerge at the level of the text signalled by the absence, emphasis or de-emphasis of sensitive material.[26]

Elaine Miller's article on Charlotte Brontë and Ellen Nussey in *Not A Passing Phase* also re-presents us with a lesbian author. She exhumes Brontë's intense relationships with women from correspondence and memoirs that have been variously suppressed, edited and destroyed. Miller questions the relentless critical construction of Brontë as the 'apparent goddess of heterosexual romance' and inserts the omitted details of lesbian biography. Whilst she emphasises the lesbian content in the novels, she acknowledges – but defers discussion on – the complex 'organic connection' between Brontë's life and her novels. She claims that there is:

> no essential contradiction between the type of novels she wrote and the loving relationship with a woman which was the centre of her emotional life.[27]

My only quibble with this well-researched article is that the resolution of this possible contradiction is seen in terms of making a more realistic match between life and text by highlighting the lesbian textual content. Miller introduces Brontë's lesbian experience more representatively into the biographical accounts and shows that it is possible to make the same-sex relationships of the novels as significant as – or more significant than – those heterosexual relationships which are so frequently read as traces of Brontë's life. Miller is clear that 'the fiction can be used to support most, if not all, interpretations of Charlotte Brontë and her life', but counters this with the assertion that the letters, 'not being fiction, can yield more direct evidence'.[28]

It is tough to give up on the hope that letters will tell us the truth about hidden lesbian heroines but, again, we have to regard the 'non-fictional' representations of the letters as differently registered but not necessarily more true or more determining of meaning than the novels. They offer us, along with contemporary criticism and our own readings, additional information with which to analyse the production of oppositional currents within apparently traditional heterosexual romance. The traces of lesbian experience can be inserted as one among other determinants of the text's narratives of resistance to heterosexual and patriarchal ideology. Many feminist critics have read Brontë's novels as proto-feminist and socialist texts containing veiled and overt assaults on male domination and the exploitation of women and the working class. I have read them in relation to imperial mechanisms of racial and cultural difference. The lesbian themes should be incorporated into a multilayered reading of the texts that relates all these social and psychic formations to each other – in the work of all critics, not only those with a specifically lesbian brief.

Elaine Marks explores this problem in her 1979 article 'Lesbian inter-textuality'.[29] She unites author and text in a discussion of the relationship between 'real' lesbians and textual representations of them. This is a 'double heritage' by which features of a certain high-profile lesbian set come to function as the markers of homosexuality in the text. This allows Marks to focus on the texts themselves, including those which are un-sympathetic or written by men, as a transcript of society's attitudes to lesbians and women.[30] But she marginalises the text's productivity for the reader: she assesses how life experience is codified into textual signifiers, but not how readers may use the meanings read from/into the text to structure life experience. This approach maximises attention to text and author, but leaves out the reader.

Although there is in Marks's writing an implied belief in the innate truth of the word, I am interested in the way she transforms the emphasis on authors into an emphasis on texts and authors within texts. Her approach can help us to dispense with author-centred criticism, and work instead with texts as producers and transformers of meaning. We can do this by drawing on her view of lesbian texts as a genre, something that can be analysed structurally regardless of the author's gender or sexuality. Her morphology of the lesbian text allows us to see 'structural similarities between diverse fictions' that tell us as much about lesbian lives as something as apparently straightforward as a heart-rending interpretation of thwarted love on the part of a reclaimed passionate friend/lesbian.

The politics of scarcity and the positive images debate

Like any other oppressed, marginalised and under-represented group, lesbians want images of themselves, and in keeping with cultural politics of the last twenty years, we have demanded that images be, like us, out and proud. This is understandable, but limiting; the scarcity of lesbian images, teachers and courses produces a field of high expectations marked by defensiveness and the demand for positive images. For lesbian critics, the involvement in an academically marginal and under-funded practice encourages an identification as heroic women warriors fighting back on the establishment's own terrain. For lesbian readers, the emphasis on positive images limits the sort of writing that is acceptable.[31]

Since writers in lesbian studies work in a field that aims to be both popular and critical, they are generally keen to find out what readers want. Quite often readers want positive images and experiences with which they can identify, based on a traditionally unified subject and a singular reading of the text. This does not mean that lesbian readers have not taken on the complications and challenges of postmodernist fiction (witness the popularity of writers like Sarah Schulman and Kathy Acker), but there remains a desire to avoid the insecurities of multiple readings. It can be unpalatable to deal with the implication that we, like texts, are contradictory and unable to control our own narratives. The strand of lesbian literary criticism that asserts its alternative interpretation of texts as the one, true reading (*Villette* is really, and only, a lesbian romance . . .) rebuts the possibility of subjectivity as contradictory and fragmented.

The desire to control our own critical narratives can be related to the popular and critical predilection for autobiography and the accompanying valorisation and deconstruction of categories of experience.[32] In order to promote a mobilising sense of collective critical consciousness we must be wary that the defensive position of lesbian studies does not leave us caught in the quagmire of positive images.

Catharine Stimpson sees the desire for positive images and a singular identification as retrograde, and argues that such 'formally staid' qualities of the lesbian novel are politically dangerous. Lesbians who 'struggle against the hostilities of the larger world can find comfort in the ease of reading' positive images which, rather than motivating them to articulate their experience and rebel against repression, may give a false sense of security and encourage inactivity. For the straight reader these easy textual pleasures may allow a retreat from the challenge of 'unfamiliar and despised material'.[33] Stimpson suggests that by perpetuating the hegemony of traditional literary orders one may endorse the 'continued strength of the larger [heterosexual] community's norms', so that for her the comforting 'sense of community' between text and self craved by readers and offered by traditional narrative forms is dangerously reactionary.

Not surprisingly, several writers are adamant that their skills and scope go beyond the literary placebos of positive images. Jane Rule, in an essay in *Outlander*, refuses to be either limited in this way or identified with her characters.[34] She insists on her right to represent a realistic range of human experience, and questions the ethos of reader/character identification. More prosaically, she points out that it is impossible to please all sections of the gay community with one text. As anyone who has discussed any of the scant television representations of lesbian and gay life will know, there is a high level of expectation that what we see should reflect our lives. The scarcity of lesbian and gay images means that any one text is overloaded with expectation far in excess of the expectations audiences have of mainstream images.

June Arnold and Bertha Harris debunk the protective myth surrounding positive images by arguing that in refusing to represent the unpalatable and contradictory elements of lesbianism, writers are disenfranchising lesbians from their own experience.[35] They cogently assert that the (mid-1970s) spate of sisterly and sanitised positive image novels can leave (particular young) lesbians with no representation or validation of their own negative feelings such as envy, betrayal or anger. If novels have no relation to the less beatific aspects of lesbian experience, there is a risk that readers will end up feeling like perverts all over again because they do not fit into the textual mode of lesbian, any more than the previous generation fitted into the stereotyped Doris Day mode of heterosexual feminity.[36] However, this demand for a variety of lesbian images is still tied into the desire for identification with textual characters that Jane Rule implicitly refuses.

Critics have to break the habit too. Some have worked the tropes of identification across texts to include the author herself as a point of identification, along with historical and fictional figures. The Lesbian

History Group's book provides us not just with a new reading of Charlotte Brontë's novels but also with a series of newly discovered lesbian writers with whom to identify. Harris and Arnold demand realistically varied prototypes in text. What is common to these approaches is the assumption that a straightforward one-to-one identification between reader and textual character is at play.

Fantasy

Cultural studies has focused extensively on mechanisms of fantasy. This often draws on Freudian psychoanalysis to suggest that fantasy works by a series of contradictory and shifting identifications rather than an allegiance to a single character.[37] But one of the effects of scarcity is that these ideas are slow to take hold in the critical and popular response to lesbian texts, where writers are still involved in the earlier stages of compiling a canon to criticise. The enormous significance of reader identification with textual representations of lesbians, alongside the critical emphasis on authorial sexual identity, posits a set of correspondences for the reader between herself, the text and the author that seals them all into a closed circuit of unified subjectivity. I would argue for a theory that opens up these identifications and lets us explore our conflicting selves without losing the thrill of camaraderie with lesbian characters or authors.

   Jean Kennard specifically addresses the issue of fantasy in relation to the lesbian reader by adding the theory of polar reading to the Jungian psychoanalytic view that subjectivity is formed out of a series of internalised oppositions.[38] In this scenario the subject accepts desired characteristics and denies those perceived as negative – thus, 'I am generous, I am not mean' or 'I am lesbian, I am not het'. Polar reading argues that the process of reading allows a fantasy identification with both sides of the pairing. Kennard expands the idea of the polarity into one of a 'spectrum of differences'. Thus the opposite of lesbian could be heterosexual female, homosexual male or heterosexual male. There are two gains in this approach: first, the reader can explore elements of herself that she may suppress because they don't fit in with her self-image, her politics or her community; second, it offers an explanation of how lesbians can derive pleasure from heterosexual and reactionary texts without losing their sense of identity. If we are careful to stress these oppositional spectra as socially produced and not innate, this approach gives us a flexible theory of reading and writing.

Conclusion

The scarcity effect of overrated expectations is in operation at both ends of the reader–writer relationship. As I have shown, the critic, too, wants a great deal from the text. Critics are, after all, readers as well and, as a reader of critical texts, I also have unreasonable expectations. Just as lesbian fiction/cultural production is both tormented and encouraged by the urgent needs of its readers, I want what I read to do everything at once, and get it right.

For the lesbian critic it is hard to risk unpopularity in the lesbian community by demanding critical standards of reading, and risky to force lesbian texts – never mind the lesbian self – onto the critical and academic community. But for all that, I bemoan the prioritisation of identification and positive images in lesbian reading. I know that my efforts as a teacher to introduce lesbian and gay issues into a heterosexual syllabus would be impossible without the support of lesbian, gay and interested students demanding points of contact with the material they study. But inclusion is not enough: we must demand that lesbian and gay culture be treated critically in both forums – the literary and academic establishment must raise its awareness of lesbian culture, and the lesbian reader must recognise her contradictory demands on the lesbian text.

It is possible to challenge the desire for an inflated sense of identification without losing the possibility of an appropriate culture and critique. Like the song says, we don't need another heroine.

I would like to thank Francis Mulhern, Sue Hamilton and Karen Adler for reading and commenting on various drafts of this essay, and the postgraduate seminar groups at Middlesex Polytechnic and Birkbeck College for discussing the initial draft.

Notes

1. On the trends of research, see Joan Nestle, *A Restricted Country: Essays and short stories*, London: Sheba, 1988; Sheila Jeffreys, 'Butch and femme now and then', in Lesbian History Group (LHG), ed., *Not A Passing Phase: Reclaiming lesbians in history*, London: The Women's Press, 1989 hereafter (B&F); Martha Vicinus, '"They wonder to which sex I belong": The historical roots of the modern lesbian identity', in Altman, ed., *Homosexuality, which Homosexuality?*, London: GMP, 1989.
2. The phrase is borrowed from Benedict Anderson, *Imagined Communities: Reflections on the origin and spread of nationalism*, London, 1983.
3. F. R. Leavis, *The Great Tradition*, Harmondsworth: Penguin, 1980.
4. See Rolande Barthes, *Image – Music – Text*, London: Fontana, 1977.

5. See Michel Foucault, 'What is an author', *Screen*, **20**, 1, 1979; Griselda Pollock, 'Agency and the avant-garde: Studies in authorship and history by way of van Gogh', *Block*, **15**, 1989.

6. For an examination of this in the visual arts, see Griselda Pollock, 'Modernity and the spaces of femininity', in Pollock, *Vision and Difference: Femininity, feminism and histories of art*, London: Routledge, 1987.

7. Martha Vicinus, '"They wonder to which sex I belong"', p. 172.

8. On the political and theoretical limitations of civil liberties and the rhetoric of rights, see Jeffrey Weeks, *Sex, Politics and Society*, Harlow: Longman, 1981; Parveen Adams and J. Minson, 'The "subject" of feminism', *m/f*, **2**, 1978.

9. For more on this point, see Adams and Minson, 'The "subject" of feminism', p. 60.

10. For developments on the subject of essences, see Diana Fuss, *Essentially Speaking: Feminism, nature and difference*, London: Routledge, 1989.

11. For the benefits to literary practice of a contingent approach to identity politics and the construction of political subjects, see Joseph Bristow, 'Being gay: Politics, identity, pleasure', *New Formations*, **9**, 1989, pp. 61–82.

12. For a critique of the voluntarism of the lesbianism debate and an exploration of its discursive effects on lesbian culture, see Reina Lewis and Karen Adler, '"Come to me baby": Or what's wrong with lesbian sm', in ~~Lon Flemming, ed., Sex and Violence (forthcoming).~~ Women's Studies International Forum, 1995

13. For a clear rehearsal of the debates, see Anja van Kooten Niekerk and Theo van der Meer, 'Homosexuality, which homosexuality?', introduction to Altman, *Homosexuality, which homosexuality?*, pp. 5–12.

14. This often draws on Michel Foucault's influential theory that a homosexual identity was discursively constructed out of a series of previously unrelated acts at the time of the trial of Oscar Wilde. See Michel Foucault, *The History of Sexuality: Volume One*, Harmondsworth: Penguin, 1979. For various critiques of Foucault's emphasis on the nineteenth century and examples of earlier homosexual behaviour, see Randolph Trumbach, 'Gender and the homosexual role in modern Western culture: The 18th and 19th centuries compared', in Altman, *Homosexuality, which homosexuality?*; Judith C. Brown, 'Lesbian sexuality in Renaissance Italy: The case of Sister Benedetta Carlini', in *ibid.*

15. I am using the different nomenclatures – lesbian, gay and homosexual – for their various and specific meanings in the different discourses with which they are associated.

16. See Vicinus, 'They wonder to which sex I belong', p. 186; and Jeffreys (B&F), p. 163.

17. For examples in pre-twentieth-century Europe, see Lillian Faderman, *Surpassing the Love of Men: Romantic friendship and love between women from the Renaissance to the present*, London: The Women's Press, 1981.

18. See, for example, Evelyn Blackwood, 'Sexuality and gender in certain Native American tribes: The case of cross-gender females', in Freedan *et al.*, eds, *The Lesbian Issue, Essays From Signs*, Chicago: Chicago University Press, 1985; Saskia Wieringa, 'An anthropological critique of constructionism: Berdaches and Butches', in Altman, *Homosexuality, which homosexuality?*

19. Witness, for example, the massive interest in the oral histories of older lesbians and the writings of Black lesbians in, for example, Grewal *et al.*, *Charting the Journey: Writings by Black and Third World women*, London: Sheba, 1988.

20. Introduction to Lesbian History Group, *Not a Passing Phase*, p. 15.

21. Adrienne Rich, 'Compulsory heterosexuality and lesbian existence', in Ann Snitow *et al.*, eds, *Desire: the politics of sexuality*, London: Virago, 1984.

22. Sheila Jeffreys, 'Does it matter if they did it?', in LHG, *Not a Passing Phase*, p. 22.

23. Catharine R. Stimpson, 'Adrienne Rich and feminist/lesbian poetry', in Stimpson,

Where The Meanings Are: Feminism and cultural spaces, New York: Methuen, 1988, p. 141.

24. See Bonnie Zimmerman, 'What has never been: An overview of lesbian feminist literary criticism', in Elaine Showalter, ed., *New Feminist Criticism: Essays on women, literature and theory*, New York: Methuen, 1985.

25. Pam Johnson, '"The best friend whom life has given me": Does Winifred Holtby have a place in lesbian history?', in LHG, *Not a Passing Phase*, pp. 141–57.

26. A contemporary example of this might be the startling absence in lesbian feminist novels of lesbian characters doubting their gay identity as counterposed to the abundance of hets on the turn within the genre. This suggests something about the difficulty of imagining lesbians having a sexual identity that is fluid. Sexual change is a one-way flow in contemporary urban dykedom, and anyone who says otherwise will find herself swimming against the imagined tide.

27. Elaine Miller, 'Through all changes and through all chances: The relationship of Ellen Nussey and Charlotte Brontë', in LHG, *Not a Passing Phase*, pp. 31–2.

28. *Ibid.*, p. 44.

29. Elaine Marks, 'Lesbian intertextuality', in Stambolian and Marks, eds, *Homosexualities and French Literature. Cultural Contexts/Critical Texts*, Ithaca, NY: Cornell University Press, 1979.

30. See also Maureen Brady and Judith McDaniel, 'Lesbians in the mainstream: Images of lesbians in recent commercial fiction', *Conditions*, **2**, 2, 1980.

31. The emphasis on identification for lesbian readers has parallels in the social significance of reading a lesbian text where the possession of such a text operates as an index to the reader's sexual orientation. Who hasn't sneaked a look at someone's bookshelf to see where they're at, or experienced the dilemma of whether to read on obviously lesbian book on a crowded train?

32. There is a growing critical literature of and about autobiography. See Ronald Fraser, *In Search of a Past*, London: Verso, 1984; Biddy Martin, 'Lesbian identity and autobiographical difference(s)', in Bella Brodzki and Celeste Schenk, *Life/lines: Theorizing women's autobiography*, Ithaca, NY and London: Cornell University Press, 1988; Carolyn Steedman, *Landscape for a Good Woman*, London, Virago: 1986; Laura Marcus, '"Enough about you, let's talk about me": Recent autobiographical writing', *New Formations*, **1**, 1982, pp. 77–94.

33. Catharine R. Stimpson, 'Zero degree deviancy: The lesbian novel in English', in Elizabeth Abel, ed., *Writing and Sexual Difference*, Brighton, Harvester, 1982.

34. Jane Rule, 'Reflections', in Rule, *Outlander*, Tallahassee: Naiad, 1981.

35. June Arnold and Bertha Harris, 'Lesbian fiction: A dialogue', *Sinister Wisdom*, **1**, 2, 1976.

36. For a discussion of why Doris Day's challenging and transgressive female roles are marginalised in favour of the characterisation of her as the perfect housewife, see Judith Williamson, 'Nice girls do', in Williamson, *Consuming Passions: The dynamics of popular culture*, London, 1986.

37. See, for example Cora Kaplan's analysis of *The Thorn Birds* in which she uses Laplanche and Pontalis's notion of the de-subjectification of the subject in fantasy. This suggests not only that the reader makes multiple and contradictory rather than unitary identifications, but that the subject may not feature in any recognisable or complete form at all, being instead subsumed into the scene of the fantasy itself. See Cora Kaplan, '*The Thorn Birds*: Fiction, fantasy, femininity', in Kaplan, *Sea Changes: Culture and feminism*, London: Verso, 1986.

38. Jean E. Kennard, 'Ourself behind ourself: a theory for lesbian readers', *Signs*, **9**, 4, 1984, p. 652.

'SOMEWHERE OVER THE RAINBOW . . .'
Postmodernism and the Fiction of Sarah Schulman

/Sally/Munt/

What does it mean to sing 'somewhere over the rainbow' and release balloons? It made her feel something very human; a kind of nostalgia with public sadness and the sharing of emotions. But then what? (Sarah Schulman, *People in Trouble* [1990], p. 44)

'What is all this postmodernist shit, anyhow?' has been the Left's *cri de cœur* (kneejerk?) response, ever since it became necessary to launch this latest French theory into the political arena. Partly because there is no 'grand narrative' which is postmodernism, a great deal of conceptual confusion and consumer scepticism have characterised its reception. At a conference at the University of Sussex, one of its British protagonists was accused of 'word magic' – a heartfelt complaint from one of the many punters who had thought they had come to a conference about *politics*. The sometimes bitter contestations over postmodernism's 'radical versus reactionary' status have been played out in fields such as social theory and philosophy. Feminists in particular have expressed antagonism towards its distancing, parodic stance, seeing its abandonment of generalisations and its rejection of coherent identities (such as woman) as a luxury only men can afford, given their historical precedence as definers. To argue that all Big Theory is out, and small theories are in, would seem to encourage the view that difference will endlessly proliferate into a relativist, selfish individualism; Linda Nicholson dubs it 'the view from everywhere'.[1] She goes on to say that 'postmodernism must avoid any simple celebration of difference or of particularity for its own sake',[2] stressing the crucial importance of situating diversity within political contexts.

Lesbian culture, in some ways, is the ideal forum for playing out postmodernist fantasies. Lesbians as a group tend to be highly self-conscious, being impressed by the perpetual need to make visible differences, from each other and dominant heterosexuality. Even on the most intimate 'private' level, sexual desire requires the inventive reconstruction of roles.[3] (This self-interrogation, though, is double-edged: to what extent are we implicated in the dominant construction of homosexuality as *the* site of inquiry into identity, which is underwritten by presumptions of what is 'normal' and therefore beyond examination?) Postmodernist fiction has to some extent slotted into a well-established space in the literary hype(r)-market, that of experimental writing. Given the combination of these two favourable contexts in the fiction of Sarah Schulman, I will explore, using close textual analysis, how identities are liberated, multiplied and shifted through her works, how Schulman manages to extract the best from postmodernism in its playful unfixing; yet concomitantly, how the generation of these texts through time reflects a developing discomfort with the de-politicising tendencies within postmodernism. Schulman's fiction can help us to sift out our own political trajectories from this confusing critical field.

Jim Collins, in *Uncommon Cultures: Popular culture and post-modernism*, argues how postmodern fictions present new forms of textuality; they are:

> responses to the complexities of contemporary cultural arenas. . . . The tensions and conflicts within the semiotic environments that are the focus of so many Post-Modernist texts result, in large part, from the struggle of individual discourses to 'clear a space' within a field of competing discourses and fragmented audiences.[4]

In a sense, lesbian and feminist fictions are likewise competing in this space, within an ideological terrain which is populated with historical shifts in definition, and conceptual uncertainty. Geographically speaking, the readers are also fragmented and dispersed, their act of reading their only collective, unifying gesture. This interconnecting textuality is problematic, if we take Chris Weedon on lesbian fiction, for example:

> If we are searching for positive lesbian role models or for a recognizable lesbian aesthetic, then a fixed concept of lesbianism is important.[5]

In 1988 I wrote an article about lesbian crime fiction[6] concerning the tension between generic conventions and the emancipatory agendas of these lesbian feminist texts. I argued that the best of these novels play with identity and succeed in offering the lesbian reader a vision of community. Sarah Schulman's books are paradoxically part of this subgenre, yet partly distanced by the employment of a postmodernist perspective which sets her novels apart from the political realism, positive images school of lesbian crime writing. By writing against this, Schulman could be said to be constructing lesbian identity around the landscape of a modern urban condition – changing, fluid, complex and fragmented, fighting for a space juxtaposed with and superimposed on other cultural identities – Jewish, Black, working-class and so on, but difficult to fix in any pragmatic way.

These 'ethnocentricities' have been described as 'other' within an oppositional structure most commonly arranged with the state as the dominant term. Jim Collins is keen to argue that crime fiction offers a critique of the state. According to him, crime fiction affirms an alternative sense of justice; he goes so far as to suggest that its proliferation in the nineteenth century represented a widespread disillusion with the state, and that 'the class of the detective is considered morally superior'.[7] Thus we may see why disempowered, struggling subcultures may be drawn to the genre, since living on the margins necessarily creates a specifically distrustful attitude to the dominant doxa. Collins goes on:

> . . . collisions between quite different forms of discourse become basic structuring principles of those texts. These collisons share a common purpose – to demonstrate that our cultures are so thoroughly discourse-based that we cannot even hope to encounter 'real life' unless we investigate the ways discourses fundamentally shape our experience.[8]

Focusing specifically on the first of these novels, then: *The Sophie Horowitz Story* was published in 1984 by the lesbian Naiad Press of Florida, USA. Schulman's first novel, set in Lower Eastside New York, reveals a cornucopia of literary and political conventions skewered on a sharp satiric wit. The eponymous hera is a writer on a low-budget women's monthly, *Feminist News*, started collectively three years previously. With a circulation of seven thousand (plus one thousand distributed free to women in prison), the publication is a parochial forum for feminist exposition and expostulation. Sophie's column is called 'On the Right and Left'. She is stimulated into this stint of investigative reporting by the arrest of a notorious terrorist and her teenage exemplar Germaine Covington, symbol of American disaffected youth. Party to a bungled bank raid, Germaine is first captured, then a faked death frees her. The plot is further enriched by another fabled feminist, Laura Wolfe, who escapes from the scene of this crime and is pursued by the worshipful sleuthing of Sophie Horowitz; as another remarks, 'looking for Laura Wolfe is a personal journey' (p. 81).

The book has certain thematic similarities with *Killing Wonder* by Dorothy Bryant.[9] In presenting two icons of feminist intervention, elevated to mythical status by an idealising subculture, Schulman addresses the same awed construction of heras. By constantly satirising the process of sanctification that such self-made martyrs condone, Schulman parodies the resultant disempowerment of the more humble feminist hack. Laura Wolfe was part of a group called Women Against Bad Things, who had 'some kind of politics which none of us understood. Whatever we did, they didn't like it . . .'. She addresses the moral prescriptiveness which can emanate from such censorious campaigns, and there is some resonance with the then contemporary movements in feminism which were perceived by some lesbians as anti-pornography and seemingly anti-sex. Laura uses sex as ideological recruitment: 'Laura made me do a whole song and dance just to get a little feel' (p. 7). The novel is, in part, a reaction against this feminist prescriptivity, exposing political hypocrisy.

Germaine Covington turns out to be implicated in framing Laura Wolfe, together with a coterie of accomplices with inverted identities: the District Attorney, who is a fence; a respected journalist, who is an s/m clone; a doctor, who ODs an immigrant; an academic, who is a cocaine dealer; along with winos who are FBI agents and a radical lawyer who is an avaricious status-seeker. Laura Wolfe, terrorist, appears in the guise of a nun. *The Sophie Horowitz Story* is a parody of 'types', whose ascribed meanings are constantly shifting. The stereotypes derive from both the dominant and the alternative cultural arena, and the only stable point in this satirical onslaught – this literary *carnival* – is Sophie. In her ironic humour she distances herself (and the reader) from the semantic cacophony.

Identity is foregrounded in the novel: Sophie is looking for Laura, and for 'herself'. The reader's pleasure derives from the recognition not of selfhood, but of roles. Schulman deploys metafictional frames to obfuscate these binaries of self/roles, authentic/inauthentic, truth/fiction. Traditional detective fiction is a predictable, highly formalised genre offering pleasure and release of tension through the affirmation of received and uncontested meanings. For the Jewish/feminist/lesbian reader of *The Sophie Horowitz Story* there is some pleasurable complicity with the text in its representation of familiar (sub)cultural signs. However, the reader becomes disconcerted as these are undermined by parody. The reader's resultant unease reflects realistically her social positioning, allowing expression to the constant, unconscious shifting of roles/selves necessary for social interaction.

Sophie's first-person narration creates the illusion of a central, stable, reliable disseminator of information. Relying on the convention of the detective as confidant and arbiter of truth, the text seduces the reader into a fantasy world, a semiotic *jouissance*, a carnivalised urban crime novel. Even Sophie, however, fails to stay in character at times, missing vital clues and relying on an intertextual construction of fictional frames within frames to keep her investigation going. One of these operates through the character of King James (a literary pun on the Authorised Version), a prolific mystery-writer whose heroes are 'real professionals', 'smooth and daring' (unlike Sophie); they 'always know just what to do' (p. 44). The author – who, in key crime-writing tradition, is a woman writing under a male pseudonym – takes another apartment in Sophie's building, which overlooks hers in the manner of Hitchcock's *Rear Window*.

Mrs Noseworthy first permeates Sophie's consciousness through the incessant noise of her typing – a metonymic reference, perhaps, to the pervasiveness of fiction. She is a parody of the spinster sleuth, an impeccably polite, bespectacled pastiche of the patriarchally defined Miss Marple/Pym/Silver:

> She was, what else can I say, a little old lady. . . . Her hair was grey, her face was wrinkled, her dress went down below her knee. (p. 78)

However, she extrapolates their subversive strengths:

> '. . . don't underestimate me because I have grey hair. We needn't be macho to be powerful, my dear.' (p. 99)

Sitting in her rocking chair, stroking her cat, Mrs Noseworthy proceeds to dissect the process of the investigation and advise her juvenile disciple in a reversal of the classic Holmes/Watson dialogue. She rejects the persona of the detecting superhero, faultless in every deduction, claiming that even 'Henrietta Bell, my greatest detective, makes mistakes'. In giving Sophie a copy of one of her adventures, *Murder in the Missionary Position*, Schulman enacts another gibe at convention. When Mrs Noseworthy pulls up at the scene of the final denouement, whisking Sophie away in her lavender BMW, it transpires that her tip-off to the police (in her best Italian accent) ensured the judicious capture of the murderer, a mercenary, Mukul Garg. Another recapitulation ensues, suffused with a comically contrived fictional self-reflexivity.

Writing, intertextuality, literary self-consciousness: *The Sophie Horowitz Story* is unrelentingly metafictional. Sophie's investigative trajectory is driven by her nose for a journalistic scoop, and this story is continually remaking itself as one level of interpretation is supplanted by another. Towards the end, Sophie stumbles home and muses on the inter-relatedness of the primary characters; they have 'become each other's art' (p. 143):

> The story was almost over. Soon I'd have to sit down and write it. There's a certain relief when that moment comes. I'd lived with these people and this information and now that time was almost up. I could say goodbye to them.
> (p. 143)

Sophie writes as the author, creating a boxlike world into which the reader is inculcated too. The impression is that once the book/box is closed, the characters cease to exist. Indeed, they all seem to disappear within the narrative – Germaine Covington (in a classic thriller cliché) goes into a toilet stall, climbs out through the window and is seen no more; Vivian and Laura Wolfe drive off into deepest New York; Sophie herself, in the final line, is swallowed into the city skyline. Her manuscripts, 'written off' by *Feminist News* as male-identified, are consequently binned. Even the text will disappear.

Writing is seen as a commodity, demystifying the bourgeois romance of expression-as-art. Sophie's motivation for The Story is at least partly based in the status and career enhancement such a scoop would bring. Writing sex, though, is a more commercial prospect; Sophie needs to make money quickly, so she attacks the typewriter as The Lesbian Pornographer. Private enterprise is cramped by the intention to make it 'real'; none of the words is right, and Sophie is stymied at first base. This text thus connives with other lesbian fictions to articulate the gap between the experience and the expression of lesbian sex. Whilst the passage could be read as prioritising experience and 'the body' over writing and language (as an inauthentic construct), I feel the point made here is that of 'man-made language', which alienates women from similar processes of construction. Women are socialised, however, into reading and writing male subject positions – Sophie swops from lesbian to gay porn, typing a short 'stroke' story of two motorcycle men and a sailor, sellable for fifty dollars. When Evan, her Boy America misfit lodger, tries, however, his 'What Makes a Woman Good in Bed' makes three thousand dollars. His ability to exchange subject positions is an expression of his own gender identity, which defines the available options.

The commodification of identity can also be seen in the way Schulman chooses to depict ethnicity, in particular Jewishness, expressed metonymically through food. Caught in Pizza Hut playing Pac-Man with her brother, Sophie observes:

Suddenly Ms Pac-Man appears on the electric screen. She's in a maze. She has to gobble up as many little blue dots as she can before the monsters catch her. It's social realism about women and over-eating. (p. 67)

It is a pertinent remark; the prevalance of food in the novel metonymically asserts its Jewishness, but also provides a cultural reference point for all women preoccupied with the inevitable appropriation, treatment, distribution and fetishism of food. Sophie's investigations are punctuated not by bourbon or Black Label but by blintzes, borscht and bagels.[10] Even her Jewish identity is foregrounded as a kind of fiction. In Chapter 37, Sophie takes the day off from investigating. In an attempt to reassure herself she visits the Jewish museum. Her understanding of the Holocaust and other systematic pogroms is mediated through exhibitions, films, shows, newspapers and books, the fictionality underscored by describing leading Nazis as an 'infamous cast of characters' (p. 145).[11] Sophie sits down in front of a television which presents a short piece called 'Grandma', unintelligible to the Gentile reader:

What are you doing wearing that *shmata*? You're a *shanda* for the *goyim*. You should only get a good job and earn a living so you shouldn't be a *schnorrer*. (p. 147)

Blending a mass-media technology with such a symbol of authentic Jewishness together in a framework labelled art, for common consumption, is indeed postmodern, and for the Gentile reader its use of strange nouns renders it almost science-fictional. The novel also concentrates on various aspects of sexual identities and the vagaries of lesbian culture, 'a certain cynicism developed collectively' (p. 112). As one Black character puts it: 'Well Sophie, we all seem to have our ethnocentricities' (p. 89).

Thus *The Sophie Horowitz Story* can certainly be categorised as parody and excess. The society depicted is indeed caught in a consumerist spectacle which renders political opposition difficult, if not purely representational. Affiliated to different, intersecting subcultures, the subject is constantly being reconstructed by consumption, but the mechanism being employed here is one not of meaningless oppression but of *pleasure*. The *Sophie Horowitz Story* is not a depressing book; Schulman's satire is sharp, and the more salient aspects of investigation are tempered, like many mystery novels, by romance. The relationship between Sophie and her lover Lillian is not mythical perfection. Together they are funny, kind, irritable, loving and sexy – an 'ordinary' couple. Humanity is ultimately left with the personal rather than the political, and in this way too the text can be described as postmodern – it finishes on such an insular note:

> Sometimes I worry about what's going to happen to me. Sometimes I fantasize about the easy life, but really I don't expect it. I just want to enjoy things, have friends and keep my life interesting. If I stick to my instincts, the world will follow. (p. 158)

Schulman's second novel, *Girls, Visions and Everything*, was published in 1986 by the feminist publishing company The Seal Press of Seattle, with the help of the National Endowment for the Arts. It is not a crime novel, but I wish to discuss it briefly as an adjunct to *The Sophie Horowitz Story* and the third novel, *After Delores*. *Girls, Visions and Everything* lacks the ontological direction of a thriller; its movement is less compulsive and more perambulatory. It is set in the same Lower Eastside – the protagonist walks the streets, marking out the geography of an urban landscape punctuated by a city mapped out with emotional happenings. Locations are symbols of connection, and constant references to crisscrossing streets remind the reader of the systematic patterns of neighbourhood and community. *Girls, Visions and Everything* is about Lila Futuransky's New York, 'the most beautiful woman she had ever known' (p. 177).

The social realism of the hardboiled thriller embodies the perspective of the underworld; the streets have to be mean, and filled with crime and corruption. The detective himself is an outlaw, a man in search of a hidden truth, as Raymond Chandler has described him: 'a complete man and a common man, yet an unusual man . . . a man of honor'.[12] Lila Futuransky is that man. Her position as a poor Jewish lesbian, pitted against the burgeoning bourgeoisification and consequential breakdown of her urban community, places her in honourable antipathy to the white, Gentile, middle-class conventionalists instigating gentrification and upward mobility. Lila Futuransky envisages herself as On the Road with Jack Kerouac; her adventure is similarly self-exploratory, but based on the *female* experiences a city offers. Her comparison with Jack is the dream of being an outlaw, reconstructed by a feminist consciousness captured within her separate subculture; Lila's trip is her constant circling between lovers, friends and compatriots.

A similar sort of sardonic wit to *The Sophie Horowitz Story* suffuses *Girls, Visions and Everything*, but there is also sadness: a sense of decaying nostalgia for streets filled with sisters and brothers sitting languidly on the stoop, swopping stories and cementing *communitas*. This is the feminisation of the street, the underworld with a human face, with its own moral and family code. It is rich kids who beat the gays and harass the poor, the prostitutes and the pushers.

The lesbians are on the streets, working the burger bar, cruising the ice-cream parlour and clubbing it at the Kitsch-Inn, currently showing a

lesbian version of *A Streetcar Named Desire*. Lila meets Emily here, performing as Stella Kowalski. The shows change every weekend; they are
more for the cast than for any audience, the art consumed by its own
production. The romance between Lila and Emily is ostensibly the main
development in the novel, structuring its five parts – one to three depicting
its ascension, and four and five its conflicts. The final chapter sees Lila
torn between the 'masculine' trajectory of On the Road individualism,
the expression of the urban street-poem, and the 'feminine' stability of
emotion and relationship commitment, which is depicted as static. The
dream of adventure has been symbolically transferred to her friend Isabel,
to whom she has given her copy of the book, and who now urges Lila:

> '. . . you can't stop walking the streets and trying to get under the city's skin
> because if you settle in your own little hole, she'll change so fast that by
> the time you wake up, she won't be yours anymore. . . . Don't do it buddy.'
> (p. 178)

This constant engagement/disengagement with change and transformation is signified by the urban landscape, which is out of their control. Even
the protective zones are folding, yet there are pockets of resistance which
pierce the city's metaphorical paralysis with parody: Gay Pride is one
such representation, fifty thousand homosexuals of every type parading
through the city streets, presenting the 'other' of heterosexuality, from
Gay Bankers to the Gay Men's Chorus singing 'It's Raining Men'.

Each Schulman novel contains a secondary hypodiegetic[13] world of
performance which further fictionalises the primary level of narration.
The highly parodic Worst Performance Festival in *Girls, Visions and
Everything* is a two-fingered salute to the liberal avant-garde, earlier
depicted in the description of an off-Broadway show which Isabel and Lila
see, and identify as 'fake social realism':

> All were pretending that they were dramatically interpreting the reality of
> New York street life. The actors strutted around, jiving like bad imitations of
> Eddie Murphy imitating a Black teenager imitating what he saw Eddie
> Murphy doing on TV the night before. The lesbian characters kissed each
> other and hit each other. The gay male characters made jokes about the sizes
> of each other's penises. The Black characters ran around with afro-picks in
> their pockets and occasionally stopped combing their hair long enough to play
> three-card monte while saying 'motha-fucka' a lot and grabbing their own
> crotches. All of this provided an appropriately colorful background for the
> white heterosexual characters to expose their deeply complex emotional lives.
> (p. 18)

Lila, dressed in a tight black T-shirt that says 'Soon To Be A Major Homosexual', comperes the Worst Performance Festival to an audience she derides, opening with the words:

> 'I want to remind you that all of us here together tonight, well, we are a community, a community of enemies. And we have to stay close to each other so we can watch out and protect ourselves. . . . Tonight we are proud to introduce our panel of minority celebrity judges from competing cliques to vote down each other's friends.' (p. 149)

It is this level of ironic distance which structures the reader into a fidgety self-consciousness; there are passages of apparently direct emotional verisimilitude between Lila and Emily which suture them into a kind of kitchen-sink realism; then the reader's identification is undercut by an unrelentingly parodic perspective which reappears in the guise of meta-fictional performance. Schulman tries to juxtapose a jumble of readerly responses, almost jerking the reader into some consciousness of her activity of creating imaginative space. She reinvents New York from her position of 'other' as a heterotopia of cultural intertextuality; she *is* Jack Kerouac – the character, not the author – claiming, even as a Jewish lesbian, that 'the road is the only image of freedom that an American can understand' (p. 164).

Thus Schulman uses the idea of a perceiving subject caught in some spatial construct which is organised around her/his consciousness; but she inhibits the sense-making process (or narrative hermeneutic) by constantly invoking and corrupting the conventional literary topology. For example, by the use of an imaginary and metaphorical 'Zone of the Interior',[14] Schulman creates a civilised zone of 'others' which is being encroached upon by the moral wilderness of capitalistic aggrandisement.

The street is an image of freedom and, paradoxically, of violence – Lila walks unmolested until the final part of the book, where she is sexually harassed by Hispanics and saved from serious injury from potential queer-bashers by the sick Black drug-dealer Ray. Lila's zone is breaking down: 'People's minds were splitting open right there on the sidewalk' (p. 14). The fictional worlds start clashing together: Blanche DuBois appears to Emily, aged eighty-five and begging for a dollar. Lila resorts to Emily with a resignation that can only be anti-romance, knowing it is the wrong decision and nostalgically lamenting the end of the road of self-hood: '*I don't know who I am right now*, she thought. *I want to go back to the old way*' (p. 170).

This whimsical nostalgia also highlights some disillusionment with the postmodernist models of space, wherein public and private are collapsed on to the street, and the same space is being used by different people in different ways. Hierarchies still exist. Being part of a bigger spectacle, being visible as one subculture among many, may not necessarily create empowerment, only more competition over a diminishing resource.

After Delores, first published by E. P. Dutton in 1988 and by Sheba Feminist Press in Britain in 1990, is another urban crime novel set in the Lower Eastside. A treatment of *After Delores* was broadcast on the British lesbian and gay magazine programme 'Out On Tuesday' in March 1990.[15] Introduced by another New York writer, Storme Webber, as a 'Manhattan microcosm' portraying the 'good dreams and the bad dreams of our neighbourhood', the introductory cameo consisted of Webber's prose poem, listing the many marginalised people resident in Lower Eastside – multicultural refugees rejected by all parts of the country, and the world.

Schulman, interviewed on the programme, commented on how this battle between disenfranchised subcultures and the bourgeoisification of the Lower Eastside forms the backdrop to all her novels. Describing artists stepping over the homeless on the way to the gallery, she observes:

> Society is so stratified that people can occupy the same physical space and never see each other, and also have completely different experiences of that space.

This would seem to be a geographical manifestation of the literary Chinese-box structure, with Schulman arguing for an actual separation of cultural locations within the same material site. As Brian McHale[16] has pointed out, postmodernist fiction makes literal the Bakhtinian metaphor of 'worlds' of discourse, and within the novel this polyphonic synchronisation of difference produces the effect of *heteroglossia*. Historically, more cosmopolitan cultures with competing subcultures have been heterogeneous, the languages or discourses struggling ideologically for precedence[17] or mutual coexistence. They are paradoxically exclusive and interrelated, zones of experience within a heterotopian space. New York is perhaps the paradigmatic example of a modern heterotopia; hence *After Delores* enacts these spatio-semiological 'combat zones'. Identity becomes fraught with definition; in one minor example the protagonist and her Hispanic friend Coco Flores see a friend's son, Daniel:

> 'That's no Daniel,' Coco said. . . . 'That's Juan Colon. Last year he was Juan Colon at any rate. This year he changed his name to Johnny. He's from PR' [Puerto Rico].

'That's no Juan Colon, I'm telling you, . . . his name is Daniel Piazzola.
He's from Argentina.'
. . . Johnny Colon, what a liar. (p. 108)

Apart from the ethnic and cultural heteroglossia, there are also continual
instances of dramatic, fictional worlds inside the supposedly real, primary
level of narration dictated in the first person, the mode historically associated with expressive realism. Schulman self-consciously obscures any
unitary monological referent to 'reality' by interlacing the text with
framing devices which foreground its instability. Coco Flores is always
telling stories; two major characters, Beatriz and Charlotte, are theatrical
actors perpetually locked into their own psychodrama; the *murdered* friend
Punkette is the character described as 'the most real' (p. 30). The narrator
is, according to Schulman speaking on 'Out On Tuesday', occupying her
own 'place of sadness that pushes people into a hallucinatory relationship
to the world'.

The narrator's space is separate and interpretative, subjected to being
'on the edge' both emotionally and discursively. Her life as an alcoholic
working-class waitress is suffused with neglect; she is nailed by despair,
a breaking, boundary-less despondency which is the result of Delores
leaving her for another lover. The narrator has no name; in another effort
to problematise the demarcation of zones and spaces, Schulman deprives
the text of a clearly defined speaker, intending that the extremity of her
pain will inculcate the reader into 'an unclear space between them and
her'.[18]

The reader's identification, then, becomes another site of contestation for
autonomy. Within the postmodernist text these constituent elements of
interconnecting space seldom cohere at the psychological or cultural level,
as Peter Currie has argued:

> discontinuities of narrative and disjunctions of personality cannot be
> overcome – by an appeal to the logic of a unifying metalanguage, a dominant
> stable discourse, settled hierarchy, or the constituency of the core self.[19]

Hence, perhaps, the fact that by the conclusion of the novel the central
emotional predicament of lost love is unresolved and unchanged, as the
last lines intimate:

> None of it means anything to me. There was only one thing I really missed. I
> missed Delores. (p. 158)

This novel, characterised by a nihilistic resignation, resists the convention of closure and re-established normalcy which is an essential prerequisite of classic crime fiction. Nevertheless, the narrative trajectory of investigation, tinged with jealousy and revenge, motivates the reader's need for revelation. The protagonist's motivation to find Punkette's killer is confused by her private outrage at being spurned, and instead of being a self-appointed neutral arbiter of social justice she reveals a flawed moral imperative (perhaps an implicit message to the more masculine murder mysteries). The book is punctuated by many verbal interactions and internal musings on murder. She will kill Delores, or the rival, or herself, or Charlotte, or Daniel. The clear categories of detective fiction – or 'functions', to quote Propp[20] – are obfuscated by being resident in the same person, hinting towards their interdependence, perhaps. Finally she does kill Punkette's murderer, who is a taxi-driver, and she comments:

> The thing about a cab is that you sit back in the leather like a movie star and instead of being part of the street and the life of the city, you only watch it, you don't come into contact. (pp. 150–51)

She annihilates the person who is not part of the city.

Textually, the reader's desire for revenge is satisfied and the mechanism of moral comeuppance is employed. However, the narrator's triumph is curtailed:

> 'I got the guy who killed Punkette. I made everything right. I suffered but I never gave up and now I have a victory, do you hear me? I have a goddamn victory. I won.'
> 'What are you talking about?' Beatriz said. 'You weren't going through all of this to find some man. You are just a lonely person who had absolutely nothing better to do. Don't fool yourself.' (p. 152)

After Delores punctures the transcendent moral prerogative of the hard-boiled dick with this pastiche of proud victory. An injection of the self-absorbed mundanity of human emotion and motivation is a symbolic stripping-down for the likes of Mickey Spillane and his *I, the Jury* ilk. As the protagonist plaintively laments, 'Who's going to get justice for me?' (p. 125); she is a loser, an antihero, denuded even of the romance of outlaw status.

Whereas *The Sophie Horowitz Story* seemed to represent a reasonably positive view of lesbian love, *Girls, Visions and Everything* contained ambivalences which have become articulated as anti-romance by *After Delores*. The lesbian novel has been restrained by its readership's need and expectation that it will represent lesbianism as an affirming lifestyle. *After Delores* resists this romantic enhancement and reproduces an urban realism evoking the hardboiled tradition. This protagonist does not transcend her environment, however, and remains removed from any emotional or sexual reward. Even the displaced romance between her and Delores does not satisfy the reader, as Coco Flores says:

> 'It doesn't matter who Delores was, why you loved her then and why you hate her now. Delores is a hallucination . . .' (p. 103)

The protagonist has a few sexual encounters which are notably unromantic: she constructs her own fantasy of Charlotte, who actually fucks her brutally, leaving her with welts and bruises. Looking for her later, she peers through the peephole of Charlotte's apartment to see her making love passionately with Beatriz, a scene calculated to underscore her own exclusion. Sexually excited, she rushes round to see a lesbian drag-queen, Priscilla Presley:

> She put on rhumba records and we danced around laughing and drinking from the bottle in between sloppy, drunken kisses. Then Elvis sang, 'Wise men say, even fools fall in love'.
> That's when I murmured 'Don't be cruel', and fell on my knees at Priscilla's feet, burying my face in her polyester. (pp. 128–9)

The sex is non-threatening by being displaced and enacted at a distance within a parodic eroticisation of difference. By synthesising a 1950s bar culture of butch and femme roles with the mythical incarnation of its two most totemic heterosexuals, Schulman blends the postmodernist revival of romantic irony with lesbian kitsch. Romance is impacted with fantasy with a literary vehemence, determinedly made raw by the erstwhile Delores, as she so bitterly insists:

> You always fall for someone thinking they're someone they're not. Sometimes I think that fashion was made for Delores, because it's so dependent on illusion. (p. 11)

After Delores, by finishing as it began, with the same emotional pain which the narrator has not managed to transcend or learn from in the classical realist epistemological manner, rejects the 'grand narrative' of self-improvement. She does not interpret her experience, she has lost the ability to locate herself. Whilst briefly striking a feminist note by the obliteration of a perpetrator of male violence ('It was a man. A man did it':

p. 136) the narrator still remains positioned as victim. The more extreme feminist ideologies of the universal removal of men are not going to effect change for women. By also so strongly rejecting romance, by rejecting truth in favour of performance, by refusing the representation of an emancipatory parable, Schulman can be said to be expressing suspicion of such universalising metanarratives. The paralysing sense of loss which suffuses *After Delores* is doubly painful – not only is romance revealed as yet one more fiction, but there is also the grief experienced by the loss of the utopian dream of the 1970s: that you *can* have a relationship with women, and that women are better.

The sadness resulting from this loss of the specificity of gay pride, of lesbian community, of a strong, unified identity, is the flip side of post-modernism, registering with progressively more impetus in these texts. Perhaps this mirrors a wider view. In this essay I do not wish to argue that feminism and postmodernism are one and the same, but there are important points of juncture: first in the desire to de-naturalise dominant ideology, and secondly in the injection of cultural difference as a field of operation. However, feminism, as Linda Hutcheon[21] points out, is a political force which desires material change; postmodernism is only a critique, with no real theory of agency or political resistance. There is a sense in which a postmodernist analysis does not do justice to Schulman's work – it must be seen as an intersection, along with Schulman's feminism; to read her work in this way must be to open up possibilities, not close them down. The three areas of postmodernism/feminism/authorship inform each other in these texts, but there are inevitably spaces, other strands which are not chased. For example, using the interpretative perspectives I have chosen makes it difficult to communicate the strong political spirit present in all the books: is this caused by a textual disjuncture or, more likely, by the limits of critical method? Or is it, perhaps, that the political impetus of these novels actually *clashes* with a postmodernist aesthetic? Fragmentation and diversity can also cause alienation and apathy, and anaesthetise activism.

In Schulman's latest novel, *People in Trouble* (Sheba Feminist Press, 1990), postmodernist styles and themes continue to be represented, but self-critically. In form the book comes closer to realism than her previous works, hinting perhaps at a creeping disillusionment with parody and play. Three central characters work out their relationship to each other, sexuality, and gender: Kate, an artist, is married to Peter; she is also lovers with Molly. Kate's political awakening takes place through her relationship with Molly, who is 'watch[ing] her friends die of AIDS' (back cover). One such friend, Scott, causes Kate to observe:

> 'Sometimes a person has to stop talking about art for a moment and take a look around.' (p. 166)

This novel has the effect of mirroring postmodernism back on itself, as though stepping back, encouraging the reader, Janus-like, both to employ and to destroy its own cultural practice. For example, *People in Trouble* expands the apocalyptic tone typical of writers such as Baudrillard, taking this as an opening moment:

> It was the beginning of the end of the world but not everyone noticed right away. Some people were dying. (p. 1)

and then, through a narrative of political enlightenment, proceeds to reject ironic, depressed disengagement in favour of a compulsion to act, an imperative to change, which is, after all, dependent on some hope of material revolution. 'Resistance', ultimately, replaces ironic reflection as the key theme. Kate sets fire to her own artwork (metafictionally entitled 'People in Trouble'), killing the billionaire developer who was also its commissioner. Ronald Horne's emporia are incarnations of the postmodernist spirit; his luxury hotel The Castle is modelled on Early Modern Colonialism, his Downtown City, consisting of sky-rise condominiums grouped together as 'Freedom Place' or 'Liberty Avenue', has 'all the elements of a made-to-order American shrine' (p. 28). By incinerating Horne, the text disposes of postmodernism's emptiest excesses. The representation 'People in Trouble' is replaced by a concrete array of 'real' people in trouble, in a distinctly didactic parting shot:

> On the way to his apartment [Molly] was thinking about how sometimes the city gets so beautiful that it's impossible to walk even one block without getting an idea. The idea she got was to try to remember the truth and not just the stories . . .
> 'Suffering can be stopped', James said. 'But it can never be avenged, so survivors watch television. Men die, their lovers wait to get sick. People eat garbage or worry about their careers. Some lives are more important than others. Some deaths are shocking, some invisible. We are a people in trouble. We do not act.' (pp. 227–8)

Schulman's novel is a warning not to confuse style with political transformations. She manages to express the doubts of those of us who are suspicious of postmodernism's ironic detachment, which threatens to anaesthetise political subjects. I feel some sympathy for the reader staggering through 'word magic' in order to construct a political praxis; postmodernism can indeed seem like a spell cast to mystify and immobilise. What draws Schulman's work together, however, is a playful exploration of the precarious state of identity, which also manages to implicate political responsibility for action.

Schulman's view of identity as unstable, as fiction, does not *dispose* of identity as a useful category for political change. Her fiction lays bare 'the fear . . . that once we have deconstructed identity, we will have nothing (nothing, that is, which is stable and secure) upon which to base a politics.'[22] Jane Gallop addresses this dialectic in *The Daughter's Seduction*:

> I do not believe in some new 'identity' which would be adequate and authentic. But I do not seek some sort of liberation from identity. That would lead only to another form of paralysis – the oceanic passivity of undifferentiation. *Identity must be continually assumed and immediately called into question.*[23] [emphasis added]

Although she apparently presumes, in saying this, that there is a simple, stable position from which we can choose or discard an identity; that we can occupy a neutral identity-free space to begin with; and that there are no imposed identities generated by society, rejecting the liberal fallacy of stability should not prevent a positive assumption of identity, and action being taken. One can also, by an expedient extension, exchange the term 'identity' for 'politics': knowing that 'politics', too, is a fiction fraught with contradiction should not deprive the individual subject of a desire and responsibility for change. In this struggle:

> we need both to theorize essentialist spaces from which to speak and, simultaneously, to deconstruct those spaces to keep them from solidifying.[24]

It is this doubling movement which Schulman's fiction narrativises so lucidly. Perhaps it is not yet time to turn postmodernism into postmortemism.

With thanks to Lois McNay, Janet Harbord and Linda Rozmovits for reading and commenting upon earlier drafts.

Notes

1. Linda J. Nicholson, ed., *Feminism/Postmodernism*, London: Routledge, 1990, p. 9.
2. *Ibid*, p. 10.
3. Here I would disagree with theorists such as Sheila Jeffreys who propose a model of the eroticisation of sameness and equality as true homosexual desire – see Sheila Jeffreys, *Anticlimax*, London: The Women's Press, 1990.
4. Jim Collins, *Uncommon Cultures: Popular culture and post-modernism*, London: Routledge, p. 27.
5. Chris Weedon, *Feminist Practice and Poststructuralist Theory*, Oxford: Basil Blackwell, 1987, pp. 160–1.
6. Sally Munt, 'The inverstigators: Lesbian crime fiction', in Susannah Radstone, ed., *Sweet Dreams: Sexuality, gender and popular fiction*, London: Lawrence & Wishart, 1988.
7. Collins, *Uncommon Cultures*, p. 35.
8. *Ibid.*, p. 60.
9. Dorothy Bryant, *Killing Wonder*, London: The Women's Press, 1981.
10. Feminist fiction, like much women's fiction, is full of food – see Joanna Russ, 'Somebody's trying to kill me and I think it's my husband: The modern Gothic', *Journal of Popular Culture*, **6**, 1973, Ohio: Bowling Green University Press, pp. 666–91. Often in lesbian crime fiction, after a scene of narrative suspense, the sleuth cooks a delicious meal which serves to placate the reader's tension, to normalise the fictional realm, and thus to ensure continuing identification with the protagonist.
11. Presumably this structure is not intended to convince the reader, in the manner of neo-fascist groups and intelligentsia, that the Holocaust was a Jewish conspiracy myth peddled for sympathy and political power. Perhaps it is a comment on a culture's alienation from its own history, and the impossibility of retrieving Truth.
12. Raymond Chandler, *The Simple Art of Murder*, New York: Ballantine, 1972, pp. 20–1.
13. See Brian McHale, *Postmodernist Fiction*, London: Routledge, 1987 for an excellent elucidation of postmodernist literary structures, despite its masculine bias and occasional homophobic remarks.
14. Thomas Pynchon, *Gravity's Rainbow*, New York: Viking, 1973, p. 711.
15. 'Out On Tuesday', Tuesday 27 March 1990, Channel Four.
16. Brian McHale, *Postmodernist Fiction*.
17. For an example of this see Dick Hebdige, *Subculture: The meaning of style*, London: Methuen, 1979.
18. Schulman speaking on 'Out On Tuesday'.
19. Peter Currie, 'The eccentric self: Anti-characterization and the problem of the subject in American postmodernist fiction', in Malcolm Bradbury and R. O. Sigmund, eds, *Contemporary American Fiction*, London: Stratford Upon Avon Studies, E. Arnold, 1987, pp. 53–71 (p. 54).
20. Vladimir Propp, *The Morphology of the Folk Tale*, Austin: University of Texas Press, 1968.
21. Linda Hutcheon, *The Politics of Postmodernism*, London: Routledge, 1989.
22. Diana Fuss, *Essentially Speaking: Feminism, nature and difference*, London: Routledge, 1990, p. 104. This is a familiar worry which emanates from what some see as the disintegration of the national Women's Liberation Movement during the early 1980s.
23. Jane Gallop, *The Daughter's Seduction: Feminism and psychoanalysis*, Ithaca, NY: Cornell University Press, 1982, p. xii; quoted in Fuss, *Essentially Speaking*.
24. *Ibid.*, p. 118.

AUDRE LORDE'S LACQUERED LAYERINGS
The Lesbian Bar as a Site of Literary Production

/Katie/King/

> From a feminist poststructuralist perspective authorship cannot be the source of the authority of meaning any more than the individual speaking subject, the agent of discourse, is its origin. This is not, however, to say that there is no place in feminist criticism for a study of authors, provided the critics recognize that accounts of authors are themselves discursive constructs and not a key to meaning. . . . In choosing a mode of reading we need to ask what useful political questions it answers. To be politically effective a reading needs to address the ideological and political concerns of the present-day reader. (Weedon, 1987, pp. 162–3)

> History is not kind to us/we restitch it with living/past memory forward/into desire/into the panic articulation/of want without having/or even the promise of getting. (Lorde, 'On my way out I passed over you and the Verrazano Bridge', 1986, p. 57)

Producing biomythography

This essay is an inquiry into literary ideology and feminist practice. It begins an examination of what I call 'the apparatus of literary production', the intersection of art, business and technology which currently determines literature – both literary works and the disciplines of literature. Looking at the apparatus of literary production resituates the author in the discursive fields producing literature. Interpretation, one form of the consumption of literature, is itself an element within the apparatus. A study of the apparatus of literary production potentially locates our cultural expressions in a global economy of language, technology, and multinational capital.

This is also an essay about reinscription, the creation and erasure of historical memory and literary identity within fields of power invoked and deployed by texts. It follows from an earlier discussion of contesting origin stories about current women's movements in the United States (King, 1986). There I argued that lesbianism has served as a constantly shifting sign in our histories of feminism, and that to sharpen our sense of its momentary specificity in conflicting discourses is to accept new forms of political accountability and new possibilities of political meaning.

The essay here continues this analysis by identifying the lesbian bar of the 1950s as a site of the production of historical memory and literary identity for feminist and gay movements. McCarthy's America, intertwining the spectres of homosexuality and communism, focuses another set of origin stories which also make collective political and institutional identities. Two contemporary but divergent texts exemplify competing meanings of the lesbian bar and of the 1950s in the USA, Audre Lorde's *Zami: A new spelling of my name* (1982) and John D'Emilio's *Sexual Politics, Sexual Communities: The making of a homosexual minority in the United States, 1940–1970* (1983). I superimpose texts and histories in order to tease out webs of action, collusion, misread codes, alliances; in other words, instances of political courage and political judgement shifting across time which oppositionally address race, sex and politics in renewed and repositioned contexts. Audre Lorde and her term 'whitelisting' come to attract these ranges of texts and histories in this essay, serving to focus and to proliferate concerns for political accountability.

Audre Lorde is a black lesbian feminist poet, novelist and essayist whose work has slowly gained prominence in the USA and Great Britain since the 1960s. She was nominated for the National Book Award in the USA in 1973 for her volume of poetry *From a Land Where Other People Live*, and has been and currently is published by both small arts presses and commercial mainstream publishers. Lorde's poetry and prose have had increasing impact on feminist theory in the United States. A powerful speaker and reader of poetry, she mobilises audiences beyond aesthetic appreciation into political action through her performances. Her various genres of writing and performance – pamphlets and polemical essays, novels, speeches, interviews, published letters, poetry, prose-poetry, taped poetry readings – create and reflect her various audiences and her multiple identities – black woman, lesbian feminist, socialist activist, cancer survivor, single mother – passionately focusing deep commitments to global feminism and the international struggle against apartheid.

Lorde's work raises helpful questions about the apparatus of literary production, offering some examples of aspects of its operation. Her publication in small arts and mainstream presses and her manipulation of genres highlight the convergence of 'audience' and 'market' in their political, racial and gender distinctions, and in the codes of elite and popular culture. Studying the apparatus of literary production necessarily debunks the use of the term 'reading' as a gloss for the academic practices of 'interpretation' which construct and reflect systems of power-charged value. Instead, it requires of us the acknowledgement of the cultures and varieties of literary consumption.

My interpretation here deliberately uses some of the strategies of academic close reading in order to appropriate their forms of authority and to empower Lorde's texts; in short, to enable their literary canonisation. Yet the politics of consumption cannot be erased by such academic practice. Lorde's public and private writing identity is as 'poet', and the political investments in the object, 'poetry', in feminism tend to naturalise the author as the source of authentic experience and to privilege poetry whose language is immediate and seemingly transparent (Clausen, 1982; King, 1987). What I have done, then, is to de-centre Lorde's ideological investments in poetry by looking at her self-designated 'prosepiece', to focus on historical specificity as a political practice and on the multiplicity and heterogeneity of *Zami* as a text, as texts interweaving its literal rewritings with its ideological reinscriptions, and to embed Lorde's and D'Emilio's texts in current controversies in US feminism over identity and sexuality.

In this first section I set the context for the meanings of the lesbian bar, suggesting implicit contemporary political agendas, including my own. Then I move to Lorde's *Zami*, investigating the process of rewriting with its proliferation of texts and the use of race and sex in the field of power located as the lesbian bar. This first close reading is joined by some theoretical comments on the construction of 'biomythographies' of gay pasts, introducing strategies for examining gay historiography. Finally I return to *Zami*, interlacing and contrasting its/my investments in 'white-listing' with the events recounted in *Sexual Politics*, *Sexual Communities*, and with its alternative conversations.

1982, the year of the first publication of Audre Lorde's 'biomythography', *Zami: A new spelling of my name*, was also the year of another feminist landmark, the controversial Scholar and the Feminist IX Conference, 'Towards a Politics of Sexuality', held on 24 April at Barnard College,

New York City (Vance, 1984). Both *Zami* and the Barnard conference 'wrote down' struggles over sexual identity that had been simmering within US feminist communities and conversations, struggles which today might be described by terms like 'the politics of identity' and 'the politics of sexuality'.

Today these two terms stabilise a variety of contesting feminist discourses in the United States, discourses which I call 'conversations' in order to heighten their momentary, local specificity. Often unselfconsciously generalised, 'conversations' are continually rewritten or reinscribed with new meanings by feminist practitioners as they attempt to describe ideology theoretically, to construct specific feminist ideologies, and to ground feminist action and practice in ideology.

'The politics of sexuality' – or, alternatively, 'the sexuality debates', or even 'Sex Wars' – intertwines a feminist reappraisal of sexual practices, the sex industry, sexology, and sex laws with a critique of the anti-pornography movement and of feminist sexual orthodoxies (Linden *et al.*, 1982; *off our backs*, June, July, September, November 1982; Snitow *et al.*, 1983; Vance, 1984; B. R. Rich, 1986). Also prominent in this reappraisal of sexuality is the valorisation of sexual minorities, particularly lesbian sadomasochism (SAMOIS, 1981) and the feminist recuperation of butch/femme roles in lesbian practice and history. Top/bottom, butch/femme coalesce and separate in historical specifics and ideological conflations. At stake are competing images of 'the lesbian' – as Outlaw (Rubin, 1981; Wittig, 1981; Nestle, 1984), as Mother (A. Rich, 1976), as Woman (A. Rich, 1980; Irigaray, 1977), as what I call 'magical sign' (King, 1986) – and competing periodisations in the United States of recent feminist history, rewriting 'the radical feminist', including the taxonomic system producing the category 'socialist feminism' (Echols, 1983a, 1983b, 1984; Vance, 1984; Jaggar, 1983).

The other term, 'the politics of identity', begins in the emerging discourse on anti-racist practice. It elaborates the notion of 'difference', now often associated with cultural particularism and with race and class criticism of 'the white women's movement' (Moraga and Anzaldúa, 1981; Smith, 1983; hooks, 1984). Audre Lorde's formulations of difference have been particularly powerful in this theoretical/practical elaboration (1984, see esp. 1977, 1979a; and Moraga and Anzaldúa, 1981; Joseph and Lewis, 1981). The work of Lorde and other women of colour requires and permits feminists to recognise and practise theory in literary/philosophical genres other than the rationalist essay. 'Difference' deconstructs the category 'white' as it continues the deconstruction of the category 'woman' (Reagon, 1983). Models of racial ethnicity and of sexual identity provide strategies proliferating non-unified, contingent identities: Jewish lesbian,

Chicana as La Mestiza, poverty/disability (Beck, 1982; Bulkin *et al.*, 1984; Moraga, 1983; Connors, 1985).

These feminist conversations problematise present taxonomies of feminism (liberal/radical/socialist), now unable to describe adequately the terrain of ideologies, either historically or currently; they also call into question any unitary 'history' of 'the women's movement', suggesting instead the simultaneity of women's movements, interlacing struggles for social justice (King, 1986). Chicana theorist Chela Sandoval has described the movement of power over these discursive fields, these 'conversations', in her work on oppositional consciousness (n.d.; see acknowledgements in Haraway, 1985). Participating in these conversations and knowingly contesting for the meanings created and employed in them, I want to make it difficult to see the political ranges represented by 'the politics of identity' and 'the politics of sexuality' as mutually exclusive. I want to use *Zami*, in fact, to suggest some of the contesting contradictions and often playful, often painful productions of meaning that these phrases connote. And I shall do this by looking to a particular place, mythic and historic, with specific signifying practices: the lesbian bar of the 1950s.

For Lorde, the gay bar stands for the contradictions of identity and solidarity/solitariness. Her individual statements about 'the gay-girl scene' often sound definitively descriptive or evaluative, but when compared from one section of *Zami* to another, these descriptions and evaluations change. In this processually fragmented work, constantly deferring key meanings, Lorde keeps rewriting the focus, the meanings of the bar scene, and especially the significations of butch/femme codes in the nexus of race and sex.

The current controversies in 'the politics of identity' and 'the politics of sexuality' come together in the work of Third World feminists like Cherríe Moraga, where the specific sexualities of the intersections of race, ethnicity, language, religion, culture, class and education are particularised and made flesh (Moraga, 1983, 1985). Lorde's return to the complexities of race and sexuality in the gay-girls' bar is also best understood in the intersections of 'the politics of identity' and 'the politics of sexuality'. Over and over, Lorde has to re-create the possibilities of being both gay and black – this in a bar culture dominated by white women, in which black women have powerful reasons for making connections, sexual and strategic, with white women and not with other black women.

Throughout *Zami*, Lorde uses the idea of 'women who work together as friends and lovers', uses it although we do not know its meaning until the next-to-the-last page of the book ('my life had become increasingly a bridge and field of women. *Zami. Zami. A Carriacou name for women who work together as friends and lovers*': Lorde, 1982, p. 255). In the bar, 'Zami' is the field of difference that structures the power-charged relationships among women: not just white women with black women and black women with black women and white women with white women, but Ky-Ky white women with Ky-Ky black women, white and black women together outside the codes of role, femme white women with butch black women, femme white women with butch white women, black women together beyond codes. (Ky-Ky is the stigmatised term for lesbians who don't adopt the identities of butch or femme in a bar scene dependent upon these meanings; while 'women together beyond codes' represents simultaneously a historically later judgement about this hegemony, and a utopian hope for relationships innocent of power.)

How to return to this scene, how to enter into the relations of power and visibility and collusion and rejection and attraction/repulsion and lust and loving is Lorde's event – an event not possible except in piling historical moment on top of historical moment. This is not one instance of time–space particularity, nor is it the utopian construction of a trans-historical myth, but instead the layerings of instance, of political meanings constrained in particularity, lacquered over so finely that they are inseparable and mutually constructing while distinct. I want to try here in this essay to show some of the grain of that finely lacquered 'history', 'restitched' 'past memory forward/into desire'. But first a deep involvement with Lorde's rewritings is necessary.

Zami rewritings: The field of power and difference

Gay girls selectively reveal and conceal the paradoxes of race and sex. Lorde wants to remember the connections among women; doing so requires putting together the sexual and psychic attractions to white women with the realities of racism and survival. A little desperately, since the assurance is only partial, but also generously, Lorde offers: 'Lesbians were probably the only Black and white women in New York City in the fifties who were making any real attempt to communicate with each other' (1982, p. 179). Writing it over at another point, Lorde adds qualifications and alters emphasis – '*So far as I could see*, gay-girls were the only Black and white women who were even talking to each other' – and generalises beyond New York City ('*in this country* in the 1950s') while dismissing the possibilities of other political solidarities: 'outside of the empty rhetoric of patriotism and political movements' (1982, p. 225; emphasis added). The sacred bond of gayness, always insufficient, is still motivating and hungry. Inside the lesbian bar the meanings of the intersections of race and sex implicitly shift from circumstance to circumstance, and these shifts are reflected in subtle rewritings, partial repetitions, revealing editings, reordered valuations and reordered connections. These shifts destabilise the oppositions black/white, butch/femme, Ky-Ky/role-playing, celebration of women's community/internalisation of homophobia.

One could easily read *Zami*'s depiction of the bar as an indictment of role-playing, even as a 1982 historical reinscription, a response against lesbian s/m with an assimilation of 1950s role-playing into a paradigm of dominance/submission that must be politically rejected.[1] This is surely one lacquered written layer of history in *Zami*. Some of Lorde's judgements and interpretations of the meanings of role-playing are straightforwardly rejecting and certainly spoken from the early 1980s in retrospective analysis:

> For some of us, role-playing reflected all the depreciating attitudes toward women which we loathed in straight society. It was a rejection of these roles that had drawn us to 'the life' in the first place. Instinctively, without particular theory or political position or dialectic, we recognized oppression as oppression, no matter where it came from. (Lord, 1982, p. 221)

As Lorde writes on here, she offers two simultaneous connections, connections both retrospective and historically separated out. First, she puts role-playing in association with 'the pretend world of dominance/submission'. At the same time, she also depicts its former hegemony in lesbian culture, a hegemony effectively routed now as reflected in the current weight of judgement against it. Lorde continues: 'But those lesbians who had carved some niche in the pretend world of dominance/subordination, rejected what they called our "confused" life style, and they were in the majority' (1982, p. 221).[2]

Lorde dramatically utilises this play of ground/foreground, of dominant ideology/heterodoxy, in the service of making complex, passionate and uneasily honest the terrors and attractions of the intersection of race and sex. These same sentiments are recast in another version of this paragraph (published separately, 1979b, p. 34; maybe directly a pre-write, or possibly simply an earlier editing), where Marion and Audre ('Marion' becomes 'Muriel' in *Zami*) – an interracial couple, young and a bit 'out of it' – are protectively nursed in this 'pretend world' and by these butch/femme women, and where the judging and the judged shift back and forth across time:

> As a couple Marion and I were out of it a lot since much of the role-playing that went on was beyond us. It seemed to both of us that butch and femme

role-playing was the very opposite of what we felt being gay was all about – the love of women. As we saw it, only women who did not really love other women nor themselves could possibly want to imitate the oppressive and stereotyped behaviour so often associated with being men or acting like men. Of course, this was not a popular view. There were butches and there were femmes but Lesbian, like Black, was still a fighting word.

Yet, Gerri's friends never put us down completely. Yes, we were peculiar, Marion and I, from our different colors right down to our raggedy-ass clothes. We had no regular jobs and queer heads – inside and out. The Afro hadn't been named yet, much less become popular, and Marion's shaggy-bowl haircut was definitely not considered dyke-chic.

But we were also very young at 19 and 21, and there was a kind of protectiveness extended to us for that reason from the other women that was largely unspoken. Someone always checked to see if we had a ride back to the city, or somewhere to stay over for the night. There was also some feeling that as self-professed poets we could be a little extra peculiar if we needed to be.[3]

Complications beyond those of age and nurturance are found in the troubling and sometimes tormented relationships among black women:

> The Black gay-girls in the Village gay bars of the fifties knew each other's names, but we seldom looked into each other's Black eyes, lest we see our own aloneness and our own blunted power mirrored in the pursuit of darkness. Some of us died inside the gaps between the mirrors and those turned-away eyes. (1982, p. 226)

Here our feelings are focused on a world in which black women are separated from each other by external and internalised racism. As a picture standing for the whole of black lesbian community, it is bleak and haunted by death. This picture of racism as essence and presence is pulled apart in three directions in other tones and writings in *Zami*. On the one hand, the power of the structures keeping black women from each other is represented by the colour-coding of butch/femme, the codes of race and power:

> The Black women I usually saw around the Bag were into heavy roles, and it frightened me. This was partly the fear of my own Blackness mirrored, and partly the realities of the masquerade. Their need for power and control seemed a much-too-open piece of myself, dressed in enemy clothing. They were tough in a way I felt I could never be. Even if they were not, their self-protective instincts warned them to appear that way. By white america's racist distortions of beauty, Black women playing 'femme' had very little chance at the Bag. There was constant competition among butches to have the most 'gorgeous femme' on their arm. And 'gorgeous' was defined by a white male world's standards. (1982, p. 224)

Here Lorde opens up some of the permutations that the combinations of black/white and butch/femme reveal, and she displays the field of difference as a net of power. She faces her own fear of her own blackness, a fear of power and control and their needs internalised as the objects of the realities of racism and the effective strategies of survival. She also faces the attraction and terror of the roles which seem to have no place open in them: Audre is not 'white woman "gorgeous"' enough for a femme, and fears to identify with butch-control.[4]

But the second direction which resists racism as essential uses the field of power to reveal the field of difference, difference haunted by lack of connections but prefiguring new meanings of multiplicity for Lorde:

> *Being women together was not enough. We were different. Being gay-girls together was not enough. We were different. Being Black together was not enough. We were different. Being Black women together was not enough. We were different.* (1982, p. 226)

The permutations of race and sex construct this 'difference' – which offers new possibilities for connection, opposition and resistance:

> It was a while before we came to realize that our place was the very house of difference rather than the security of one particular difference. (And often, we were cowards in our learning.) It was years before we learned to use the strength that daily surviving can bring, years before we learned fear does not have to incapacitate, and that we could appreciate each other on terms not necessarily our own. (1982, p. 226)

The 'litany of difference' leading to 'the very house of difference' supplies another lacquered historical interpretation of the past, creating it new in the deployment of the meanings of role-playing.

The final chapter of *Zami* suggests a third pulling away from racism as presence in the celebration of a party of black lesbians together and a new black lesbian lover. A happy conflation of food and sex and sensual descriptions of the physical codes of black butches and femmes – touches, smells, textures – make up and break up the negative contours of role-playing, dissolving the powers of butch/femme codes to represent essentially white/black domination:

> the centerpiece of the whole table was a huge platter of succulent and thinly sliced roast beef, set into an underpan of cracked ice. Upon the beige platter, each slice of rare meat has been lovingly laid out and individually folded up into a vulval pattern, with a tiny dab of mayonnaise at the crucial apex. The

pink-brown folded meat around the pale cream-yellow dot formed suggestive
sculptures. (1982, p. 242)

Femmes wore their hair in tightly curled pageboy bobs, or piled high on their
heads in sculptured bunches of curls, or in feather cuts framing their faces.
That sweetly clean fragrance of beauty-parlor that hung over all Black
women's gatherings in the fifties was present here also, adding its identifiable
smell of hot comb and hair pomade to the other aromas in the room.
   Butches wore their hair cut shorter, in a D.A. shaped to a point in the back,
or a short pageboy, or sometimes in a tightly curled poodle that predated the
natural afro. But this was a rarity. (1982, p. 242)

Zami begins its ending with conflations of sex and 'exotic' . . . no,
tropical . . . no, actually, West Indian market food: cocoyams, and
cassava in dreams, red finger bananas, avocado. Kitty, Audre's lover, is
simultaneously mundanely particularised and mythologically elaborated.
Around Kitty Lorde rewrites black women's choices: from 'Tar Beach' in
conditions five to *Zami*, Lorde reinterprets the locations of black women's
struggles outside the places of their particular strength. In 'Tar Beach' she
writes:

[of Kitty's 7-year-old daughter living in Georgia with her grandmother] 'She's
going to be able to love anybody she wants to love,' Afrekete said, fiercely,
lighting a Lucky Strike. 'Same way she's going to be able to work any place
she damn well pleases. Her mama's going to see to that.'
   Once we talked about how black women had been committed *by choice* to
waging our campaigns in the enemies' strongholds, too much and too often,
and how our and our sisters' psychic lands had been decimated and scar-
wearied by those repeated battles and campaigns. (Lorde, 1979b, p. 44;
emphasis added)

In *Zami* this changes to:

Once we talked about how Black women had been committed *without choice* to
waging our campaigns in the enemies' strongholds, too much and too often,
and how our psychic landscapes had been plundered and wearied by those
repeated battles and campaigns. (Lorde, 1982, p. 250; emphasis added)

Kitty's offhand introduction of herself is drawn in *Zami* as ordinary and
specific:

'Audre . . . that's a nice name. What's it short for?'
   My damp arm hairs bristled in the Ruth Brown music, and the heat. I could
not stand anybody messing around with my name, not even with nicknames.

'Nothing. It's just Audre. What's Kitty short for?'
'Afrekete,' she said, snapping her fingers in time to the rhythm of it and giving a long laugh. 'That's me. The Black pussycat. . . .' (1982, p. 243)

But of course we already have some idea that Afrekete is portentously named: in the dedication of *Zami*:

To Helen, who made up the best adventures
To Blanche, with whom I lived many of them
To the hands of Afrekete
In the recognition of loving lies an answer to despair

at the end of the extended epigraph preceding *Zami*'s prologue

To the journeywomen pieces of myself.
Becoming.
Afrekete

(1982, p. 5)

and in the mingling of romantic/mythological/erotic imagery surrounding sexuality with Kitty, in dreams of gifts of food (1982, p. 249) and ecstatic invocations:

Afrekete Afrekete ride me to the crossroads where we shall sleep, coated in the woman's power. The sound of our bodies meeting is the prayer of all strangers and sisters, that the discarded evils, abandoned at all crossroads, will not follow us upon our journeys. (1982, p. 252)

And like the meaning of the word *Zami*, which we encounter only in the epilogue to the 'biomythography', so we learn the meaning of *Afrekete* as included in that epilogue in the litany of 'women who helped give me substance':

Ma-Liz, DeLois, Louise Briscoe, Aunt Anni, Linda, and Genevieve; MawuLisa, thunder, sky, sun, the great mother of us all; and Afrekete, her youngest daughter, the mischievous linguist, trickster, best-beloved, whom we must all become. (1982, p. 255)

Racism as deadly essence and presence is deconstructed in the deployment of the complexities of the meanings of role-playing, its presence and absence. The colour codes of butch-femme reveal and play with power, thus structuring desire; this play of power is transformed into the strangely awesome-dangerous 'very house of difference'. There, no unitary self resides but instead selves mapping the field of power and difference.

Finally, the deeply troubling/fascinating lesbian bar is left behind for the home of celebrating black lesbians who, in wonderful contradiction, suddenly and without explanation become both butch and femme. Their use of these codes becomes distinctively black in sensory description and seems unmarked by the destructive corrosions of 'the gaps between the mirrors and those turned-away eyes'. Rather than a bar scene in which the white lesbian community covers over black women's survival in separation, instead mundane and inspiring worlds are superimposed in Lorde's creation of Audre's new lover, Kitty. In these superimposed worlds, possibilities are not 'mythologised' as choices but made mundane in the recognitions of histories. At the same time distinctly black myths give meanings to a reconceived world of newly produced substance, where they 'shine through' the details of everyday life: making 'biomythography' – a writing down of our meanings of identity (for Lorde, as black woman, as poet, as lesbian) with the materials of our lives.

Making histories and sexual identities: 'the passing dreams of choice . . . at once before and after'

> For those of us who live at the shoreline/standing upon the constant edges of decision/crucial and alone/for those of us who cannot indulge/the passing dreams of choice/who love in doorways coming and going/in the hours between dawns/looking inward and outward/at once before and after. ('Litany for Survival', in Lorde, 1978, p. 31)

'Biomythography' might well name a variety of generic strategies in the construction of gay and lesbian identity in the USA. In his 1983 call for 'a new, more accurate theory of gay history' John D'Emilio remarks that current ideas about gay people's past are mythologies marked by particular political struggles and assumptions: 'in building a movement without a knowledge of our history, we instead invented a mythology. This mythical history drew on personal experience, which we read backward in time' (D'Emilio, 1983b, p. 101).[5]

While I too would like to see a more accurate and historically specific account of the gay 'past', I'm also interested in remarking on the resources and materials out of which all our histories are made, including D'Emilio's own fascinating work. As feminists, as gay people, we are accountable for our historical reinscriptions which are produced inside particular political moments, their 'accuracy' another dream of choice . . . looking inward and outward/at once before and after'. It is in this spirit that I would like to use Lorde's term for her autobiographical novel, 'biomythography', to refer to the histories (in the plural) of lesbian and gay pasts, as they all construct our momentary identities, our current 'us'. This use of biomythography also creates a continuum across Lorde's own distinctions between poetry and prose and across the 'letters' of literature and history.

The generic strategies of the biomythography of lesbian and gay history currently include historical monograph and book, polemical critique, film and video and slide show, oral history, review essay, introspective analysis, academic/polemical anthology, novel and poem and short story, and undoubtedly others as well.[6] My focus on the lesbian bar in the 1950s in Lorde's *Zami* is an example of a kind of examination of the resources and strategies out of which these biomythographies are produced and an example of how genres are 'made', here from the feminist political practices of lesbianism and anti-racism. I'm pulling out the lesbian bar in the 1950s as a site of production of a range of biomythographies, of which Lorde's *Zami* is exemplary.

The lesbian bar of the 1950s and the meanings of the codes of butch/ femme roles are used productively in the current controversies named as 'the politics of identity' and 'the politics of sexuality'. Allan Bérubé's and John D'Emilio's work defines gay identity, for lesbians and gay men, as 'a product of history' coming 'into existence in a specific historical era' (D'Emilio, 1983b, p. 101). That era is framed, on the one hand, by World War II and, on the other hand, by the McCarthy era. The lesbian bar figures prominently in this originary moment. I think it is no accident that Lorde's biomythographical construction of her identity as lesbian and poet, the story of *Zami*, looks to this originary era – where current gay histories powerfully make collective political and institutional identities. It is in this currently contested time/place where 'the passing dreams of choice' are mobilised that Lorde looks for the secrets of the making of her personal identity; the passing dreams of choice, where sexual identity is neither an existential decision nor biochemically/psychoanalytically prog-rammed, but instead produced in the fields of difference constructed individually *and* collectively.

Whitelisting in the McCarthy past: Rereadings through power-charged codes

Noticing 'whitelisting' at the origins, in the McCarthy past, reinscribes race as a significant feature in the intersections of sexuality, radical politics and class which provide the elements mobilised in current biomythographies of gay identity. Lorde's sensitivities and making of her own person require that so-called 'blacklisting' be permutated, its transformation becoming a new lens making and exposing contact with people and the world.

CONTACT LENSES

Lacking what they want to see
makes my eyes hungry
and eyes can feel
only pain.

Once I lived behind thick walls
of glass
and my eyes belonged
to a different ethic
timidly rubbing the edges
of whatever turned them on.
Seeing usually
was a matter of what was
in front of my eyes
matching what was
behind my brain.
Now my eyes have become
a part of me exposed
quick risky and open
to all the same dangers.

I see much
better now
and my eyes hurt.
             (Lorde, 1978, p. 94)

'Whitelisted' in *Zami* are the white 'single women of moderate means, mostly from California and New York', who make up 'the american colony in Cuernavaca'. Their economic circumstances map their class and educational resources, their sexual and political histories, as some:

> owned shares in the little tourist shops that lined the Plaza; others supplemented whatever income they had by working in those shops, or teaching and nursing a few days a week in Mexico City. Some of these women were divorced and living on alimony; others were nurses . . . who had served in the Lincoln Brigade and run into trouble with the american government because of it. . . . There were members of the red-baited Hollywood Ten and their families, whitelisted out of work in the movie industry, and eking out a living in less-expensive Mexico by editing and ghostwriting. There were victims of other McCarthyist purges, still going on in full swing. (Lorde, 1982, p. 159)

Lorde's witty permutation on 'blacklisting', like the reversal of a Necker cube, juxtaposes and exposes the power relation between marked and unmarked categories – here, 'black' and 'white'. Using the lens of 'whitelisting', she places in focus both the white agents enforcing political sanctions and the race-conscious membership of the progressive circles Lorde connects and disconnects with. The permeable edges of these circles, the source of persecution, the actual relation to the Communist Party, are still (protectively?) ambiguous in *Zami*. The phrase 'Communist Party' itself is used only once, only in recounting the terrorising Question: 'Are you or have you ever been a member of the Communist Party?' (1982, p. 149). In this context, 'whitelisting' also alludes to the intersections of multiple oppressions in the recognition of multiple identities.

Sexuality, class, politics are all complex threads in Lorde's biomythography and in the biomythography of gay identity (exemplified by D'Emilio's *Sexual Politics, Sexual Communities*, 1983). Pointing out 'whitelisting' deepens this history by its consistent inscription of race into the webs of power. Between New York and Mexico the shifting meanings of political affiliation and sexual preference are recentred. In 1953 Audre leaves New York, escaping from both 'emotional scrapes' and 'the deepening political gloom and red-baiting hysteria' (1982, p. 148) after working with other 'progressives' in the Committee to Free the Rosenbergs. There Lorde notices the play between race and sex:

> The Rosenbergs' struggle became synonymous for me with being able to live in this country at all, with being able to survive in hostile surroundings. But my feelings of connection with most of the people I met in progressive circles, were as tenuous as those I had with my co-workers at the Health Center. I could imagine these comrades, Black and white, among whom color and racial differences could be openly examined and talked about, nonetheless one day asking me accusingly, 'Are you or have you ever been a member of a homosexual relationship?' For them, being gay was 'bourgeois and reactionary', a reason for suspicion and shunning. Besides, it made you 'more susceptible to the FBI'. (Lorde, 1982, p. 149)

Similarly overdetermined elements of sexuality and politics are woven and rewoven in D'Emilio's complex biomythography of the contemporaneous Mattachine Society. First we learn of the political, cultural equations made by McCarthy conservatives *between* communism and homosexuality: a demonology in which both poison the minds and bodies of American youth, both are invisible and infiltrating, both mock morality and social values and finally effeminise American manhood (D'Emilio, 1983a, p. 49). Then we learn the secret 'true' history of the radical origins of the Mattachine Society, founded by individuals who were indeed CP members (1983a, p. 53). These first secret meetings occurred in 1950, the same year in which both the Internal Security Act was passed and the Senate reported on 'sexual perverts' in government – in the last, claiming homosexuals were more susceptible to the blackmail of Soviet agents (1983a, pp. 41–2).

But we also learn from this secret history that the two CP members, Henry Hay and Bob Hull, severed their party memberships in 1951. Hay had also reported his organising of homosexuals to the CP (1983a, p. 69). The CP had no interest in a homosexual-rights movement – indeed, no longer had tolerance for homosexuality in its ranks since the 1930s reversal under Stalin of Soviet policy on homosexuality (1983a, p. 59). So the gay 'demons' were unwanted in any political camp, scapegoated between McCarthy America and the American CP; compromised, on the one hand, as more 'susceptible to the FBI' and, on the other, as more susceptible to communist blackmail; equally caught between terrorising Questions of affiliation: 'Are you or have you ever been . . .?'

The 1953 electrocution of the Rosenbergs – which made 'the idea of Mexico' shine 'like a beacon' for Lorde (1982, p. 1487), an escape from hostile America – occurred on the east coast; on the west coast – still partially underground – the Mattachine Society reached its peak membership and attracted the corrosive attention of the red-baiting press (D'Emilio, 1983a, pp. 75–91). D'Emilio narrates the events of the west-coast public 'democratic' convention in which the newly elected gay leaders of Mattachine purged their own organisation of 'communist infiltration'. Notice the profound differences between 'radical origins' – D'Emilio's potent location – and these new leaders' cannibalising history of 'communist infiltration.'[7] D'Emilio points out that the women and men who joined Mattachine after 1954 knew nothing about early radical or CP connections; this information was withheld by Mattachine officers (1983a, p. 90). As the 'progressives' purged themselves of homosexual associations (Lorde, 1982, p. 148), so the homosexuals purged themselves of those 'seeking to overthrow or destroy any of [American] society's existing institutions, laws or mores', unrealistically imagining themselves as being able 'to be assimilated as constructive, valuable, and responsible citizens' (D'Emilio, 1983a, p. 84).[8]

D'Emilio's biomythography redraws the lesbian bar. Bar life in general stands for the possibilities of militant community and community and collective identity promised by the 'radical origins' of Mattachine. This vision of militant action and a political definition of gay identity formed the basis of the opening remarks made by the radical leaders of Mattachine at the 1953 founding convention in LA. But D'Emilio's history paints this vision as betrayed by gay people themselves, desperately longing for respectable membership in a patriotic America.[9] The lesbian version of this respectability is especially class-bound, according to D'Emilio. He historicises the butch/femme codes of the lesbian bar, and its place as a public expression of gay identity:

cross-dressing promised economic independence as well as allowing lesbian couples to live together under the guise of husband and wife.

After the 1920s, working-class lesbian life assumed a more public, undisguised expression that included as its central feature bars for gay women. As a subcultural institution, bars for lesbians appeared later than bars for male homosexuals. . . .

As the only clearly identifiable collective manifestation of lesbian existence, the bars filled a unique role in the evolution of a group consciousness among gay women. They alone brought lesbianism into the public sphere. (D'Emilio, 1983a, pp. 97–9)

When the Daughters of Bilitis (DOB) began to organise lesbians in 1955, the organisation's leaders offered it as an *alternative* to the bars. Butch/ femme roles were among the aspects of bar culture from which DOB wanted lesbians to be 'weaned' (D'Emilio's term 1983a, p. 106). 'Gay women "aren't barhoppers", one officer declared, "but people with steady jobs, most of them with good positions"' (D'Emilio, 1983a, p. 113). These class prejudices reflected not *lesbians* as a group but *DOB* as a group, made up of 'white-collar semi-professionals disenchanted with a bar subculture whose population included many women who labored in factories and appeared butch in dress and behavior. The Daughters looked askance at both bar life and the butch lesbian' (1983a, p. 106). DOB also enforced anti-butch dress codes.[10] D'Emilio suggests that these middle-class values were what kept DOB from becoming a successful location for lesbian community and political action.

I want to intertwine these kinds of complexities too with 'whitelisting', expanding its meaning to include the betrayals and survival skills which put oppressed people at odds with each other in their needs to survive and to align with points of power; the permutation, 'whitelisting', reminds us in this context *who really has power* when marked groups are caught in the webs of collusion, intended and unintended. Lorde emphasises that this activity of naming who has the power is both dangerous and essential.

The bewildering and collaborating dance of disassociation, the struggle to survive in spiralling circumstances of possible betrayals, creates the environment whose effects Lorde judges among the expatriates in Cuernavaca, the environment in which gay identity is a riddling object of gossip, and a secret of the experienced:

The women I met through Frieda were older and far more experienced than I. I learned later that they speculated at length in private as to whether or not I was gay, and whether or not I knew it. It never occurred to me that they were gay, or at least bisexual, themselves. I never suspected because a large part of their existence was devoted toward concealing the fact. These women pretended to be straight in a way they never would have pretended to be conservative. Their political courage was far greater than their sexual openness. To my provincially New York and naïve eyes, 'gay-girls' were just that – young, obvious, and definitely bohemian. Certainly not progressive, comfortable, matronly, and over forty, with swimming pools, dyed hair, and young second husbands. As far as I knew all the american women in the Plaza were straight, just emancipated.

Weeks later, I mentioned as much to Eudora on our way to the pyramids at Teotihuacan, and she almost laughed us off the road into a ditch. (Lorde, 1982, p. 160)

The joke that amuses Eudora so much, the network of codes that Audre misreads in Cuernavaca, maps out politics, age, regionalism, lifestyle, class, heterosexual privilege (which becomes visible at the intersection of these various codes; Lorde's oppositional judgements are reflected in the coolly evaluative nuance in paralleling 'political courage' and 'sexual openness'), and (unspoken) race.

The judgements shifting across time, revealed in the play of background/foreground that the dimension of time offers and Lorde's style of writing/rewriting persists in, expose their own inconsistencies. These elements are the traces of 'whitelisting' and its responses, responses easily liable to error and requiring constant reassessment.

Lorde's connection to and judgement of the 'gay-girl' bars *follows* her experiences in Mexico; the butch/femme rituals are matched alongside the whitelisted political codes of 'the progressives'.[11] Race, sex and politics offer backdrops for each other, for evaluation and judgement. In one scene (the gay bar) Lorde suggests that lesbians are the only black and white women talking to each other, dismissing discussion inside what she calls 'the empty rhetoric of patriotism and political movements' (1982, p. 225); while in another scene (among the New York left) she judges ('whitelists'?) 'these comrades, Black and white, among whom color and racial differences could be openly examined and talked about', yet who cannot be trusted one day not to confront her 'accusingly, "Are you or have you ever been a member of a homosexual relationship?"' (1982, p. 149). Lorde's inconsistent location of talk about race only foregrounds the highly charged interlacings of systems of power and the need to address oppositionally race, sex and politics, each in renewed and repositioned contexts.

Layers of meanings, layers of histories, layers of readings and re-readings through webs of power-charged codes mark biomythography. My series of superimposed histories here is intended to tease out these layers and, indeed, to add to them. My discussion, first of the gay-girls' bars and then of the collaborating codes of political identity, reverses Lorde's own sequences, while I also append to *Zami* D'Emilio's history of the construction of public gay identity in the McCarthy years. All of this interweaving is meant to elucidate those 'passing dreams of choice' – to show how the lesbian bar functions as a site of the production of sexual identities currently, and to demonstrate how it is that sexual identity is neither an 'existential decision' nor, as I said before, 'biochemically/ psychoanalytically programmed', but rather profoundly constructed in the meshings of individual and collective identities.

In my hands, the exploration of 'whitelisting' becomes a cautionary description of the judgements mobilised by the progressives and the gay-girl scene in *Zami* and the gay movement in D'Emilio. They also encode elements of debate today, particularly within the conversations on the politics of sexuality. I think it is important to read Rubin's 'The leather menace' (1981) as a critique of internalised homophobia within lesbian feminism, as an injunction that lesbians and gay men have political interests in common, something that 'lesbianism as feminism's magical sign' (King, 1986) denies.[1]

D'Emilio's biomythography tells a story of the formation of the social and cultural resources that were eventually mobilised in the 1970s by gay liberation and lesbian feminism. He suggests that the class prejudices of DOB, sufficient to prevent lesbians' organising in the 1950s and 1960s, were manipulatable by 1970s feminism, as lesbian feminists were re-cruited not from the lesbian bar 'but from the heterosexual world, with the women's liberation movement as a way station' (D'Emilio, 1983a, p. 237). The success of (a middle-class?) lesbian feminism overshadowed the earlier terms and strengths of a largely working-class gay women's identity formation in the 1950s (1983a, p. 240).

Audre Lorde's biomythography *Zami*, with its focus on the intersection of race and sexuality in the lesbian bar, does not at all reflect the same story as D'Emilio's history *Sexual Politics, Sexual Communities*, which is told at the intersection of class and political affiliation. None the less, *Zami*, with its lacquered histories – restricted, salvaged, dreaming of choice and its absence, even at times also 'whitelisting' the gay past – constructs lesbian

---

[1] Continuing this elucidation of historical reinscriptions of the lesbian, and exploring as 'biomyth-ographics' the events, texts, persons and interests that make up the conversations creating 'the politics of sexuality', my next article in this series of three connects deployments of power suggested by the term 'whitelisting' here and these issues of political accountability raised in the first (King, 1986). My current book project responds more specifically to the issues I raised at the beginning of this essay on the apparatus of literary production and the work of Audre Lorde, and will more directly address politicised publication sites and markets, literary consumption, and the ideological uses of poetry as well.

personal and political identity out of many of the same resources and materials. These resources, materials, and also political investments mark our current productions of gay identities. *Zami* manages too to exemplify what Chicana theorist Chela Sandoval calls 'oppositional consciousness'[12] – in the *rewritings themselves* of the meanings of the bar scene and in the transparent *processes* of rewriting which reveal the locations of the intersections of race, sexuality, language, culture, class, education, age and politics.

The value of this kind of process-bound political specificity I have learned about most clearly from Sandoval and Cherríe Moraga. I believe these two theorists describe especially convincingly the complexities of political identity, as they use creative and intellectual tools made within those overlapping feminist territories, 'the politics of identity' and 'the politics of sexuality'. Lorde belongs with these and other political workers, often women of colour, who are now powerfully reconstructing feminism.

Notes

1. This first and easiest reading can be contextualised by Susan Leigh Star's interview with Audre Lorde in *Against Sadomasochism* (Linden *et al.*, 1982, pp. 66–71). *Against Sadomasochism* is a polemical response to the notorious (and more risky) book *Coming to Power: Writings and graphics on lesbian s/m* (SAMOIS, 1981), which contains the influential essay by Gayle Rubin, 'The leather menace: comments on politics and s/m', critiquing lesbian sexual orthodoxies, suggesting the shared interests of lesbians and other 'perverts', and valorising lesbian s/m. Both *Coming to Power* and *Against Sadomasochism* pre-date and set the agendas for the Barnard conference (see pp. 53–4).
2. The significance of the stigmatised label Ky-Ky becomes clearer in this context: 'We were both part of the "freaky" bunch of lesbians who weren't into role-playing, and who the butches and femmes, Black and white, disparaged with the term Ky-Ky, or AC/DC. Ky-Ky was the same name that was used for gay-girls who slept with johns for money. Prostitutes' (Lorde, 1982, p. 178).
3. These three paragraphs appear in an earlier version of the final chapter of *Zami* (Chapter 31) in *conditions five: the black women's issue* (Lorde, 1979b, p. 34), as '"Tar Beach" from *Prosepiece*, part iii'. They do not appear in the version published in *Zami*. (They are related, however, to writing in *Zami* on pp. 221 and 206.) The contributor's notes to *conditions five* say: 'This piece is an excerpt from her [Lorde's] forthcoming fiction entitled *I've Been Standing On This Streetcorner A Hell of A Long Time!*' When *conditions five* was re-edited (by Barbara Smith) as *Home Girls: A Black feminist anthology* (Smith, 1983), *Zami* had already been released and, instead of the version that appeared in *conditions five*, Chapter 31 from *Zami* was substituted (and the contributor's notes were re-written).
4. However, she mentions her earlier desires to make love to others, not be made love to, which lover Eudora in Mexico challenges (Lorde, 1982, p. 169). Even so, many of

Lorde's sexual descriptions are of this love-making *to* another woman. Notice that Newton and Walton (1984, pp. 242–50) identify this 'behavior' as 'dominant', signalling the 'erotic role' of 'top'. Audre's own self-description can be mischievously reread with this terminology; in contrast, Lorde's descriptions are generally more subtle and complex than is allowed for by this simple top/bottom distinction.

5. The time periods and audiences for this essay are explained in D'Emilio's endnotes: 'This essay is a revised version of a lecture given before several audiences in 1979 and 1980.' The essay's audiences were 'the Baltimore Gay Alliance, the San Francisco Lesbian and Gay History Project, the organizers of Gay Awareness Week 1980 at San Jose State University of California at Irvine, and the coordinators of the Student Affairs Lectures at the University of California at Irvine.'

6. Examples are John D'Emilio's exciting book *Sexual Politics, Sexual Communities: The making of a homosexual minority in the United States, 1940–1970* (1983); Alice Echols's powerful polemics in 'The taming of the id: Feminist sexual politics, 1968–83' (1984); films like *The Word is Out*, videos such as *Before Stonewall*, and the slide show *Marching to a Different Drummer*, which Allan Bérubé says funded his research, for example, 'Marching to a different drummer: lesbian and gay GIs in World War II' (1981/1983). Oral histories contributing to a number of these efforts have been collected by, among others, the San Francisco Lesbian and Gay History Project. B. R. Rich's review essay in *Feminist Studies* (1986), Amber Hollibaugh's and Cherríe Moraga's 'What we're rolling around in bed with: Sexual silences in feminism' (1981/1983), and Esther Newton's and Shirley Walton's 'The misunderstanding: Toward a more precise sexual vocabulary' (1984) are examples of introspective analysis. The two anthologised (Snitow *et al.*, 1983; Vance, 1984) are both academic and polemical. Finally, Lorde and Moraga exemplify a proliferating literature in novel, poem and story on the histories of gay identity.

7. D'Emilio's narrative depends upon his interviews with convention participants and examination of their personal papers (see footnotes, 1983a, pp. 77–91).

8. Quoted by D'Emilio from the text of a pamphlet entitled 'Aims and principles', released by the Southern California Area Council of Mattachine; see D'Emilio (1983a, p. 84, footnote 28).

9. Like a tolerated membership in a patriotic military during the height of World War II? See Bérubé and D'Emilio (1984).

10. 'Barbara Gittings, who joined DOB in 1958, recalled an incident in which "a woman who had been living pretty much as a transvestite most of her life was persuaded, for the purpose of attending [a DOB convention], to don female garb, to deck herself out in as "feminine" a manner as she could, given that female clothes were totally alien to her. Everybody rejoiced over this as though some great victory had been accomplished – the "feminizing" of this woman' (D'Emilio, 1983b, p. 106; bracketed inclusion is D'Emilio's).

11. Lorde's description in *Zami* of her involvement in progressive politics and her trip to Mexico overlaps her description of the lesbian bar scene. A *Zami* chronology (which may or may not reflect Lorde's own chronology – remember this is 'biomythography') would suggest that Audre's close connection with progressive politics is first remarked when she moves in with an acquaintance, Rhea, in 1953, a bit before Audre visits Washington demonstrating in support of the Rosenbergs. The Rosenbergs were electrocuted in June 1953. The internal events of *Zami* suggests that Audre's visit to Mexico is in 1953. (Lorde's own vita are inconsistent about the dates here by a year: cf. entry in Shockley and Chandler [1973, p. 101] and entry in Evans [1984, p. 292]; *Zami*'s history and Lorde's history simply may not be rigidly parallel.) *Zami* history suggests that Audre returns to New York City on 4 July 1953, and becomes more involved in bar life (as

described earlier) during 1954. It is in 1955 that her room-mate Rhea leaves New York, after being denounced to the Communist Party for her association with a black lesbian. A chronology of the events described by D'Emilio (to which I have referred extensively) goes something like this: the Internal Security Act is passed by Congress in September 1950, and the Senate Report on 'sexual perverts' is copyrighted in 1950 too. In November 1950 the first secret meetings of Mattachine take place. By 1951 open meetings of study groups for Mattachine are occurring, and Hull and Hay sever their party connections. By 1953 the CP origins have become a real liability, subject of newspaper speculation, while Mattachine's membership peaks and an organisational convention is held in LA. There a new, anti-communist leadership is elected. So effective is the suppression of the radical origins of Mattachine that after 1954 those joining know nothing about it. In 1955 the women's organisation, the Daughters of Bilitis, is formed. Both Mattachine and DOB are firmly 'respectable' politically, and focus efforts on 'education' through the mediation of social science experts, offering their memberships as populations for scientific study.

12. Commenting and theorising on events at the NWSA's annual meetings in 1981, Chela Sandoval makes an argument for a political stance which she calls 'oppositional consciousness' (Sandoval, n.d.). See also Sandoval (1984).

Works Cited

Beck, Evelyn Torton, ed. (1982) *Nice Jewish Girls: A lesbian anthology*. Watertown, MA: Persephone. (Repr. Trumansburg, NY: Crossing Press, 1984.)

Bérubé, Allan (1983) 'Marching to a different drummer. Lesbian and gay GIs in World War II', in Snitow *et al.*, eds, (1983), pp. 88–99. (Originally published in *The Advocate*, 15 October 1981.)

Bérubé, Allan and John D'Emilio (1984) 'The military and lesbians during the McCarthy years.' *Signs*, **9**, pp. 759–75. (Repr. in Freeman *et al.* [1985], pp. 279–95.)

Bulkin, Elly, Barbara Smith and Minnie Bruce Pratt, eds (1984) *Yours in Struggle: Three feminist perspectives on anti-Semitism and racism*. New York: Long Haul.

Clausen, Jan (1982) *A Movement of Poets: Thoughts on poetry and feminism*. Brooklyn: Long Haul.

Connors, Debra (1985) 'Disability, sexism and the social order', in Susan E. Browne, Debra Connors and Nanci Stern, eds, *With the Power of Each Breath: A disabled women's anthology*. Pittsburgh, PA: Cleis, pp. 92–107.

D'Emilio, John (1983a) *Sexual Politics, Sexual Communities: The making of a homosexual minority in the United States, 1940–1970*. Chicago: University of Chicago Press.

D'Emilio, John (1983b) 'Capitalism and gay identity', in Snitow *et al.*, eds (1983), pp. 100–13.

Echols, Alice (1983a) 'Cultural feminism: Feminist capitalism and the anti-pornography movement.' *Social Text*, **3**, pp. 34–53.

Echols, Alice (1983b) 'The new feminism of yin and yang', in Snitow *et al.*, eds (1983), pp. 439–59.

Echols, Alice (1984) 'The taming of the id: Feminist sexual politics, 1968–83', in Vance, ed. (1984), pp. 50–72.

Evans, Mari, ed. (1984) *Black Women Writers*. Garden City, NY: Anchor/ Doubleday.

Freeman, Estelle B., Barbara C. Gelpi, Susan L. Johnson and Kathleen M. Weston, eds (1985) *The Lesbian Issue: Essays from SIGNS*. Chicago: University of Chicago Press.

Haraway, Donna J. (1985) 'Manifesto for cyborgs: Science, technology and socialist feminism in the 1980s.' *Socialist Review*, **80**, pp. 65–108. (Repr. *Australian Feminist Studies*, **4** [1987], pp. 1–42; to be repr. in Elizabeth Weed and Joan Scott, eds, *Feminism/Theory/Politics*. Pembroke Center for Research on Women, forthcoming.)

Hollibaugh, Amber and Cherríe Moraga (1983) 'What we're rolling around in bed with: Sexual silences in feminism', in Snitow *et al.*, eds (1983), pp. 394–405. (Originally published in *Heresies*, **12** [1981], 'The sex issue'.)

hooks, bell [Gloria Watkins] (1984) *Feminist theory: From margin to center*. Boston, MA: South End.

Irigaray, Luce (1977) *This Sex Which Is Not One*. Ithaca, NY: Cornell University Press.

Jaggar, Alison M. (1983) *Feminist Politics and Human Nature*. Sussex: Harvester; Totawa, NJ: Rowman.

Joseph, Gloria I. and Jill Lewis (1981) *Common Differences: Conflicts in black and white feminist perspectives*. Garden City, NY: Anchor/Doubleday.

King, Katie (1986) 'The situation of lesbianism as feminism's magical sign: Contests for meaning and the US women's movement, 1968–1972.' *Communication*, **9**, pp. 65–91. Special issue: 'Feminist critiques of popular culture', ed. Paula Treichler and Ellen Wartella.

King, Katie (1987) 'Canons without innocence: Academic practices and feminist practices making the poem in the work of Emily Dickinson and Audre Lorde.' Unpublished dissertation, University of California, Santa Cruz.

Linden, Robin Ruth, Darleen R. Pagano, Diana E. H. Russell and Susan Leigh Star, eds (1982) *Against Sadomasochism: A radical feminist analysis*. Palo Alto, CA: Frog in the Well Press.

Lorde, Audre (1973) *From a Land Where Other People Live*. Detroit, MI: Broadside.

Lorde, Audre (1977) 'Poetry is not a luxury.' *Chrysalis*, **3**, (Repr. in Lorde [1984], pp. 36–9.)

Lorde, Audre (1978) *The Black Unicorn*. New York: Norton.

Lorde, Audre (1979a) 'The master's tools will never dismantle the master's house.' Personal is Political Panel, The Second Sex Conference, New York, 29 September 1979. (Repr. in Moraga and Anzaldúa, eds [1981], pp. 98–101. Repr. in Lorde [1984], pp. 110–11.)

Lorde, Audre (1979b) '"Tar Beach" from *Prosepiece*, part iii.' *conditions five: The black women's issue* (Autumn).

Lorde, Audre (1982) *Zami: A new spelling of my name*. Watertown, MA: Persephone. (Repr. Trumansburg, NY: Crossing Press, 1983.)

Lorde, Audre (1984) *Sister Outsider*. Trumansburg, NY: Crossing Press.

Lorde, Audre (1986) *Our Dead Behind Us*. New York: Norton.

Moraga, Cherríe (1983) *Loving in the War Years: lo que nunca paso por sus labios*. Boston, MA: South End.

Moraga, Cherríe (1985) 'The rape scene, excerpt from "Giving Up the Ghost", a play in progress.' *Conditions*, **11/12**, pp. 110–16.

Moraga, Cherríe and Gloria Anzaldúa, eds (1981) *This Bridge Called My Back: Writings by radical women of color*. Watertown, MA: Persephone. (Repr. New York: Kitchen Table: Women of Color Press, 1984.)

Nestle, Joan (1984) 'The fem question', in Vance, ed. (1984), pp. 232–41.

Newton, Esther and Shirley Walton (1984) 'The misunderstanding: Toward a more precise sexual vocabulary', in Vance, ed. (1984), pp. 242–50.

Reagon, Bernice Johnson (1983) 'Coalition politics: Turning the century', in Smith , ed. (1983), pp. 356–68. (Originally spoken at the West Coast Women's Music Festival, Yosemite National Forest, California, 1981.)

Rich, Adrienne (1976) *Of Women Born: Motherhood as experience and institution*. New York: Norton.

Rich, Adrienne (1980) 'Compulsory heterosexuality and lesbian existence.' *Signs*, **5**, 4, pp. 631–60.

Rich, B. Ruby (1986) 'Feminism and sexuality in the 1980s.' *Feminist Studies*, **12**, pp. 525–61.

Rubin, Gayle (1981) 'The leather menace: Comments on politics and s/m', in SAMOIS (1981), pp. 192–225.

SAMOIS (1981) *Coming to Power: Writings and graphics on lesbian s/m*. Palo Alto, CA: Up Press.

Sandoval, Chela (n.d. [probably 1983]) 'Women respond to racism: A report on the National Women's Studies Association Conference, Storrs, Connecticut.' Occasional paper series: *The Struggle Within*. Oakland: Center for Third World Organizing [4228 Telegraph Avenue, Oakland, CA 94609].

Sandoval, Chela (1984) 'Comment on Krieger's "Lesbian identity and community: recent social science literature".' *Signs*, **9**, pp. 725–9. (Repr. in Freeman *et al.*, eds (1985), pp. 241–8.)

Shockley, Ann Allen and Sue P. Chandler, eds (1973) *Living Black American Authors*. New York: Bowker.

Smith, Barbara, ed. (1983) *Home Girls: A Black feminist anthology*. New York: Kitchen Table: Women of Color Press. (Originally published as *conditions five: The black women's issue*, 1979.)

Snitow, Ann, Christine Stansell and Sharon Thompson, eds (1983) *Powers of Desire: The politics of sexuality*. New York: Monthly Review Press/New Feminist Library.

Vance, Carole S., ed. (1984) *Pleasure and Danger: Exploring female sexuality*. Boston, MA: Routledge.

Weedon, Chris (1987) *Feminist Practice and Poststructuralist Theory*. New York: Blackwell.

Wittig, Monique (1981) 'One is not born a woman.' *Feminist Issues*, **1**, pp. 47–54.

AUDRE LORDE AND THE AFRICAN-AMERICAN TRADITION
When the Family is Not Enough

/Anna/Wilson/

The ordeal of recitation at the local church is a scene that recurs in contemporary African-American reconstructions of childhood. Two recent versions, when juxtaposed, suggest that encoded within the account of this ritual speech to the community lie intimations of how another tradition, that of African-American literature, is currently constructed, and of how writers are placed and place themselves within it. The first retelling is from an essay in Alice Walker's *In Search of Our Mothers' Gardens*:

> When I rise to give my speech I do so on a great wave of love and pride and expectation. People in the church stop rustling their crinolines. They seem to hold their breath. I can tell they admire my dress, but it's my spirit, bordering on sassiness (womanishness), they secretly applaud.
>
> 'That girl's a little *mess*,' they whisper to each other, pleased.
>
> Naturally I say my speech without stammer or pause, unlike those who stutter, stammer, or, worst of all, forget. . . . '[I]sn't she the *cutest* thing!' frequently floats my way. 'And got so much sense!' they gratefully add . . . for which thoughtful addition I thank them to this day. ('Beauty: When the other dancer is the self', pp. 385–6).

The second account is from Henry Louis Gates's article in the *New York Times*, 'Whose canon is it, anyway?':

> . . . the church . . . was packed – bulging and glistening with black people, eager to hear pieces, despite the fact that they had heard all of the pieces already, year after year, like bits and fragments of a repeated master text . . .
>
> And then the worst happened; I completely forgot the words of my piece. Standing there, pressed and starched, just as clean as I could be, in front of

just about everybody in our part of town, I could not for the life of me remember one word of that piece.

After standing there I don't know how long, struck dumb and captivated by all of those staring eyes, I heard a voice from near the back of the church proclaim, 'Jesus was a boy like me,/And like Him I want to be.'

And my mother, having arisen to find my voice, smoothed her dress and sat down again. The congregation's applause lasted as long as its laughter and I crawled back to my seat.

What this moment crystallizes for me is how much of my scholarly and critical work has been an attempt to learn how to speak in the strong, compelling cadences of my mother's voice. (*NYTBR*, 26 February 1989, p. 45)

Alice Walker's reminiscence is of an Edenic moment *before* she loses her sense of self and her capacity to voice that self: the scene in the church thus functions as the state of grace, of full consciousness of the self-in-community that Walker must struggle to recapture after a series of silences imposed upon her as she grows up. Gates, on the other hand, never has a voice to lose – first his mother ventriloquises his voice for him, then he declares his own mission as that of learning to speak, himself, in her 'compelling cadences'. What might it mean for how the African-American tradition is imagined that the writer-as-girl has a voice conceived as naturally as her own, while the writer-as-boy must reconstruct one, and that his mother's? Another difference one might notice here lies in the child's relation to its community: Gates's memory is of a community in which he fails and is forgiven; if the failure is painful, he is none the less able to recuperate it as an adult by an act of ventriloquism of his own – by claiming his right, capacity and duty to voice his mother's speech, neatly turning the tables and memorialising her at the same time. Walker's memory is of success, and of the approval that doing what is expected of one can bring. It feels good to be a good girl. The voice that Walker remembers as her originary one is saying what has been said before, and what the church mothers want to hear.

In a necessary act of reappropriation, African-American literature – a literature that has emerged from the experience of a people whose heritage and familial structures have been distorted and suppressed by slavery and white cultural imperialism – founds its tradition of cultural transmission in familial and generational metaphor. I think there are concerns that can legitimately be raised about the recuperation of the family as model of development and structure for African-American women writers, however, and I attempt this here through Audre Lorde who, by virtue of her self-identification as a Black lesbian, is always only with difficulty to be accommodated within a communal or literary structure that is conceived as based in the family.[1] I also want to suggest, as a parallel to this argument, that Lorde's position within the feminist canon bears examination, albeit for different reasons.

The question arises, of course, as to the fitness of the additional act of ventriloquism, as conducted by a white feminist, that this essay represents. Lorde's multifaceted liminality as a Black lesbian intersects somewhere with my own quite differently nuanced marginality as a white feminist who is also a lesbian – but this of itself hardly authorises my project. Lorde, in person and in her work, chooses to speak to white lesbians at times; at other times she refuses to do so. Her theoretical commitment to dialogue across differences, much quoted in both academic and activist circles, is combined with a various and complex practice of speech and silence towards a range of audiences, a practice that acknowledges that dialogue does not happen except between equals.[2] I animate her voice here, then, in the knowledge that the fiction of her speech that I create is my own, produced in service of dialogic purposes which will inevitably run at a tangent to Lorde's. But my use of Lorde raises other issues than whether or not we are in dialogue. I use my reading of her work to address two different audiences, audiences whose stances in relation to the work with which I am specifically concerned here, *Zami: a new spelling of my name*, have been divergent. As Valerie Smith has pointed out, African-American criticism has not on the whole felt the need to make what she calls totalising gestures whereby lesbian experience is included within an emerging African-American canon. In so far as African-American criticism has recognised lesbian writing, it has been as a subgenre of women's fiction – something that opens up the area of women's sexuality and enables appreciation of the bonds between heterosexual women – rather than as texts that emerge from a discrete area of experience or angle of vision. On the other hand – as the inclusion of two essays on Lorde in this volume neatly demonstrates – *Zami* is on the verge of canonisation within white feminist academia as the token Black lesbian voice.

For feminist academia Lorde is particularly effective as a token: since she is Black, lesbian and a mother, her work compactly represents that generally repressed matter towards which white feminists wish to make a gesture of inclusion – but since Lorde conveniently represents so much at once, she can be included without her presence threatening the overall balance of the white majority vision. As a token of particular identities, moreover, Lorde is included as one who speaks for the marginal, not for the mainstream. Paradoxically, in other words, Lorde occupies diametrically opposed positions in two literatures: in one her words are consumed for the light they can shed on the mainstream of Black female possibility; in the other her work stands alongside, but is not read as directly bearing upon, the mainstream white feminist consciousness. It is my project here to challenge both these ways of reading Lorde, to suggest that *Zami* produces a way of seeing that has significance as a commentary on how the Black community as a whole both lives and theorises itself, and that Lorde's textual practice also has the power to address not merely the problems of identity politics but also the issues of lesbian aesthetics.

When Gates suggests that the current task of the Black (male) critic is 'learning to speak in the voice of the black mother', he is seeking to move to the centre of the African-American tradition what Black women writers and critics have been doing for some time. I use Alice Walker as my example of this process of the creation of a tradition and its structure here, because her writing in general – and her description of her own sense of a literary tradition in particular – have been so influential. Walker describes being aware of her need of Zora Neale Hurston's work before she knew Hurston existed; it is Hurston who can authenticate both Walker's own work as a writer and the tales her mother tells about Black folklore, underpinning a literary and a familial tradition at once. Walker specifies the mission of the artist as recovery of female forebears: 'we must fearlessly pull out of ourselves and look at and identify with our lives the living creativity some of our great-grandmothers were not allowed to know' ('In search of our mothers' gardens', p. 237). The authentic art of the Black woman, then, produces not only her own voice but also that of her matrilineal line. Both continuity and individuality are celebrated in this account of a tradition of Black women's creativity, a seamless continuum that flows on underground unheeded but which, when tapped by Walker and her fellows, comes to brilliant gushing life, confirming and legitimating the new by the sameness of the old.

Such a sense of oneself as positioned within the arms of an embracing, if invisible, history assumes an unproblematic relation to the community in which one finds one's identity. While Walker neither ignores nor is unaffected by those elements of her historical moment which seek to silence her, she essentially lays claim to a community that always recognises her and in whom she always recognises herself. It is this tradition that Michael Awkward articulates in his recent study of African-American women writers, *Inspiriting Influences*. While Awkward agrees with Gates's suggestion of a 'signifying' relation between African-American men's texts and their precursors (one, that is, of competitive revision), he finds that African-American women 'seem to form a more harmonious system' (p. 4). As a comparative model for white women authors, Awkward employs the 'anxiety of authorship' version of literary history originally constructed to describe British nineteenth-century novelists by Gilbert and Gubar, one in which writing is produced as dissimulated rage by women artists oppressed and silenced by patriarchal culture. Less contentious than Black men, less embittered than white women, African-American women writers are constructing a tradition in which bonding, a 'quest for unity and community', is the governing quality.

A similar construction of the generational relationship is given by Deborah McDowell in her essay 'The changing same' on twentieth-century Black women writers, where the move away from a public readership to a private one, a shift from white to black audiences, is explicitly described by McDowell as not 'adversarial'; the contemporary women's texts are in 'dialogue', not competition, with their precursors, despite the distinct shift in political tactics which she identifies as occurring between generations. Again, Joanne Braxton's study of Black women's autobiography identifies the speaker of female autobiography as 'the outraged mother': the outrage will be memorialised and arrested by reiteration of the mother's speech – a process that depends on knowledge that is passed down through the female line. Her literary tradition hinges on a changeless model of transmission, on daughters' recapitulation of their mothers' words. These are only a few examples of what is a dominant critical trend: the celebration of an African-American women's tradition that is both familial and gloriously affirming.[3] In interrogating this account of a tradition, I want not only to raise the problem of exclusions from the fold but also to question the idea of the family, and what can be said within it, that such a tradition implies.

How is a Black lesbian to be accommodated within a tradition that is envisaged as generational? Must she – and can she – represent herself as part of this uncontentious stream? In defining *Zami* as 'a book about Lorde's reconciliation with her mother', Barbara Christian draws an automatic connection between such reconciliation and what she calls Lorde's 'attemp[t] to place her lesbianism within the context of black women's culture' ('No more buried lives', p. 199). In order to come within that context, Christian implies, one *must* reconcile with one's mother. While I would agree that Lorde intends to connect her sexuality to Black women's culture, it seems to me that *Zami* suggests something more difficult, something both more challenging for the Black community and more suggestive for African-American literature than reconciliation. Rather than the wayward child who returns to the acknowledged safety of her mother's terms of reference, Lorde suggests the necessity for both rejection and acceptance of her mother's truths:

> When the strongest words for what I have to offer come out of me sounding like words I remember from my mother's mouth, then I either have to reassess the meaning of everything I have to say now, or re-examine the worth of her old words. (*Zami*, p. 31)

By tracing the trajectory of Audre's search for identity in *Zami*, I hope to suggest what this doubled move of re-examination and reassessment might mean not just for the Black lesbian but for other African-American women writers.[4]

If re-entry into the Black family is likely to be problematic, one might wonder whether there is a lesbian literary family within which Lorde could figure. The lesbian literary tradition, however, is almost entirely white. While African-American lesbians have laid claim to historical continuity, and a 'lesbian theme' has recently been identified in the writing of contemporary African-American women, the literary model set out by Radclyffe Hall in *The Well of Loneliness* is still the mainstream, for all that is has been radically revised, and it is a model that focuses on expulsion rather than inclusion.[5] The tradition which the lesbian fashions or imagines cannot, by this definition, be a familial one: the term 'coming out' describes a movement away from the culture of one's birth and towards a re-cognition of one's identity within a different, non-generationally structured, group. A lesbian 'history' is thus always self-consciously a fiction, an imagined heritage. As a result of the necessity for departure from the culture of origin, the lesbian fictional journey has tended to be an individualistic one wherein identity-formation is envisaged in terms of the self-fashioning of the *Bildungsroman*. Journey's end – 'lesbian nation', as Bonnie Zimmerman has called it – is figured, however, not as return and accommodation to an existing social structure but rather as an entry into a new kind of social formation, one which is outside heterosexual society and history. The society into which the questing lesbian is absorbed reflects the needs of her new identity rather than her cultural origins. As the trajectory of this journey suggests, there are strong ahistorical and utopian elements in lesbian self-fashioning. The lesbian imagination is focused on the future, on 'what has never been'; while the past may be mined for mythicised foremothers, Amazons, Sapphos and rich Parisiennes, the lesbian's foreshortened history – her name itself a coinage that has no etymology going back beyond the pathologising of early-twentieth-century sexologists – requires that full identity and self-knowledge are always in some sense postponed into the future, into the utopia into which the fully fashioned lesbian would escape.

The Black lesbian literary tradition is one that has no natural existence; it can only intermittently be created. Lorde's search for precursors lacks the affirmatory tone so familiar from Walker, whose recoveries seem somehow to bring the dead to life. Lorde's lost precursors stay lost:

> I think a lot about Angelina Weld Grimké, a Black Lesbian poet of the Harlem Renaissance who is never identified as such . . .
>
> I often think of Angelina Weld Grimké dying alone in an apartment in New York City in 1958 while I was a young Black Lesbian struggling in isolation at Hunter College, and I think of what it could have meant in terms of sisterhood and survival for each one of us to have known of the other's existence: for me to have had her words and her wisdom, and for her to have known I needed them! It is so crucial for each one of us to know she is not alone. ('A burst of light', p. 73)

Unlike Walker, who literally uncovers the remains of the Hurston that she needs, Lorde could not imagine Weld Grimké into being: there is no basis on which she can 'know' she is there before she finds her, so that the finding could be not surprise but confirmation. In this absence of precursors, the knowledge of community must be created and re-created in fragile acts of repetition, rather than rediscovered.

In the absence of a Black tradition, then, Lorde's biomythography *Zami* initially constructs a lesbian existence that has needs and features in common with the lesbian myth produced by white Ango-American novelists. Her sexual coming out is described within a series of metaphors for recognition familiar from that tradition: making love is 'like coming home to a joy I was meant for' (*Zami*, p. 139); the act of lesbian sex is naturalised through being presented as a return to an original knowledge that the protagonist has temporarily forgotten: 'wherever I touched, felt right and completing, as if I had been born to make love to this woman, and was remembering her body rather than learning it deeply for the first time' (p. 139). This is a country of the body rather than of a people. Audre's community as a young lesbian in New York is defined by sexuality, and it is a community that attempts the utopian separation and newness of lesbian nation: 'We were reinventing the world together' (p. 209); 'we had no patterns to follow, except our own needs and our own unthought-out dreams' (p. 211). Yet membership in such a community is purchased at the price of non-recognition of Blackness; Lorde repeatedly describes Audre's 'invisibility' to the white lesbian community as Black; she is admitted only under the assumption of sameness. The lesbian community believes in itself as obliterating difference, 'that as lesbians, we were all outsiders and all equal in our outsiderhood. "We're all niggers," [Muriel, Audre's white lover] used to say' (p. 203). Yet in Lorde's analysis the lesbian community is not elsewhere but is rather a microcosm of the world outside, as her description of the lesbian bar the Bagatelle shows:

> The Rosenbergs had been executed, the transistor radio had been invented, and frontal lobotomy was the standard solution for persistent deviation . . .
> The society within the confines of the Bagatelle reflected the ripples and eddies of the larger society that had spawned it . . .
> The breakdown into the mommies and the daddies was an important part of lesbian relationships in the Bagatelle. . . . And you were never supposed to ask who was who, which is why there was such heavy emphasis upon correct garb. The well-dressed gay-girl was supposed to give you enough cues for you to know. (p. 221)

In the white model, the real world recedes before the lesbian community's power to redefine: one reclothed oneself in a new identity and a new way of relating. It is one of Orlando's freedom in Virgina Woolf's imaginary biography that s/he is able effortlessly to switch between costumes; her sexual fluidity is signalled by this flexibility, and in the same moment it indicates a crucial aspiration: the capacity both to switch between costumes and to cross-dress stands for freedom from gender imprisonment. George Sand said of her experience of cross-dressing, 'My clothes knew no fear.' But for Audre a rigidly stratified dress-code, each item signifying a particular class or role position, expresses not freedom of play but her imprisonment within a system of hierarchised differences. The 'uncharted territory' that she finds in trying to discover new ways of relating in 'a new world of women' is not just uncharted but inaccesible: there is no pathway for the Black lesbian that leads from the actual lesbian community, where class distinctions are precisely observed and race is unmentionable, to lesbian nation. It is from this experience that Lorde constructs the 'house of difference' that she finally articulates as 'our place'; it is a refusal of the aspiration to unity that lesbian nation encodes. The 'house of difference', then, is a movement away from otherworldliness. It accepts the inevitability of a material world where class, race, gender all continue to exist. It is, therefore, a step back towards acknowledging the necessity of reasserting ties of identity with the Black community.

Yet Audre has already moved away from her familial ties, for her means of survival is explicitly at odds with her mother's teaching: 'When I moved out of my mother's house . . . I began to fashion some different relationship to this country of our sojourn. I began to seek some more fruitful return than simple bitterness from this place of my mother's exile' (p. 104). Lorde's route to a sense of self that both acknowledges her mother and frees herself from her is encoded in the phrase 'this country of our sojourn'. 'Sojourn' is neither home nor exile; lexically it is located, perhaps, on the hyphen between 'African' and 'American'. Yet even this liminal position seems too absolute, for Lorde's sense of place is always multiple. In order to achieve 'sojourn', Audre must at once embrace and distance herself from her mother's concept of 'home'. The positionings of 'home' are themselves complex, both geographical and metaphysical at once: 'Once *home* was a far way off, a place I had never been to but knew well out of my mother's mouth'; here Grenada is that unknown and yet familiar other that exists to put the 'real' world of Harlem into relation, to rid it of inevitability and naturalness. Grenada renders Harlem 'bearable because it was not all . . . some temporary abode, never to be considered forever nor totally binding nor defining' (p. 13). This – her mother's – definition of 'home' is that of the exile who yearns for a definite but unrecoverable place and time, and it is a home that Audre must abandon if she is to live 'here'.

Yet Carriacou, the island of her mother's birth, becomes for Lorde a metaphor for her maternal heritage, one which is the more powerful for apparently being unmapped, 'a sweet place somewhere else which they had not managed to capture yet on paper, nor to throttle and bind up between the pages of a schoolbook' (p. 14). It is problematic, none the less, that Carriacou will be 'throttled' – its voice silenced – if it is charted, for if it remains *only* magical, a place of metaphor alone, then Audre's tenuous, multiplied sojourn will tend to become a simple opposition, the real world of New York and the mythic community of Carriacou. Audre finally finds Carriacou on a map, the *Atlas of the Encyclopaedia Britannica* which, Lorde writes, 'has always prided itself upon the accurate cartology of its colonies'. The reality of Carriacou as a mapped space indicates the inexorable colonisation of the world; but it also reinforces the need for Lorde to redescribe it, to give it a voice and significance that is not the strangled one of the former colony. In rejecting her mother's home, Audre is at the same time rescuing it for herself. She must rework the originary myth, putting it at a different relation with 'here' to construct, between the two, a new 'fruitful' country.

But sojourn is created not only through geography. Paradoxically but inevitably, Lorde constructs an identity as both Black and lesbian by thinking back through her mother. In the 1950s there was no sense of tradition for Black 'gay-girls': 'There were no mothers, no sisters, no heroes. We had to do it alone, like our sister Amazons, the riders on the loneliest outposts of the kingdom of Dahomey' (p. 176). Here the narrator imposes upon the loneliness of the young Black lesbian a retrospective connection to a mythicised African past that is not available in the present of the text. The analogy thus has literary but not experiential force, precisely because the Amazons were *not* accessible as heroes; it has power over the future rather than the past. What Lorde attempts in *Zami*, however, is a redescription of the experience of growing up as a Black lesbian without heroes and models in terms of rediscovery of a heritage and a tradition for protagonist as well as reader. Lorde's reconstruction can never amount to the celebratory rediscovery that Walker pronounces: although Audre re-cognises her mother as a 'Black dyke', this reclamation of her mother's strength is double-edged, for if Audre recognises the connection, her mother would not:

> I believe that there have always been Black dykes around – in the sense of powerful and women-oriented women – who would rather have died than use that name for themselves. And that includes my momma. (p. 15)

When Audre leaves her mother's house, then, it is in order to find a different relation between here and elsewhere; it is a journey that takes her, initially, away from the Black community: 'the land of Black people seemed very far away and hostile territory' (p. 177). It also takes her into a series of a relationships that, with one exception, are with white women. When the strands of what Lorde calls pieces of the 'real me' are finally woven back together, however, Audre reunites herself with the Black community and specifically with the Black community as family: she is able to move back into the lineage from which she has had to detach herself, the lineage that Walker has been able seamlessly to claim. Audre's return is through a mythicised relationship with the Black woman Kitty, who is also Afrekete, the goddess, 'the mischievous, linguist, trickster, best-beloved' (p. 255). The sex between the two women, which Lorde describes in loving detail, is not merely suffused with natural imagery, it is a specific Africanised naturalness, one of warm oceans and plantains and tropical fruit. Afrekete possesses the power to reintegrate Audre into the Harlem where those by whom she must be recognised live. When the two women go out after making love it is not, Lorde points out, into an African night that they descend:

> with cocopalms softly applauding and crickets keeping time with the pounding of a tar-laden, treacherous, beautiful sea. It was onto 113th Street that we descended after our meeting under the Midsummer Eve's Moon, but the mother and fathers smiled at us in greeting as we strolled down to Eighth Avenue, hand in hand. (p. 253)

Finally, then, Audre is re-established in the generational line, a child smiled upon in its choice of companion by the 'mothers and fathers' of

Harlem. That her return to the community is envisaged as a return to the family is reinforced by the reinscription of lesbianism in the closing lines of *Zami* as something that can, after all, be passed down the matrilineal line once Carriacou is recognised as a place of origin: 'There it is said that the desire to lie with other women is a drive from the mother's blood' (p. 256). The familial ties that Audre takes up again are to a community that has been refashioned: the return is not to the same place.

The return to the family is enabling partly because it is not, and can never be, absolute. It is only when Audre has achieved the sense of self that acknowledges both her mother's heritage and the need to refigure that legacy into a newly imagined culture that she can listen to the truths that come not only from her mother's mouth but also from the mouth of the woman whose place in the family is dubious, who says things that no one wants to hear. Audre's visits to Afrekete also enable a memory of her friend's stepmother, Ella:

> who shuffled about with an apron on and a broom outside the room where Gennie and I lay on the studio couch. She would be singing her non-stop tuneless little song over and over:
> Momma kilt me
> Poppa et me
> Po' lil' brudder
> suck ma bones . . .
> And now I think the goddess was speaking through Ella also, but Ella was too beaten down . . . to believe in her own mouth, and we . . . were too arrogant and childish . . . to see that our survival might very well lay [*sic*] in listening to the sweeping woman's tuneless song. (p. 251)

Gennie, Audre's first love, dies a child suicide, unable to articulate the truth of her father's abuse: she dies because she and Audre cannot hear the song which tells of violence within the family. The adult that Audre has become has the power to hear and speak both the good news of family as tradition and the bad news of family as site of abuse.

In suggesting that a familial and cultural tradition has to be reconceived before Audre can find a place of sojourn, I am contesting both heterosexual and lesbian interpretations of the structure of an African-American women's tradition. The Black lesbian critic Jewelle Gomez represents Lorde's writing as seamlessly coincident with her roots: '*Zami* takes place in the bosom of the Black community . . . it reveals how Black lesbians can and do maintain a connection to their culture and families in order to survive' ('A cultural legacy denied and discovered: Black lesbians in fiction by women', p. 119). Gomez's drive to inclusion prompts her to require of the Black lesbian writer a commitment to a tradition that is steeped in familial metaphor:

> The Black Lesbian must recreate our home, unadulterated, unsanitized, specific and not isolated from the generations that have nurtured us . . . so that we, who have been lost in the shadows of the past, can be revealed and appreciated for the powerful legacy that we bear. (p. 122)

While this presents itself as a call to truth-telling, it is in effect a call to the creation of a myth of Black lesbian origins that has only hope to sustain its vision of the family as suddenly without transformation, able to include those it has excluded. It seems to me that, as with the heterosexual female tradition with which Gomez here seeks to align lesbian writers, there is an element here of the necessary blindness that goes with a desire to accommodate oneself to preexisting structures. While nurturance and legacies need to be both recognised and fantasised where they do not exist, celebration cannot tell the whole story or, indeed, provide a substantial basis for – to remain with the metaphor – future generations.

As Deborah McDowell has pointed out in 'Reading family matters', the idea of the Black family is a nostalgic construction as much as it is a place of refuge; the reality is a site of exploitation as much as it is the locus for the preservation of culture. African-American women writers have consistently opened the family myth up for scrutiny, yet a tradition is now being constructed in which Black women novelists embody a harmonious familial relationship that has escaped both their Black brothers and their white female peers. Unlike white women, African-American women are good daughters and good girls. They don't argue with their mothers, they have 'dialogue'; they speak their mothers' words and they are good. Must a reassertion of female worth lead to a sentimental gloss being put on women's function in the family? If African-American women writers are to be corralled into a position in which the authenticity of their membership in a cultural tradition is to be assessed by means of the extent to which they say what their mothers before them have said, there will, I suggest, be some important things that are unsayable. In the public ritual space of church or text, is success to be achieved by repetition of the 'master text'? Should Gates really have remembered his piece, given that Jesus was not, after all, '"a boy like [him]"' in some important respects? And is his mother's speaking of these words, an act that requires a voice at a still greater distance from her own reality, to be uncomplicatedly celebrated?[6]

That Lorde herself reinvests in 'mothers and fathers', albeit as categories which she has comprehensively redefined, is in itself prob-lematic, suggesting a crucial lack of alternative conceptualisations through which to imagine community. Lorde's reinvented family is self-consciously denaturalised, however, and acquires the shiftiness of ventriloquised performance. The use of the familial as structuring metaphor for critical thought limits our capacity to theorise in important ways. Traditions are not, after all, families; and we may be able to think differently and usefully about how texts interact with each other if we can abstract ourselves occasionally from a way of thinking that marks certain relations as legitimate. To categorise literary conflict, for instance, in terms of filial acquiescence or rebellion – in terms, that is, of power recognised as natural or unnatural through its siting in the metaphoric family – encodes a myriad of unexamined assumptions about not only how texts work but how they should work. We should hesitate before we construct traditions in terms that unflinchingly re-create social structures in the same moment as they create meaning.

And thus I return to the ways of meaning that are currently being constructed within feminist criticism. With feminism's shift away from the political activism of the 1970s to the current institutionalisation within academia have come two cultural phenomena: a shift in those texts which are seen as relevant to feminist concerns, and the beginnings of a narrative whereby this shift itself is explained and the lesbian novels written since the beginning of the second wave of the women's movement are placed in their historical context.[7] The form of this narrative has been influenced by its authorship: the telling of history has passed into academic rather than activist hands, and the slant towards a particular kind of text that this brings has been furthered by the pressures brought to bear on feminist academics by their need to maintain institutional position – to write about, for instance, texts which score highly in other academic value systems. An early example of the position that produces this sort of history is Catharine Stimpson's account of the lesbian novel, where the novel's awareness of itself as a deviant form, which makes authorial (or stylistic) neutrality impossible, is taken as a mark of literary unsophistication; while Stimpson is tolerant of the political necessities that produce positive self-assertion (*Rubyfruit Jungle*) or gloomy self-justification (*The Well of Loneliness*), she longs for something more like what modernism has done for other novel-ists who are not lesbians. Broadly speaking, the history of the lesbian novel as told in academia is of a progression from the necessary crudities of the early years, when believe was strong and identity new and to be celebrated at all costs, through a period of doubt when the only safety was the privacy of the essential self, to a contemporary period of play and experimentation wherein self, identity and narrative are all put into question in search of a subversion that is textually rather than socially located.

An example of a historical reading of the first two stages of the process is Yvonne Klein's account of changes between the form of lesbian nation that seems plausible in novels of the 1970s and in those of the 1980s, the latter replacing the external 'world elsewhere' of the first wave of novels of development, where lesbian nation is concrete, if marginal, with a privatised, interior sense of community. Lacking the optimism of the 1970s, the protagonists of the 1980s reach a nation which, according to Klein, has no 'literal extension in a political or social reality'. In both these two stages, the search for identity is paramount; what is at stake is the construction of an oppositional community, whether public or private, and the criterion for evaluating these novels will tend to be the 'reality' of the experience depicted. Thus Barbara Smith's survey of literature about Black lesbians prizes *Zami* above all other representations she examines, on the grounds that Lorde achieves both 'verisimilitude' and 'authenticity' – conveying, roughly, both the events of Black lesbian life *and* what it feels like to live it.

The third stage in the lesbian novel's progress depends in the first instance upon readings of theory rather than of fiction; for the patriarchal social structures which the 1970s novels sought to escape are substituted the patriarchal structures of narrative form, the escape from which is now seen as necessary to lesbian expression. If narrative exists to reproduce culture – and specifically gender difference – as we know it, only a refusal of its impulse, this theory goes, will do.[8] The exit from this impasse is figured by Marilyn Farwell, searching for a way of reintroducing the possibility of desire between women into language, as 'trangressive sameness'. Female desire, the quality that narrative is ignorant of, can be conceptualised only as independent of a categorisation system that is grounded in distinction through difference. Where boundaries blur – where, instead of trying to redefine difference, confusion begins – this is where Farwell locates 'lesbian narrative space'. A similar conclusion is reached in Penelope Engelbrecht's search for 'a metaphysic of lesbian-(ism)': constructing a theory of lesbian subjectivity that posits a similarity between subject and 'Other/self'. Engelbrecht finds this aesthetic inscribed in 'fluid' works – in other words, those 'more radical postmodern lesbian texts' in which 'the Subject need not occupy a static "position"'. What this might mean for the lesbian novel, or even for lesbian consciousness, is suggested by Farwell's location of the site of boundary confusion back where it used to be, at moments of intimacy between 'lover/beloved'. Although Engelbrecht sees the postmodern lesbian Subject's 'self-Naming' and 'self-empowerment' as acts which both create and are part of 'collective (lesbian) empowerment', the mechanism and social setting for this process are both somewhat unclear, given the very specifically textual construction of the subjectivity that she envisages. The escape from narrative seems to require a retreat from the material world: in abandoning the impurity of narrative's reiteration of the old games, politics too seems likely to be abandoned for the transgressive samenesses and confusing boundaries of the bedroom. Lesbian nation has thus shifted from its original place of mythic expectation shared by a community to a private construction, to, finally, a place of space that is present only textually, in the shifting samenesses of a postmodern text.

The consequences of this history impinge on texts as well as their readers. It is an inevitable consequence of constructing a history (a genre in which narrative has yet to be abandoned) that certain events, objects or modes of being thus become part of the past. Novels become relics of the necessities of their historical moments, only the present being granted the power to speak forward from its immediate context into the future. *Zami* has been admitted into the feminist canon as a novel that encodes a denied identity; for example, it serves the function of making vivid a Black lesbian's position in the world to students in my and some of my colleagues' Women's Studies classes. However, as an example of an early stage of development, a step in the history of the lesbian novel, *Zami*'s strength becomes its limitation: its power to exemplify the struggle to find a self, and a way of living that self, in the available world, becomes also the reason why it cannot speak beyond its moment – into, for instance, the new pessimism of postfeminism. For how can the verisimilitude that Smith celebrates be relevant to an assault on narrative structure? *Zami* is also among the texts considered by Klein as exemplary of those novels of the 1980s which seek solace in private myth-making for social absence. Yet, as I have been concerned to detail above, Lorde's project in *Zami* centrally involves the assertion of the insufficiency of any form of withdrawal from 'political or social reality'. Sojourn, as Audre seeks it, is a liminal state that draws its liveableness precisely from inhabiting both social reality and social possibility, mythic fantasy and the reality of the quotidian. Klein's analysis, as with any history, is a means to impose order. In this case, her redescription of *Zami* as a narrative of retreat serves a specific critical function: it clears a path for the orthodoxy of the moment, confining the novel within the bounds of a now outmoded strategy.

Yet Lorde's text resists this commodification as historical curiosity, despite the fact that its incipient canonicity might seem to render such a position inevitable. For Lorde can be seen to anticipate, even as her textual strategies challenge, the white lesbian aesthetic of the moment. Lorde's text surely operates both as the story of a search for identity and – in its meticulous rendition of the wilful blindness of the lesbian community to its own complicity with the world it professed to reject – as a rewriting of that 1970s utopianism which claimed the possibility of an identity un-sullied by external cultural influence. But Lorde's textual complexity also invites a reading of Audre's search as as much a subversion of the politics of identity as it is a successful grasping of 'the real me'. Audre's final repositioning within an accepting community depends, as I have shown, not on a rediscovery of Black lesbian origins but on a reimagination of them, one that is self-consciously fictive, laying claim not to the natural or essential but to the revision of these terms to provide a constructed – and therefore always at once endangered and negotiable – ground for being. On the one hand Lorde asserts that there is a difficult safety, finally, for the outsider, only in the visibility of differences, differences that require categories, distinctions and the identification of the self as participating in those categories. It seems that there is an identity to find. But this is crucially complicated by Lorde's refusal to settle on any particular difference, for within the 'house of difference' aspects of identity are always in relation each other in a pattern that is constantly shifting. Even visibility, the supposedly essential creator of difference, is reconstrued as sameness: thus it is in Mexico that Audre finally finds – and loses – herself, for in Mexico she is *seen* because she is *the same colour* as everybody else.

Lorde's challenge to current aesthetic inquiry lies in her assertion of an abiding connection between individual and social identity. This is how she is able to maintain a connection between political subversion and textual subversion, a link that in contemporary discussions of a lesbian aesthetic seems to have become an abyss. Unlike that of the postmodern lesbian Subject, Audre's identity is never established only by the transgressions of the bedroom: it is from the bedroom that Audre and Kitty emerge, and it is from this 'lesbian narrative space' that Audre goes out to refigure the Black family of Harlem as including her; but the reconstruction that happens in the street is as crucial as that conducted in the mythic bed.

Notes

1. My usage in this essay varies between 'African-American', which I adopt when discussing African-American literature in general because it is currently the preferred term of those who write it or about it, and 'Black', which I use when discussing Lorde in particular, since she has made clear her commitment to this latter term.

2. I am indebted to Zofia Burr's paper 'Dedicated form: Audre Lorde's poetics of address' for clarifying for me the consistent distinction in Lorde's work between the ideal of dialogue across any 'difference' and the practice that operates in recognition of inequities that may render speech across those differences non-dialogic.

3. The traditional construction has not been without its non-participants. Hazel Carby, in *Reconstructing Womanhood: The emergence of the Afro-American woman novelist*, has questioned whether it is useful or possible to speak of a tradition of African-American women's literature at all, given the white frame of both form and audience into which Carby sees these writers as having to insert themselves. Hortense Spillers's use of 'discontinuities' as the term to describe the pattern of formal change in African-American women's novels in 'Cross-currents, discontinuities: Black women's fiction' seems also to be an attempt to avoid the suggestion of a direct line of literary heritage. But only Michele Wallace, to my knowledge, in 'Variations on negation and the heresy of black feminist creativity', has specifically suggested that succeeding generations of African-American women may not always want to say what their mothers have said before them – or that, indeed, previous generations of the silenced may be misrepresented by those who purport to speak on their behalf.

4. In order to preserve the fictive distance that Lorde seems to intend, I use 'Audre' here for the protagonist and 'Lorde' for the narrator/writer of *Zami*.

5. Diane Bogus, in her article 'The "Queen B" figure in Black literature', traces a tradition of Black 'women-loving women' that, she claims, has been ignored both by mainstream culture and by contemporary Black lesbians; implied, however, in Bogus's argument is the suggestion that the term 'lesbian' is inappropriate to Black women's experience, representing a separatist and androphobic impulse appropriate only to white women's culture. Barbara Christian examines the 'lesbian theme' in 'Trajectories of self-definition: Placing contemporary Afro-American fiction'; her focus is rather on the community as a whole than on the position of lesbians within it.

6. Michele Wallace makes a similar point about the problems of an identification with Jesus in 'Negative images: Towards a Black feminist cultural criticism', in the course of an attack on Gates's and the canon-formers' appropriation of Black women's voices.

7. Elaine Showalter, responding to criticism of her article 'Feminist criticism in the wilderness', contests the 'fall into academia' reading of the institutionalisation of feminism on the grounds that academia *is* activism. I feel that there is a material difference in the kinds of trouble that can be made by those without allegiance to academia, even if feminist academics by definition struggle and by definition feel themselves to be outsiders.

8. The 'suspicion of narrative' theory is cogently expressed and theoretically founded by Teresa de Lauretis in her essay 'Desire in narrative'. De Lauretis's analysis of narrative structures suggests that 'a story requires sadism': narrative at its most fundamental level, that is, requires and reproduces an active male protagonist who moves across, through or over a passive female ground: he transforms, she is that which is transformed; or at best, she – figured here as 'heroine' rather than the always female-gendered ground, site of the male quest – is the reward for his labours. She does not desire, except to be desired. While de Lauretis assumes a heterosexual model for narrative in arriving at the position that narrative codifies sexual differences, Marilyn Farwell has pointed out that the insertion of a female would-be subject into the male position allows only that the female hero take on male desire: a gender-specific dualism is retained. In this reading, then, the vicelike grip of narrative relentlessly reconstitutes difference.

Works Cited

Awkward, Michael (1989) *Inspiriting Influences: Tradition revision and Afro-American women's novels*. New York: Columbia University Press.

Bogus, Diane A. (1990) 'The "Queen B" figure in Black literature', in Karla Jay and Joanne Glasgow, eds, *Lesbian Texts and Contents: Radical revisions*. New York: New York University Press, pp. 275–90.

Braxton, Joanne M. (1989) *Black Women Writing Autobiography*. Philadelphia: Temple University Press.

Brown, Rita Mae (1973) *Rubyfruit Jungle*. Plainfield, VT: Daughters, Inc.

Burr, Zofia (1991) 'Dedicated form: Andre Lorde's poetics of address'. Paper given at American Women Writers of Color Conference, Ocean City, Maryland, 28–30 May.

Carby, Hazel V. (1987) *Reconstructing Womanhood: The emergence of the Afro-American woman novelist*. New York: Oxford University Press.

Christian, Barbara (1985a) 'No more buried lives: The theme of lesbianism in Audre Lorde's *Zami*, Gloria Naylor's *Women of Brewster Place*, Ntozake Shange's *Sassafras, Cypress and Indigo* and Alice Walker's *The Color Purple*', in Barbara Christian, *Black Feminist Criticism*. New York: Pergamon Press, pp. 187–204.

Christian, Barbara (1985b) 'Trajectories of self-definition: Placing contemporary Afro-American women's fiction', in *Black Feminist Criticism*, pp. 171–86.

de Lauretis, Teresa (1984) 'Desire in narrative', in de Lauretis, ed., *Alice Doesn't: Feminism, semiotics, cinema*, Bloomington: Indiana University Press, pp. 103–57.

Engelbrecht, Penelope J. (1990) '"Lifting belly is a language": The postmodern lesbian subject'. *Feminist Studies*, **16**, 1, pp. 85–115.

Farwell, Marilyn (1990) 'Heterosexual plots & lesbian subtexts: Towards a theory of lesbian narrative space', in Karla Jay and Joanne Glasgow, eds, *Lesbian Texts and Contexts*, pp. 91–103.

Gates, Henry Louis Jr (1989) 'Whose canon is it, anyway?' *New York Times Book Review*, 26 February, pp. 1, 44–5.

Gilbert, Sandra M. and Susan Gubar (1979) *The Madwoman in the Attic*. New Haven, CT: Yale University Press.

Gomez, Jewelle (1983) 'A cultural legacy denied & discovered: Black lesbians in fiction by women', in Barbara Smith, ed., *Home Girls: a Black feminist anthology*. New York: Kitchen Table Press, pp. 110–23.

Hall, Radclyffe (1982) *The Well of Loneliness* [1928]. London: Virago.

Klein, Yvonne M. (1990) 'Myth and community in recent lesbian autobiographical fiction', in Karla Jay and Joanne Glasgow, eds, *Lesbian Texts and Contexts*, p. 330–8.

Lorde, Audre (1982) *Zami. A new spelling of my name*. Watertown, MA: Persephone.

Lorde, Audre (1988) 'A burst of light: Living with cancer', in *A Burst of Light*. Ithaca, NY: Firebrand Books, pp. 49–134.

McDowell, Deborah E. (1987) '"The changing same": Generational connections and Black women novelists'. *New Literary History*, **18**, 2, pp. 281–302.

McDowell, Deborah E. (1989) 'Reading family matters', in Cheryl A. Wall, ed., *Changing Our Own Words*. New Brunswick: Rutgers University Press, pp. 75–97.

Showalter, Elaine (1982) 'Reply to Carolyn J. Allen', in Elizabeth Abel, ed., *Writing and Sexual Difference*. Sussex: Harvester Press, pp. 304–7.

Smith, Barbara (1990) 'The truth that never hurts: Black lesbians in fiction in the 1980s', in Joanne M. Braxton and Andrée Nicola McLaughlin, eds, *Wild Women in the Whirlwind: Afra-American culture and the contemporary literary renaissance*. New Brunswick: Rutgers University Press, pp. 213–45.

Smith, Valerie (1987) *Self-Discovery and Authority in Afro-American Narrative*. Cambridge, MA: Harvard University Press.

Spillers, Hortense (1985) 'Cross-currents, discontinuities: Black women's fiction', in Marjorie Pryse & Hortense Spillers eds, *Conjuring: Black Women, Fiction & Literary Tradition*. Bloomington: Indiana University Press.

Stimpson, Catharine (1981) 'Zero degree deviancy: The lesbian novel in English'. *Critical Inquiry*, **8**, 2, pp. 363–79.

Walker, Alice (1984) 'Beauty: When the other dancer is the self', 'In search of our mother's gardens', 'Looking for Zora' and 'Zora Neale Hurston: A cautionary tale and a partisan view', in *In Search of Our Mothers' Gardens* [1983] London: The Women's Press.

Wallace, Michele (1990a) 'Negative images: Towards a Black feminist cultural criticism', in Wallace, *Invisibility Blues: From Pop to Theory*. London: Verso, pp. 241–55.

Wallace, Michele (1990b) 'Variations on negation and the heresy of Black feminist creativity', in *Invisibility Blues*, pp. 213–40.

Woolf, Virginia (1977) *Orlando* [1928]. London: Grafton Books.

Zimmerman, Bonnie (1990) *The Safe Sea of Women: Lesbian fiction 1969–1989*. Boston, MA: Beacon Press.

THE GREYHOUND BUS STATION IN THE EVOLUTION OF LESBIAN POPULAR CULTURE

/Angela/Weir/and/Elizabeth/Wilson/

Lesbian pulp or semiotext?

For one of us, lesbian romantic fiction was brought by a returning lover, straight from San Francisco: a mythical, romantic place with many names – 'Bay Area', 'Berkeley', 'North Beach', the 'Hungry I', 'Fisherman's Wharf', a place where lesbian and gay culture was supremely *Other* than what it was in London in the early 1960s. How should we respond to these luridly packaged paperbacks? They seemed to partake of the forbidden in every sense. Cheap thrills. To read one was on a par with eating a box of chocolates or gorging on a copy of *Vogue*: it was a question of unadulterated pleasure, unmodified by any pretensions to literary value or aesthetic importance. To lose oneself in these narratives was to participate more fully in a total lesbian alternative world than was ever possible by means of forays to the Gateways Club in the King's Road, or drag pubs on the Isle of Dogs. In this fantasy world work, home – and, indeed, everything about 'everyday life' – were subordinated to the fierce dictates of sexual desire. They were daydreams made palpable, and much more intensely lesbian than life could ever be. But they were also cheap fiction, with pictures of 'scantily clad' women on the front and banner headlines: 'I am a Woman . . . in love with a woman: must society reject me?'

These same novels have been reborn in the 1980s as seminal texts of lesbian feminism. Now that we are thoroughly schooled in the idea of the 'text' as opposed to 'great literature', reading *anything* can become not only permissible but part of a seriously academic piece of deconstructive analysis, and the novels of Ann Bannon, Valerie Taylor and other writers have been, as it were, transformed by a new and more consciously literary reading. *Then* they were something forbidden not only by the wider society, but by one's own (sixties) standards of what was artistically worthy and important; *now* they have become prime sites for an excavation of lesbian culture. Actually, to reread them is to be made aware that they are much better written than one had remembered; they are not 'pulp fiction', although they are written in a popular style. So deeply ingrained, however, were prejudices about 'high art' and 'low culture' in that now distant period that Ann Bannon and the rest were automatically consigned to the category of libidinised trash.

Above all, though, there was something inherently exotic and unlikely in the very existence of mass-audience books written by, for and about lesbians. How could this possibly be? In one way it was a foretaste of the way in which the United States became the land of the avant-garde, of pop art and radicalism, in the 1960s, a mecca for all those who wished to be at the cutting edge of the political aesthetic (the King's Road and Swinging London notwithstanding). This was, perhaps, especially true for lesbians and gays – *there* Warhol's avant-garde, for example, was deeply homosexual; *there* existed a lesbian and gay culture far in advance of Britain, where gay male culture was still ridden with class distinctions and the lesbian world was a relatively tentative one. At the same time one approached these pulp novels initially with a sort of suspicion, fearful that the stories might be only about the inauthenticity of deviant loves, about evil obsession or, at best, tragedy.

Amazingly, they were not. What most of the lesbian protagonists in these novels do face is the tension of being pulled between the romantic, yet inevitably ghettoised world of lesbianism – 'life in the shadows' – and the suffocating conventions of suburban marriage. In some of the novels marriage and heterosexuality win out in the end, but this is seldom because the heroine has 'matured' into normality; more often because the desire for emotional security is so great. Paula Christian's *The Other Side of Desire* (1965) ends with the heroine's recognition that she will not stop feeling sexual attraction towards other women, but that heterosexual marriage offers stability and affirmation:

> She could hold hands with him in public; she could not worry about anything she did because it was natural and acceptable to all onlookers. How much simpler, how more reassuring than a homosexual relationship.[1]

Frances, the heroine of Valerie Taylor's *Return to Lesbos* (1963), by contrast *does* eventually leave her husband, her marriage, and her stifling, small-town existence. In fact, this contrast between an authentic and challenging lesbian love and the inauthenticity and alienation of mainstream American life in the 1950s is something that must immediately strike readers in the 1990s as paradoxical and intriguing. Given that our stereotype of the fifties is of seamless repression and conservatism, how could these novels ever have been produced in such a time?

The fifties: a kitsch dystopia

As a period (not necessarily absolutely confined to the decade itself), the fifties has become a contemporary myth comprised of mixed horror and nostalgia. On the one hand we have been inundated with fifties pastiche – from Levi jeans advertisements to films, from sharp haircuts to dark-red lipstick, from pop graphics to golden oldies. The world that is thus re-created is deeply romantic – sexuality is hedged about with prohibitions, passions both personal and political are hidden, secret, threatening. A wonderful style exists to express this, a combination of Paris Left Bank and Greenwich Village, Jean Gabin and Audrey Hepburn, outlawry and bohemianism to set against the uptight heterosexuality of tight-waisted fashions inspired by Christian Dior. On the other hand we re-create the period of the Cold War, the nuclear threat, McCarthyism, spies, treason, fear, while according to our feminist folk myth, all women were pushed back into the home, all gays were persecuted; there was no chink of radical light at the end of the tunnel.[2]

The stereotype of seamless conservatism and conformity fails to capture another side to the fifties, or at least to the late fifties and early sixties, when these novels were written. Indeed, it is instructive to contrast them with *The Price of Salt* by Claire Morgan, written in 1953 (and reissued in 1990 as *Carol* by Patricia Highsmith). In *The Price of Salt* the atmosphere of paranoia and isolation is overpowering, and although this may be partly to do with Highsmith's especially bleak and menacing world-view, it surely has something to do with the *early* (as opposed to the late) fifties as well. Yet even in the early 1950s radical political and artistic communities kept dissent alive, and in the late fifties open political radicalism was growing in the United States as well as Britain, with civil-rights activities in the South, and the beginnings of opposition to McCarthy's House Unamerican Activities Committee. By 1960 also, the pioneering lesbian and gay organisations One, Daughters of Bilitis and the Mattachine Society were well established as civil-rights organisations campaigning for recognition.[3]

Salvatore Licata argues that the World War II years opened up the possibility of gay relationships and also an embryonic gay community in large cities in the United States, where women and men in the armed services could congregate away from home when on leave. The publication of the Kinsey Report, *Sexual Behaviour in the Human Male*, in 1948 was also crucial, Licata suggests. It revealed that as many as 37 per cent of American men had had at least one homosexual experience, and this led to a heightened awareness of homosexuality. Although McCarthyism and the 'Red Scare' – which, among other things, associated communism with homosexuality – were also at their height, even this resulted in more discussion and in the beginnings of indignant protest from a growing 'gay community'.[4] The period 1953 to 1960, according to Licata, was one of 'consolidated growth' for the recently formed gay and lesbian organisations. If, therefore, we start from a position that sees the 1950s as a period of unmitigated repression, we shall never understand what these novels represent, or will have at best a flawed understanding of their social context. That said, neither should we underestimate the difficulties attendant upon being lesbian or gay and 'out' in the 1950s; a recent study of lesbians in Buffalo, New York, reveals that they had to be prepared to defend themselves physically against attacks:

> Although confrontation with the straight world was a constant during this period [1940–60], its nature changed over time. In the forties, women braved ridicule and verbal abuse, but rarely physical conflict. . . . In the fifties, with the increased visibility of the established gay community, the concomitant postwar rigidification of sex roles, and the political repression of the McCarthy era, the street dyke emerged. She was a full time 'queer', who frequented the bars even on week nights and was ready at any time to fight for her space and dignity. Many . . . [are] both aware and proud that their fighting contributed to a safer, more comfortable environment for lesbians today.[5]

Economic as well as social change, and above all the growth of consumerism, also marked the period. The mass publishing market was expanding. In 1957 the Supreme Court, in its Roth decision, attempted a new and less restrictive definition of 'obscenity', which had the effect of relaxing the censorship of sexual material.[6] As a result, 'dime novels' – fiction in which a major element was sex, and destined for a male readership – poured from the presses. Lesbian eroticism could be included in these 'steamy' romances; in fact the lesbian novels were among the most popular – in 1957 Reed Marr's *Women Without Men* was in the top ten list of paperback bestsellers in the whole of the American publishing industry.[7]

Cheap paperbacks found a huge audience because, apart from anything else, they were sold not just in bookshops but in drugstores, supermarkets and railway kiosks. This is where the Greyhound Bus Station becomes significant. Women as well as men were becoming more mobile in the postwar United States. The ideology of the family might hold sway, but women, especially young women, were leaving home for the Big City, and a life (they hoped) of independence and (sexual) emancipation. Ann Bannon's heroine, Laura, comes to New York from the Midwest (admittedly Chicago); Frances in *Return to Lesbos* goes back to Chicago from her Illinois small town. In *Three Women* by March Hastings (1958) Paula's journey is only from a tenement on the Lower Eastside to the bohemian freedom of Greenwich Village, but the emotional distance travelled is just as great.

From suburb to Bohemia

Absolutely central to these novels is 'the problem that has no name'. After Paula has slept with her boyfriend for the first time, she feels far from ecstatic:

> But it wasn't what she and Phil had done together that made her anxious. It was the insistent thought that soon she would have a husband, then children, and the routine of life would be carved out for her, leaving her nothing she could do to change it.
> . . . Suddenly it had become important to discover who she – Paula Temple – really was. Her life, her individual self, seemed terribly precious now.[8]

In an interesting way, therefore, these novels are by no means marginal, as one might expect; on the contrary, they address one of the central social problems of the United States in the early postwar period: conformity versus 'self-expression' – individualism. The 1950s were indeed a politically conservative period, but also one of intense cultural and social contestation.

The issue of conformity as opposed to individualism was a general, not simply a women's question. In fact, initially it was not usually posed as a problem for women at all. In postwar American sociology the rush to the suburbs and the growth of the big corporation were blamed for the Man in the Grey Flannel Suit, the Organisation Man, the Lonely Crowd.[9] In much of the writing on both the suburbs and the metropolis there is an implicit or direct contrast with the pioneering spirit of rugged individualism. The small town, it is suggested, is at the heart of 'the American

Way'. Both the anomie and anonymity of the great city *and* the consumerist nightmare of the suburb are equally destructive of the frontier spirit which fostered individuality, yet paradoxically drew everyone into a cohesive and democratic community. Democracy, community *and* individualism all seemed to be vanishing during the Eisenhower years.

Betty Friedan's *The Feminine Mystique*, published in 1963, thus came out of a more general sociological critique of suburban life, but it was also a scathing denunciation of American womanhood's traditional role. The housewives Friedan interviewed are the same ones that Valerie Taylor's Frances meets when she moves to the small town: 'Women spilled out to meet them. . . . The Young Married ones, thirtyish, in capri pants that showed their backyard tans'.[10] Frances empathises with them: 'For a moment she shared and understood the concern of women for position, a leaky umbrella in a rainy world'. But their concerns are confined to bridge club, painting class and shopping trips to Chicago; soon she feels compelled to assert that she is different. When one of them suggests: '"This would be a good house to do in Victorian. There's even a bay window in the dining room. Victorian's very good now,"' Frances inwardly grits her teeth and then says, 'a little shrilly, "I'm afraid I like Contemporary"'.[11]

The contrast of aesthetic styles gestures economically to two opposed worlds. Male sociologists who criticised suburbia may have – at least in some cases – longed for a return to the certainties of Frontier days, but there was a radical and distinctly metropolitan alternative: Bohemia – and 'contemporary' style is a coded reference to this world, with its coffee bars and Italian chairs, its modern jazz and Beat poets. Edmund White, in *The Beautiful Room Is Empty* (1983), has recalled the importance of the Chicago bohemian subculture in providing a venue in which gays could meet, or even just exist.[12] The lesbian novels of the fifties testify just how important this was. Frances meets the woman who will become her lover in a second-hand bookshop run by a gay man. Ann Bannon's Laura discovers the vibrant alternative world of Greenwich Village, which is for artists and eccentrics as well as for lesbians and gay men.

This, of course, was part of the very situation that some of the critics of large cities dreaded. They raged against the anonymity and loneliness of huge cities such as New York, but this very anonymity made gay life possible. In theory at least, you could shed your past, your family, the expectations of small-town society; and, especially if you were a woman, you could become a person in your own right. It is true that the risks of poverty and failure were greater for women too, and this is interestingly highlighted in a novel from the immediate postwar period, *Death of a Doll*, by Hilda Lawrence (1947).[13] *Death of a Doll*, a murder mystery, is not part of the 'lesbian canon', but the villainess is a lesbian (unhinged), and the story is set in a New York City boarding hostel for single women. The hostel is run by a lesbian couple, who try to create a comfortable environment for their little community of women, although this is depicted as infantilised and suffocating. The young women who live there are tied to unrewarding, routine jobs as clerical workers or salesgirls in department stores. This novel is homophobic, yet its suggestion that the alternative to suburban conformity for many young women who sought their fortunes in the big city was merely a different kind of disappointment and greater economic insecurity must be taken seriously. Many women in the early postwar period were caught between two equally unattractive choices: poverty and spinsterhood on the one hand, suburban marriage on the other. While, therefore, it would be wrong to play down the profoundly sexual importance of the fifties lesbian novels, sexual choices are inextricably linked in this literature to the lack of economic independence for women at that time. Lesbianism stands as a metaphor for personal autonomy and, openly or implicitly, heterosexuality is posed as inauthentic for women, precisely because it involves financial dependence.

For March Hasting's Paula and Ann Bannon's Beth, if not for Laura or Taylor's Frances, sex with men is not distasteful in itself, and may on the contrary be desired; what is intolerable is the baggage that comes with it, the sense of all other possibilities being closed off for ever. Marriage for women is quite definitely an *alternative* to self-fulfilment in terms of a career or even just personal autonomy. In Ann Bannon's *Journey to a Woman* (1960) Beth, who is married, cries out to her husband, '"I want to *know* myself . . . I don't even know who I am. Or what I am."' Her husband's response, however, is unequivocal: '"You're my *wife*!", he said sharply, as if that were the argument to end them all.'[14] Paula's fiancé's biggest ambition is to run a paint store, but Paula wants to be a painter, and finds a woman lover who really is an artist.

(In acknowledging the adolescent aspect of Paula's voyage of self-discovery and love for the older woman, Byrne, March Hastings implicitly admits the possibility that love between women may be flawed, and underlines this by giving Byrne another, long-standing relationship with Greta, a crazy neurotic. Yet while appearing thus to concede ground to the Freudians who were dismissing all homosexual love as immature in the fifties, March Hastings uses her plot to show us that Greta was driven mad by social repression and the need for secrecy. The adolescent affair of the two girls is innocent and beautiful to them, so much so that Byrne naively tells her mother about it. The predictable result is that not only are they separated, but Greta is coerced into a loveless marriage, which drives her to drink and destroys her life.)

So these novels articulate the general aspirations of those – not lesbians only – who journeyed to the city, or to a city's Bohemia, in search of 'something more', a world of success as opposed to a working-class or lower-middle-class life of drudgery and sameness, a world of adventure as opposed to the tedious safety of bourgeois marriage. And although the myth of Bohemia is easily romanticised, bohemian circles were rather more democratic than small-town life had ever been – above all for women, since the social order in small-town America had always been explicitly patriarchal. For the lesbian heroine of the fifties, by contrast, the Greenwich Village world of bars and cafés is one in which barriers of class are lowered: middle-class Laura and working-class Beebo can meet, and their mutual passion transcends the social restrictions of life in the mainstream. Bohemia was no utopia, but at least it provided a more accepting ambience than mainstream society.

The problem *with* a name

Most lesbian feminist discussion of the fifties lesbian novels has concentrated on their engagement with the Freudianism which 'saturated' the United States at the time when they were written. Popularised – indeed vulgarised – psychoanalytic ideas were constantly in play to police and pathologise all those who deviated from the heterosexual and marital norm. As Diane Hamer and Suzanna Walters have shown, the result is an ambiguity, especially in Ann Bannon's work. At certain points Ann Bannon appears to accept the psychoanalytic view that lesbianism (and male homosexuality) result from childhood trauma, and especially that lesbians are 'made' by fathers. Laura's father was driven by half-suppressed incestuous desire for her; Beebo's father brought her up like a boy on their farm. In Ann Bannon's series of novels, the only positive male character is Jack Mann, a homosexual. As Diane Hamer says, Jack 'is a comic-tragic figure whose references to his "analyst", and his pet-name for Laura – "Mother" – "in honour of my Oedipus complex" provide the most constant reminders of this pseudo-Freudian culture.'[15]

The fact is that lesbians and gay men, like the pop psychiatrists, sociologists and journalists, were preoccupied with *why* homosexuality existed. Since that time, the reaction against pathologisation and the 'medical model', together with the Gay Liberation emphasis on homo-eroticism as choice, have moved us away from this preoccupation with origins. Feminist and radical gay insistence on gender as a social construct rather than as 'natural' has gained wider, although by no means complete, acceptance. Ironically, one result of this in the late 1980s, in Britain at least, was that in some quarters the homophobes returned once more to the concept of same-sex love as *sinful* – a choice, yes, but one that is abhorrent and should be stopped. It is of course still true that vulgar Freudianism was deeply repressive, and tended to increase the low self-esteem and stigmatisation of lesbians and gay men. Yet there was a more progressive side to this search for understanding, flawed as it was. From the standpoint of the 1950s, the substitution by liberals of 'understanding' for 'punishment' was not wholly reactionary. Whilst not wishing for one moment to advocate a return to the treatment model for the 1990s, its use in the 1950s needs to be understood as contradictory, rather than monolithically oppressive.

Our emphasis on the social context of fifties lesbian fiction is also an emphasis on the more radical aspects of fifties culture in general. This does not mean that we ignore the extent to which 'lesbian pulp' is determined and limited by the period in which it was written, simply that we view that period as more ambiguous and in some ways more radical than the feminist (and, indeed, general) myth of the fifties would allow. In Hollywood film, for example, as much as in these novels, there was contestation between heterosexual stereotypes (Marilyn Monroe, John Wayne, and – laughably – Rock Hudson) and an alternative model of sexual masculinity, the outlaw or rebel portrayed by Montgomery Clift, Marlon Brando and James Dean, all of whom were bisexual.[16] Doris Day worked through the contradictions of romance versus career in a number of her films – and in *Annie Get Your Gun* the attempt to 'be feminine' became overtly hysterical, although this film was made as early as 1950. Later on in the fifties *Funny Face* (1957), while poking fun at Existentialism and Beatnik Greenwich Village, also laughed at the absurdity of the *Vogue* cult of femininity. In this film Audrey Hepburn plays the part of the Village intellectual who becomes a fashion model against her will, and Hepburn had already established herself as an alternative 'Left Bank' model of the bohemian 'gamine' – the boyish girl with hair cropped short in the much-copied 'urchin cut'.

From aristocratic to popular

A further important and interesting feature of fifties lesbian novels is that they are more radical than the lesbian novels of the 1920s and 1930s, decades we think of as much more socially and politically radical than the 1950s. There is a sharp break between the lesbian romances of the 1950s and the more literary productions of the years between 1900 and 1940.

Renée Vivien and Radclyffe Hall had created, in different ways, a format for the lesbian novel. It was essentially aristocratic, and its frame of reference, particularly in Renée Vivien's case, was classical Greece and Sappho.[17] (This ambience echoed that of another semi-erotic novel about lesbians, *Les Chansons de Bilitis* (1894) by a male writer, Pierre Louys.) Both this and Renée Vivien's work were influenced by the Decadence – ideas of 'art for art's sake', and the cultivation of sensation in literature. Renée Vivien, Radclyffe Hall and their friends were mostly upper-class women of independent means, almost the only women who *could* lead an independent lesbian existence before and immediately after World War I. Radclyffe Hall's stereotype of the 'invert' has been frequently discussed by feminists in recent years,[18] and – most famously in *The Well of Loneliness* – she represented lesbians as scarred (literally in the case of Stephen, her hero(ine)) by their inborn 'difference' (for difference read defect).

It is easy to mock the aristocratic lesbians of the 1900s – as Colette did in *The Pure and the Impure* (1932).[19] Colette lived in a lesbian relationship with the Marquise de Belbœuf, known as 'Missy', for eight years, yet Shari Benstock suggests that she was uneasy with the polarities of masculinity and femininity represented by cross-dressing, and 'actually desired a female community in which femininity, of the culturally composed sort, is reinforced and where all that is male . . . has been exorcised'. Shari Benstock is equally uneasy with cross-dressing, and in her study of lesbianism in Paris both before and after World War I, *Women of the Left Bank*, she strongly condemns it:

> Female cross-dressing was not only a mark of aristocracy, it was sister to the dandyism of the period and shared, ironically, in the misogyny that supported the dandy's burlesque of the female. Female cross-dressing was indeed the mark of self-contempt. . . . Cross-dressing served as a public announcement of a commitment to lesbian relationships, but it registered this commitment in a code that specifically denied an allegiance to womanhood as societally defined (e.g. the feminine). . . . Although cross-dressing was an antisocial act that called attention to societal definitions of female homosexuals as 'inverts' and 'perverts', it nonetheless was not a sign of liberation from heterosexual norms or patriarchal domination. Cross-dressing reinforced the power of such constraints. Cross-dressing, moreover, did not acknowledge women's oppression – indeed just the opposite.[20]

This appears to us as a moral judgement coming from the cultural feminism of the 1970s, and is not really borne out by all the author's material. To denounce cross-dressing so unequivocally as inauthentic is to come close to applying inappropriate retrospective political assumptions, and is strange in a cultural historian whose work is so painstaking and detailed.

Homophobic caricatures abounded in the literature of the 1920s and

1930s. Lesbians were likely to be portrayed as men *manquées*: Evelyn Waugh made Mrs Melrose Ape, a lesbian evangelist, one of the significant characters in his *Vile Bodies* (1930); much later, Anthony Powell retrospectively mocked bohemian lesbians of the twenties and thirties in *Casanova's Chinese Restaurant* (1960):

> 'Poor old Hopkins,' Norah said. . . . 'Such a pity she goes round looking and talking like the most boring kind of man. Her flat might be the bar of a golf club.'
> . . . However, things had been very different some years before. Then, Hopkins had thrilled Norah and Eleanor with her eye-glass and her dinner-jacket and her barrack-room phrases.[21]

In the lesbian novels of the period written *by* lesbians, the 'mannish' lesbian 'invert' also appears, most notoriously in Radclyffe Hall and her heroine Stephen Gordon. Yet in some ways *The Well of Loneliness* is rather old-fashioned – it reads stylistically, for example, as an Edwardian middlebrow novel – and in some other novels the lesbian appeared, by contrast, as an androgynous figure. Gale Wilhelm's *We Too Are Drifting*, published in 1935, not only features the 'new' androgynous heroine, but is much more modernist in style.

The main character in this novel is Jan Morale, an artist. Jan is divinely good-looking in a boyish way – in fact her great friend, the sculptor Kletkin, uses her as a model for his statue of 'Hermaphrodite': '"Look, Jan! Hermaphroditus! You're lying on your belly looking down into the pool."'[22] In the Greek legend, of course, it was Narcissus who gazed at himself in a pool – and Gale Wilhelm dwells on the ambivalent beauty of her heroine in a narcissistic way, rather as Radclyffe Hall does in *The Well of Loneliness*. Narcissism may seem too harsh and pejorative a word, but we would defend its use because in both books an insistence on the ambivalent beauty of the figures with whom the authors clearly identify, coupled with deep pessimism, suggests self-pity, which is one form of self-regard. The 'feminine' partners they desire are palely drawn by comparison. The focus of attention is the tragic, noble invert:

> Her throat came strong and dark out of the robe and her face was narrow and dark and hollowed out under the cheek bones and the chin was strong. It was a strong face but it was blank as a mask. Her eyes were dark gray and you could look a long way into them, they had a marvelous depth and when she looked at you, you imagined she was seeing twice as much as anybody else did. She was thirty years old but she looked like a boy half that age until she looked at you.[23]

In Gale Wilhelm's short, allusive novel, Jan's corrosive despair is in part caused by her ill-luck in falling in love with a young woman who is basically straight, or at least unable to resist the pull of mainstream conventions; and she is pursued by a married woman with whom she has had an affair, but whom she no longer loves or even desires. The text implies that society's oppression is real, and that lesbian love is too fragile to withstand the iron laws of mainstream society. But Jan's life is yet more tragic than such a reality would explain: Kletkin, her only real friend and source of moral support, is killed in a riding accident, and her brother has been hanged for an unspecified crime. Oppression has become overdetermined, and internalised as self-hatred and consequently self-absorption.

Unlike the 'dime novels' of the fifties – and this is a significant distinction – these two novels were sold as literary productions; in no way were they intended for a 'popular' audience. *We Too Are Drifting* was published by Random House and favourably reviewed in 'quality' newspapers and periodicals.[24] The heroines of both it and *The Well of Loneliness* seek and find affirmation only through the identity of 'Artist'. This identity, however, has different connotations from those it achieves in the popular novels of the 1950s. For Radclyffe Hall and Gale Wilhelm the artistic identity is solitary, individualistic and almost religious, and operates in a world of privilege – part upper-class Bohemia, part simply upper-class. In this construction, isolation is the dominant condition of being an artist; there is little notion of the collective identity and social acceptance of 1950s Bohemia. On the contrary, Radclyffe Hall depicts the Paris *demi-monde* of the 1920s as a species of hell, peopled by freaks.

From invert to butch

What remains constant is the centrality of the lesbian and her search for identity. There continues to be a search for the 'truth' of her being, yet she and her identity have subtly changed by the time we reach the postwar period. Radclyffe Hall's Stephen and Gale Wilhelm's Jan experience love as poisoned at the source because while they are not 'real men', they can love only 'real women': in other words, they desire feminine women – and to be feminine is to be ultimately heterosexual. Their love is therefore doomed to tragedy. Also – in strong contrast to the feminine heroines of the 1950s, Laura, Frances and Paula – the women Jan and Stephen love are essentially passive. The nearest Radclyffe Hall ever gets to permitting Stephen's feminine lover to express desire is in the following passage:

Stephen was . . . grooming her hair with a couple of brushes that had been dipped in water. The water had darkened her hair in patches, but had deepened the wide wave above her forehead. Seeing Mary in the glass she did not turn round, but just smiled for a moment at their two reflections. Mary sat down in an armchair and watched her, noticing the strong, thin, line of her thighs, noticing too the curve of her breasts – slight and compact, of a certain beauty. She had taken off her jacket and looked very tall in her soft silk shirt and her skirt of dark serge.[25]

But it is Stephen's narcissistic 'look' that dominates and defines the scene.[26]

In the post-World War II lesbian subculture as described by Ann Bannon, female desire is not only explicit and acknowledged, it is active and strong. Laura fantasises about:

the big ones, the butches, who acted like men and expected to be treated as such. They were the ones who excited Laura the most, when it came right down to it. Women, women – she loved them all, especially the big girls with the firm strides and the cigarettes in their mouths.[27]

Diane Hamer suggests that in Bannon's novels the butch lesbian stands not for an imitation of manhood but for a distinct *lesbian* sexuality, a point borne out by Joan Nestle's well-known retrospective account,[28] and this active sexual desire and expression is experienced by all the lesbians in Ann Bannon's novels. Her 'butch' heroine, Beebo, not only desires women but is herself desired by them. Their gaze is as searching and imperious as hers:

For the first time in her life she was proud of her size, proud of her strength, even proud of her oddly boyish face. She could see interest, even admiration on the faces of many of the girls. She was not used to that kind of reaction in people, and it exhilarated her.[29]

The reciprocity of passion between two women, even when they are strongly cast in butch and femme roles, is equally evident in Randy Salem's *Chris* (1959).[30] Chris is one of the butchest of women and, unlike Beebo, she is powerful, independent and successful in the wider world of work, being a well-known conchologist, marine biologist and swimmer – in fact, during the course of the narrative she risks her life deep-sea diving for a rare shell. Like Jan in *We Too Are Drifting*, Chris has become enmeshed in destructive self-hatred, which is threatening her ability to work. In her case, however, it is not because of the inescapable tragedy of being a lesbian that her life has gone wrong, but because she has got involved with the wrong woman: Dizz.

Perhaps the most interesting aspect of this particular novel is the way in which it represents femme behaviour. Dizz is frigid. She won't let Chris make love to her, she flirts with men, she is neurotic, bored and empty-headed, yet content to let Chris support her financially. Then Chris meets Carol. Carol desires her, seduces her, pursues her. Also, she works in the marine biology field herself, so she can be an understanding companion as well as a passionate lover. In other words, she is everything that Dizz is not. Yet Chris cannot shake herself free of her 'sick obsession' with Dizz, and the plot revolves in part around the conflict generated by the triangle. Finally Carol, the active femme, ditches Chris, convinced that she will never leave Dizz. The ending of the novel is left to some extent open, and there is a hint that Carol might just settle for a man. Her significance as a character, however, is entirely lesbian: unlike Chris, she knows what she wants; unlike Dizz, she is happy with her sexuality; like Ann Bannon's Laura, she loves Chris for being butch, but she loves her as a woman. Poised between the contrasted figures of the 'true' and 'false' femme, Chris is by implication criticised for the very characteristics which are posed by Radclyffe Hall and Gale Wilhelm as inherent to the lesbian's lot. It is Jan's *destiny* to love the ultimately unresponsive Victoria, just as it is Stephen's to be God's tragic mistake, but it is Chris's error and weakness to cling to Dizz and to refuse the 'rich, constructive, satisfying life' she could have had with Carol.

The significance of Dizz as a frigid femme can, of course, be read in more than one way. At a crucial moment in the narrative she sleeps with a man, but the experience only disgusts her: '"Men are just like lesbians, only worse,"' she complains. '"I let him kiss me and all he wanted was to get my pants off."'[31] This appears to express a general frustration that many women may have felt at the norms of sexual relations in the 1950s, rather than a specifically lesbian problem. Alternatively – or as well – we might read the characterisation of Dizz as an attack on femme roles generally, although this seems less likely, given the positive way in which Carol is portrayed.

Chris is closer to the prewar novels than to Ann Bannon's fictions in one respect: the novel is not set squarely in the lesbian/gay subculture (although Chris goes to bars to pick up women, it is implied that this is sordid) and the nature of her work makes Chris an isolated, although 'special' figure – something of a star – who relates mainly to men. Like Stephen Gordon, she is wounded (she sustains an injury while diving), and the sense of the butch lesbian as a wounded figure is certainly not absent from the novels of the 1950s.

Suzanna Walters has suggested that Veda in Ann Bannon's *Journey to a Woman* is scarred because of her inability to confront her lesbianism, whereas Stephen Gordon's scar was the inevitable mark of her deviancy.[32] Yet the wound also suggests, in a more general sense, the vulnerability of the apparently impervious butch. Chris is presented as wonderfully good-looking and as more attractive to women than men are. (There are not one but two episodes in the novel when men lose out in competition with her for a woman.) Nevertheless, like Ann Bannon's Beebo Brinker, she is caught to some extent in the ambivalence of her role and time, and her vulnerability to wound and injury may possibly represent an ambivalence from within the lesbian community itself towards her woman's body, or towards the desire it generates.

In the 1930s Djuna Barnes, like Gale Wilhelm a modernist writer – and one whose work has been far more highly praised – suggested that the 'invert' represented the romantic impossible object of desire:

> What is this love we have for the invert, boy or girl? It was they who were spoken of in every romance that we ever read. The girl lost, what is she but the prince found? The prince on the white horse that we have always been seeking. . . . In the girl it is the prince, and in the boy it is the girl that makes a prince a prince – and not a man.[33]

Ambivalence is also expressed in Ann Bannon's novels. Beebo, however much she is desired by other women, can break down at a time of crisis and lament her inability to marry Laura, while in a moment of cruelty Laura taunts her for wearing trousers:

> 'You're ridiculous. . . . You're a little girl trying to be a little boy. Grow up Beebo. You'll never be a little boy. Or a big boy. You just haven't got what it takes. . . . You can wear pants till you're blue in the face and it won't change what's underneath.'[34]

Beebo is at risk of appearing pathetic for choosing her work, as a lift boy, so that she can wear trousers on the job; worse, the jibe is a homophobic one, clearly referring to the lesbian's 'lack' of a prick. (How many lesbians have been asked the snide question: 'Yes, but what do you *do* in bed?' – i.e. you can't 'do' anything.) Yet on another occasion Laura shouts at a *male* lift attendant, 'Don't you know those pants won't make a man of you!'[35] – at which point the critique of gender roles reappears.

The potency and poignancy of the 1950s butch is her ability to combine the vulnerable and the invulnerable simultaneously. Ambivalence not-withstanding, however, in the end she is not the ambivalent androgyne of the 1930s. She represents a lived alternative, the possible, not the impossible object of desire. This is above all because her appeal to other women is so strongly emphasised in Ann Bannon's fiction and the other novels we have discussed. By contrast, the reader is seldom or never invited to view the inverts of the 1930s through the eyes of their feminine lovers.

From being to choosing

In the 1980s the butch/femme theme was difficult for some of a new generation of lesbian readers to take, and within the novels themselves, Suzanna Walters suggests, there is a dialogue between two opposed attitudes which even then divided the lesbian community: a dialogue between lesbians such as the women who organised Daughters of Bilitis, who argued for joining the mainstream and disliked the 'negative images' of the butch bar dykes, and the women of the bars themselves, for whom their appearance 'spoke' their lesbian desire. (This was also, to some extent, a class divide between middle-class assimilationism and working-class rebellion.)

This dialogue is one instance of the perennial dilemma of marginalised groups: assimilation or rebellion becomes, in political terms, reform or revolution, the practical versus the romantic solution. On balance the lesbian novel of the 1950s opted for the romantic rather than the reformist view. That is to say: the women in the novels of Ann Bannon, Valerie Taylor and March Hastings reject mainstream life and choose instead their own integrity, their own alternative lifestyle, thus bringing their marginality to the centre of their lives and making it the overriding value.[36] In these novels it is for the most part passionate, sexual, physical, lesbian love that wins out over all the forces ranged against it – the state, convention, traditional morality, male power. Yet in thus asserting that sexuality is at the core of our identity, they articulate a very fifties – a very Freudian – theme. At the very moment of assertion of lesbian sexual identity, they conform to the culture they were challenging, for it was in the 1950s that the idea that sexuality *does* represent the kernel of the self really took hold. These novels, too, assert that sex is the key to self, and this mainstream belief, appearing in these countercultural texts, condenses the Janus-face of the fifties.[37]

In many ways the internal lesbian struggles of the 1980s (internal to the lesbian subculture, that is), centred as they were on ultimately moralistic concerns about correct and incorrect sexualities, were much less radical than the brave challenges of the 1950s, and we will return to the novels of the fifties again and again for the sense they give of the birth and growth of an entirely new phenomenon: the startling, harsh, vibrant lesbian and gay culture which we have inherited, but perhaps do not always sufficiently cherish. At the same time we need to approach the 'dime novels' with more than nostalgia and the uncritical acclamation of 'recognising our foremothers', for we have moved on. Today we insist, in the face of a new backlash, on the importance of choice rather than the discovery of an essential self; on what we can or might become rather than what we 'really are'. Yet at the same time, many of the dilemmas of Laura, Paula and the rest remain with us. The contrary pull of security and social acceptance on the one hand and a stigmatised love on the other is still real for many, so that we must also, in deconstructing the ambience of the fifties, remember that we are still not so far from those years today.

In 1970 the (British) *Gay Liberation Manifesto* referred to butch/femme roles as a form of 'self-oppression', and hostility to the butch from those influenced by feminism was largely because everything masculine was to be rejected. In another and 'postmodern' time – the 1990s – when dusty answers have replaced former certainties and forced us into a greater recognition of complexity, we can see that lesbians, however 'butch' (and, for that matter, gay men, however 'effeminate') state in that very transgression of 'normal' sexual identities an affirmation of themselves as women and men: there is a sense in which the 'butch' is more obviously a woman than the most feminine of women – that is precisely what makes her scandalous.

Notes

1. Paula Christian, *The Other Side of Desire*, New Milford, CT: Timely Books, 1981, p. 156. (Originally published in 1965.)
2. Suzanna Danuta Walters, 'As her hand crept slowly up her thigh: Ann Bannon and the politics of pulp', *Social Text*, **23**, 1989, reproduces this stereotype of the 1950s.
3. See John D'Emilio, *Sexual Politics, Sexual Communities: The making of a homosexual minority in the United States, 1940–1970*, Chicago: University of Chicago Press, 1983.
4. Salvatore Licata, 'The homosexual rights movement in the United States: A traditionally overlooked area of American history', in Salvatore Licata and Robert Petersen, eds, *The Gay Past: A collection of historical essays*, Binghampton, NY: Harrington Park Press, 1985.
5. Madeline Davis and Elizabeth Lapovsky Kennedy, 'Oral history and the study of sexuality in the lesbian community: Buffalo, New York, 1940–1960', in Martin Bauml Duberman, Martha Vicinus and George Chauncey, Jr, eds, *Hidden from History: Reclaiming the gay and lesbian past*, Harmondsworth: Penguin, 1990, pp. 427–8.
6. John D'Emilio, *Sexual Politics, Sexual Communities*, p. 132 and Chapter 8, *passim*.
7. Suzanna Danuta Walters, 'As her hand crept slowly up her thigh', p. 84.
8. March Hastings, *Three Women*, Tallahassee, FL: Naiad Press, 1985, p. 27. (Originally published in 1958.)

9. There is a huge American literature on suburbia dating from the 1950s, when the exodus to the suburbs (begun long before, but now accelerating) generated its own critique. See, for example, Robert Wood, *Suburbia: Its people and their politics*, Boston, MA: Houghton Mifflin, 1958; John Seeley, R. A. Sims and E. W. Loosley, *Crestwood Heights*, London: Constable, 1957; and A. C. Spectorsky, *The Exurbanites*, Philadelphia, PA: J. B. Lippincott, 1955, who is an exception in dealing specifically with the difficulties women faced in the suburbs. See also novelists Sinclair Lewis (writing before World War II), Peter De Vries and John O'Hara. David Riesman, *The Lonely Crowd*, (New Haven, CT: Yale University Press, 1950) and William H. Whyte, Jr, *The Organisation Man* (New York: Simon & Schuster, 1956) critique mass society and its consequent conformity in a more general way.

10. See Betty Friedan, *The Feminine Mystique*, Harmondsworth: Penguin, 1972. (Originally published in 1963). Diane Hamer, '"I Am a Woman": Ann Bannon and the writing of lesbian identity in the 1950s', in Mark Lilly, ed., *Lesbian and Gay Writing*, London: Macmillan, 1990, also notes the connection with Betty Friedan and acknowledges Sue O'Sullivan, who pointed it out to her.

11. Valerie Taylor, *Return to Lesbos*, Tallahassee, FL: Naiad Press, 1982, p. 20. (Originally published in 1963.)

12. Edmund White, *The Beautiful Room Is Empty*, London: Picador, 1988.

13. Hilda Lawrence, *Death of a Doll*, London: Pandora, 1987. (Originally published in 1947.)

14. Ann Bannon, *Journey to a Woman*, Tallahassee, FL: Naiad Press, 1960, p. 78.

15. Diane Hamer, 'I Am A Woman', p. 10 (MS.).

16. See Graham McCann, *Rebel Males: Clift, Brando and Dean*, London: Hamish Hamilton, 1991.

17. Renée Vivien, *A Woman Appeared To Me*, translated from the French by Jeannette H. Foster, with an introduction by Gayle Rubin, Tallahassee, FL: Naiad Press, 1976. (Originally published as *Une Femme m'apparut*, 1904.)

18. See Blanche Weisen Cook, 'Women alone stir my imagination: Lesbianism and the cultural tradition', *Signs*, **4**, 4, 1979; Lillian Faderman, *Surpassing the Love of Men: Romantic friendship and love between women from the Renaissance to the present*, London: The Women's Press, 1985; Lillian Faderman and Ann Williams, 'Radclyffe Hall and the lesbian image', *Conditions*, **1**, 1978; and Sheila Jeffreys, *The Spinster and Her Enemies: Feminism and sexuality 1880–1930*, London: Pandora, 1985, all of which take a negative view; while Sonja Ruehl, 'Inverts and experts: Radclyffe Hall and the lesbian identity', in Rosalind Brunt and Caroline Rowan, eds, *Feminism, Culture and Politics*, London: Lawrence & Wishart, 1982; Jean Radford, 'An inverted romance: *The Well of Loneliness* and sexual ideology', in Jean Radford, ed., *The Progress of Romance: The politics of popular fiction*, London: Routledge, 1986; and Esther Newton, 'The mythic mannish lesbian: Radclyffe Hall and the New Woman', 1984, reprinted in Martin Duberman, Martha Vicinus and George Chauncey, Jr, eds, *Hidden From History*, all take a more complex approach.

19. Colette, *The Pure and the Impure*, translated from the French by Herma Briffault, with an introduction by Janet Flanner, Harmondsworth: Penguin, 1980. (Originally published as *Ces Plaisirs*, 1932.)

20. Shari Benstock, *Women of the Left Bank: Paris 1900–1940*, London: Virago, 1987, pp. 58, 181. Shari Benstock objects most strongly to the class connotations of cross-dressing, and goes on to state that women who had to conceal their masculine dress in public came from a different class and stood to lose everything if their deviance were discovered – yet earlier on she has told us that the upper-class 'Missy' was one of those who was forced to conceal her man's clothing under a cloak. (She is also highly critical of Gertrude Stein

and Alice B. Toklas for their role-playing.) See also Elizabeth Wilson, 'Chic thrills', in *Hallucinations: Life in the postmodern city*, London: Radius, 1988.

21. Anthony Powell, *Casonova's Chinese Restaurant*, London: Heinemann, 1960, pp. 117–18.
22. Gale Wilhelm, *We Too Are Drifting*, Tallahassee, FL: Naiad Press, 1984, p. 27. (Originally published in 1935.)
23. *Ibid.*, p. 38.
24. Barbara Grier, 'Introduction', in Gale Wilhelm, *We Too Are Drifting*.
25. Radclyffe Hall, *The Well of Loneliness*, London: Virago, 1982, p. 323. (Originally published in 1928.)
26. See Katrina Rolley, 'Love, desire and the pursuit of the whole: Dress and the lesbian couple', in Juliet Ash and Elizabeth Wilson, eds, *Chic Thrills: A fashion reader*, London: Pandora, 1991.
27. Ann Bannon, *Women in the Shadows*, London: Sphere, 1970, p. 106. (Originally published in 1959.)
28. Joan Nestle, *A Restricted Country*, London: Sheba, 1987.
29. Ann Bannon, *Beebo Brinker*, Tallahassee, FL: Naiad Press, 1986, p. 41. (Originally published in 1962.)
30. Randy Salem, *Chris*, Tallahassee, FL: Naiad Press, 1989. (Originally published in 1959.)
31. *Ibid.*, p. 172.
32. Suzanna Danuta Walters, 'As her hand crept slowly up her thigh', p. 88.
33. Djuna Barnes, *Nightwood*, London: Faber & Faber, 1963, p. 194. (Originally published in 1936.)
34. Ann Bannon, *I Am A Woman*, Tallahassee, FL: Naiad Press, 1983, p. 175. (Originally published in 1959.)
35. *Ibid.*, p. 202.
36. As a qualification to this assessment we should point out, as have Diane Hamer and Suzanna Walters, that Ann Bannon resolves the difficulties of Jack Mann and Laura by having them contract a 'gay marriage'. They have a child by artificial insemination, and both remain free to have affairs with members of their own sex. As Diane Hamer says, this is a 'parody' of marriage: a fantasy solution to some of the dilemmas of being lesbian or gay at that period, and possibly to those of the author herself, a married woman with children at the time. See Maida Tilchen, 'Ann Bannon: The mystery solved', *Gay Community News*, 8 January 1983; Jeff Weinstein, 'In praise of pulp: Bannon's lusty lesbians', *Voice Literary Supplement*, **20**, 1983; Charlotte Rubens, '50's lesbian "pulp" author: An interview with Ann Bannon', *Coming Up!* November 1983; and Tricia Lootens, 'Ann Bannon: A lesbian audience discovers its lost literature', *Off Our Backs*, **13**, 11, 1983.
37. See Michel Foucault, *The History of Sexuality: Volume One: An introduction*, Harmondsworth: Penguin, 1976; and Jeffrey Weeks, *Sexuality and its Discontents: Meanings, myths and modern sexualities*, London: Routledge, 1985.

HELL AND THE MIRROR
A Reading of *Desert of the Heart*

/Gillian/Spraggs/

In mid-seventies Britain the title was startingly, even embarrassingly, explicit: *Lesbian Images*. Stark white on a blue dust jacket, it leapt at me from a shelf of miscellaneous literary studies in the bookshop where I was, as on so many days, truanting from my thesis. The author, Jane Rule, was someone I'd never heard of: a novelist, American-born, working in Canada. Back at home, devouring the pages, I delighted in the irony, the controlled anger, the persuasive logic with which in her earlier chapters she dismantles first the negative morality of the Christian churches, and then the dubious science and still more dubious therapies – at any rate, when advocated as 'cures' for lesbians – of the practitioners of psychiatry and psychoanalysis. As an alternative to the certitudes of patriarchal science and religion, she presents the various, personal, particular, resonant images offered by a number of woman writers, mainly novelists, judging them in accordance with her estimates as to their fidelity to lesbian existence and their insights into the morality of lived experience.

Jane Rule subscribes whole-heartedly to the theory of 'expressive realism' which, in the early 1970s, was still extremely influential in British and transatlantic literary criticism, especially criticism of the novel. In *Lesbian Images*, literature is viewed as a means of communicating truths about life, and Rule confidently tackles what she sees as her business as a reader, distinguishing between the supposedly accurate perception and the inauthentic. For example, she criticises the novelist Maureen Duffy for failing, as she sees it, to 'translate truly' between experience and fiction, instead allowing her work to be 'threatened by theories of human behavior'.[1] It is not surprising, given her suspicion of psychoanalytic approaches, that she is critical of Duffy's Freudian bias, but there is considerable naivety in the implication that a novelist unencumbered by overt ideology can make of her or his imaginings a transparent window on experience. For Rule, indeed, literary 'truths' are always plural; no one person's perspective is the same as another's, and the individuality of the novelist's vision is a crucial guarantee of its authenticity and value. But this conception leaves her unprepared to acknowledge what most recent writers on literature would recognise, within certain differences of emphasis, as the central influence of language itself – not merely in controlling the form of expression, but in structuring thought by controlling the formulations from which it cannot meaningfully be separated, and even in shaping what we call our 'experience' – which, outside language, is, in important ways, quite ungraspable and unintelligible to us.[2]

If this is accepted, 'the reality of lesbian experience', as Rule calls it in her Preface, is no more directly accessible through literature than it is available through divine revelation or scientific theories of human psychology. But this hardly means that the study of literature ceases to have any purpose: rather the reverse. For if experience is radically structured by language, then the investigation of discourses, or 'domains of language-use', becomes a strategy for approaching a more critical awareness of the categories, flexible and shifting as these are, that mediate our sense of the real.[3] And among the identifiable domains of language-use, literary writing, and especially the realist novel, is one of the most insidiously potent in presenting images and narratives of human existence and relations that, as Rule's observations suggest, impress with a conviction of their 'truth'. From this perspective, a study of literary images of lesbianism, while unlikely to deliver immediate insights into 'the reality of lesbian experience', is clearly valuable as a means of illuminating the phenomenon of lesbianism and especially the formation, social and individual, of a lesbian identity.

In fact, as several critics have noted, the influence of specifically literary texts on definitions and perceptions of female homosexual desire and practice has been exceptionally strong, for reasons that probably have much to do with the silence – virtual or complete – historically maintained on these matters by most other public discourses.[4] Indeed, there is a sense in which much of recoverable lesbian history has been an account of a process of rereading and reconstructing particular literary texts – Sappho's fragments, Baudelaire's 'Femmes damnées', or *The Well of Loneliness*. As long ago as 1823, Anne Lister, Yorkshire gentlewoman and scholar, indicated in her diary the significance to her, in helping to make sense of her sexual preference, of the sixth satire of Juvenal, which contains a salacious account of the homosexual activities attributed to some upperclass women of Imperial Rome.[5] The most obvious reading of this passage would find it aggressively hostile to the whole idea of women having sex with each other; but one doubts whether this constituted its value to Lister, who seems very far from self-hating. One may guess that this woman of strong sexual drives reconstructed the poem in her reading of it in ways that stressed its explicit and even exuberant physicality.

In *Lesbian Images*, the language of 'truth' and 'translation' cannot conceal the fact that reconstructing texts, re-creating them as 'positive images' of lesbian sexuality, is a major part of Rule's approach, as she threads a path through the private codes of Gertrude Stein or the obliquities of Elizabeth Bowen. The result is a book of considerable generosity and charm. In 1976 it had a deeply affirming influence on my sense of myself as a lesbian, and a marked effect on my choice of reading. However, before I set off in determined quest of novels by May Sarton or Rita Mae Brown, I wanted to read more work by Jane Rule. Her first novel, *Desert of the Heart*, had been published in 1964. Truanting once more from my research, I tracked it down in a copyright library and read it doggedly, edgily, trying not to display emotions that didn't suit the atmosphere of quiet, abstracted study. In the mid-seventies, novels that dealt affirmatively with sexual relationships between women were very rare in my experience. Each new discovery overwhelmed me with excitement and gratitude.

On the first encounter, the book impressed me most for what I then saw as its conspicuous refusal to problematise lesbianism; a reading that now seems absurd, since for one of the two main characters the scandal and difficulty of a lesbian lifestyle is precisely the point at issue for much of the novel. At that time, however, I doubt if I could have begun to imagine a lesbian fiction, or a lesbian life, in which lesbianism was not on some level an immense and perpetual source of stress. Tension, the external resistance to ridicule and hostility, the internal battle to control anxiety, to settle self-doubt, was the atmosphere of life and, like the air, was something to take for granted. In this context, it is not strange that my reading of *Desert of the Heart* foregrounded the hoped-for but uncertain resolution, not the expected conflict. Reading now in a different moment and very different contexts – social, cultural and personal – I can re-member, but cannot recapture, that earlier excitement. Nevertheless, the memory of it will always remain for me part of the meaning of *Desert of the Heart*: a book that challenged a wilderness of silence and malice.

Desert of the Heart is a lesbian love story; it is also a reflection on the meaning of love, and of being lesbian. One of the ways in which it may be read is as a fictional counterpart to *Lesbian Images*. Like *Lesbian Images*, it directly challenges the two major discourses besides the literary that in Western culture have historically offered perspectives on sexual relations between women: the discourse of traditional Christianity and the discourse of psychoanalytic theory. However, its method is rather different. In place of argument it adopts a course of polemical reconstruction. In *Lesbian Images*, the creative reshapings of texts such as Elizabeth Bowen's *The Little Girls* are never acknowledged as such: the book presents itself as an inquiry into what they are 'really' about. Fair enough; even in these self-consciously theoretical days, it is still an advantageous manoeuvre to neglect to point out the extent to which the critic's reading invariably reconstitutes the text in patterns that, for whatever reason, are personally felt to be of service. Fiction is a different sort of game; 'detachment' is no longer one of the rules, nor is 'respect for the text'.

Desert of the Heart is set in Reno, Nevada, the town in the heart of the sterile desert whose economy is founded on casinos and quickie divorces. Evelyn is a literary scholar, an intelligent, capable woman whose strength and independence have gradually undermined her inadequate husband until he is acutely depressed. For his sake – urged on by the professionals of medicine and morals, not only her husband's doctors but her own church minister – this woman who has always believed in doing the right thing has come to Reno to seek a divorce. It is through her eyes that we first see the desert: the 'miles of burning sand' visible from the plane that later, from the ground, fill her with an irrational terror. What she sees is a vision of something she doesn't believe in, 'a Catholic desolation'[6] – specifically, to her trained scholar's imagination, the 'burning sands' (*arena arsiccia*) described by the medieval Italian poet Dante, in one section of his *Inferno*.[7] This detailed tourists' guide to the regions of the damned is the first book of *The Divine Comedy*, a massive three-part poem which is one of the major monuments of traditional Christian culture. In the passage directly alluded to in *Desert of the Heart*, it describes how those who are 'violent against God' are confined in Hell to a vast sandy desert, heated continually by huge flakes of flame which descend from above.

According to Dante, the category of those who are 'violent against God' includes 'usurers' – people who lend out money in return for interest – and homosexuals. In both cases their sin is a form of blasphemy: they are held to have rejected the gifts of God's Creation and turned aside to pursue unnatural practices.[8] The charge that homosexual acts are 'against nature' first entered Christian discourse in a passage of St Paul's Epistle to the Romans, which is also the only place in the Bible to make explicit mention of love-making between women.[9] At the time St Paul was writing, the idea that there is something unnatural about homosexual behaviour was already ancient; four hundred years earlier, the Greek philosopher Plato had criticised same-sex love-making, by men or women, in very similar language.[10] With St Paul's endorsement it acquired all the authority of primal Christian tradition, and in subsequent theological doctrine the homosexual is condemned as a sinner, because she or he refuses to be content with God's gift of procreative sex, choosing instead to engage in a sterile search for pleasure.

The association with the usurer is not so strange as it might at first appear, for historically the Church's teaching contrasted the wicked usurer with the simple honest farmer. The moneylender despises the 'natural' way to wealth, the growing of crops and rearing of stock, and with diabolical ingenuity breeds gold from barren gold. There is a great deal of unintended irony in the calls that we have been hearing over recent years from prominent members of the Conservative Party in Great Britain, with its devotion to capitalism and its dependence on business sponsors, for a return to traditional Christian values. For many centuries, the Church regarded the taking of interest as one of the more serious sins because it was felt to be a fundamental perversion, a means of becoming rich without doing any productive work or contributing to the good of the community.[11]

At the beginning of *Desert of the Heart*, Evelyn's hell is the empty, meaningless existence that she has committed herself to enduring, a woman with no purpose except to wait out the weeks until the divorce that she has not wanted, that she feels as a personal failure, can be ratified by the courts. It is a hell of remorse, too, for the damage she has unwittingly done to her husband. But as she begins to come to know Ann, younger, frankly bisexual, 'a 'change-apron' in one of the local casinos whose job is to dole out change to the crowds who come to play the slot machines, the desert town is revealed as an image of a very traditional hell – peopled, like Dante's sandy plain, not only by homosexuals but by those who seek wealth without working for it – in this case both the punters in the casinos stricken by gambling fever, and the casino owners, who make obscene amounts of money by pandering to their fantasies of luck and riches.

By this time, one of Rule's main projects is becoming clear. Within the cultural domain of traditional Christianity, there was a territory allocated specifically to homosexuals. This was the city of Sodom, mentioned in the Book of Genesis, one of the legendary 'cities of the plain', which was destroyed by fire from Heaven after an unappetising episode involving an attempted rape by its citizens on a couple of visiting angels.[12] The 'men of Sodom', or Sodomites, came to be thought of as paradigmatic homosexuals, and the fate of Sodom was an exemplary warning for anyone who might be tempted by their particular sin, which the Church knew as sodomy. Dante's barren plain with the descending flakes of fire draws heavily on the imagery of Sodom's destruction, and underlines the point that theologically, Sodom, the country of the homosexuals, is simply a particular region within the boundaries of Hell. Rule's strategy, at once daring and conservative, is to appropriate Hell, to incorporate its images in her fiction and reshape them to her own purposes, and so to change its meaning.

Desert of the Heart is neither the first nor the latest lesbian fiction to attempt such a strategy. In *The Well of Loneliness* (1928) the Roman Catholic convert Radclyffe Hall describes the gay bar run by the drug-dealer Alec, in post-World War I Paris, in terms that make of it an image of Hell: its customers are 'lost', 'tormented', 'beyond all hope, it seemed, of salvation'. Alec's bar, with its degraded clientele, is Sodom as this was pictured in Christian cultural tradition, further embellished with a few suggestions from the 'decadent' strain in nineteenth-century French poetry – which was itself heavily influenced by the imagery of Sodom and Hell. But in Hall's novel, the traditional charge against sodomites of perversity, unnatural vice, is countered by an insistence on a view of homosexuality as 'congenital inversion': so that the men who frequent Alec's are sinners not by reason of their sexual practices – for as born inverts these are natural to them – but only in so far as they have fallen into the sin of despair. Consequently, the hell that they are in is only secondarily a result of their turning away from God; its primary cause is the social injustice and persecution that have taken away their hope and caused them to seek refuge in alcohol and cocaine. In Hall's ironic revision of the Sodom myth, 'if there were a God', it is not the inverts against whom 'His anger must rise' but 'the world' that has driven them to such a desperate state.[13]

Over the last sixty years, the stranglehold of traditional Christianity over public culture in the Western world has grown gradually weaker, so that the full scandal of Hall's position has become muted. Possibly it is only people such as myself, brought up within traditionalist Christian subcultures, who can begin to interpret fully the discourse within which she was writing, and the emotional and intellectual courage needed to frame the kind of challenge she puts up. In the world I inhabited as a child, Hell was a major topographical feature. It was the place where unrepentant sinners lived, shut out from God's presence, the only true source of joy. I was a sinner; the Bible said this, and so did my parents. God was a universal Thought Policeman, who knew even more about my sins than my mother did. But God was also my Heavenly Father: he loved me, like my parents, only even more so, and if I repented my sins, he would forgive me. More – if I asked him, he would give me the strength, or grace, to stop sinning, to be transformed, a new person. But there is a nasty double-bind concealed behind this promise. If you find that your guilty hopes and wishes are just as powerful, your bad behaviour still as compulsive as always, then clearly your faith and penitence have been insufficient. The sinner who has not repented is in danger of Hell. But there is a further twist: those who ask for the grace of God and then can't believe that it has been given to them have fallen into what Radclyffe Hall would have identified as the sin of despair.

When I was fifteen, I made what I still regard as one of the most important decisions of my life: I chose, deliberately, to go to Hell. This was made slightly easier by the fact that, as my father authoritatively affirmed, many of my heroes, like Christopher Marlowe and Dylan Thomas, were there already. Moreover, while the thought of Hell was terrifying, the idea of an eternity spent in Heaven, in the company of God and my parents, afflicted me with a sickening sense of claustrophobia. Interestingly enough, from the point at which I consciously embraced despair as a way of life, I began to find it possible to believe that Hell did not exist. However, delivering my imagination was very much harder than emancipating my mind. At nineteen, I experienced a series of waking nightmares of the Hell in which, intellectually, I no longer believed. These focused less on the burning fires than on the bottomless pit of the Book of Revelation, an image that struck me with special horror and that, as I am now beginning to understand, corresponded with appalling accuracy to my sense at that time of being adrift, without firm footing, emotionally, culturally and intellectually.

Such feelings are common enough to displaced persons; and traditional Christian culture, with its closed intellectual system, its structure of hierarchically imposed morality, appears to me now like a totalitarian state, from which I acknowledge myself a driven refugee. As for Radclyffe Hall: in the context of her own internalisation of Christian ideology, and the ostentatious Christian righteousness that dominated public culture at the time she was writing, her attempt to turn centuries of judgement back again on the judges impresses me as heroic. Meanwhile, even in a society that is largely post-Christian, the landscape of Hell continues to haunt the collective imagination, just as it has haunted my bad dreams. The cosmology of Heaven and Hell still carries enough of a charge to fuel a large part of the provocativeness, the foregrounded outrageousness, of *Virgile, Non* (1985), Monique Wittig's lesbian-feminist revision of Dante's *Divine Comedy*. In a wholesale ironic reversal, Hell here becomes the hetero-patriarchy, imaged in powerful sequences of surrealistic cruelty, as demonic males find a diversity of ways to torture compliant women. The sandy desert where Dante locates his sodomites is now a no-man's-land between Hell and Limbo, and Limbo, as the narrative slides playfully closer to realism, is a dyke bar in San Francisco. Paradise appears to be a rather hearty lesbian picnic, but perhaps my imaginative shortcomings are letting down the text.[14] If Hall's more obviously conservative position commits her to retaining the rigmaroles of sin and divine anger, the rigid separatism that informs Wittig's allegory and into which she reinterprets the adversarial dualism of her source seems to me to constitute at least as much of a barrier to effecting a truly radical imaginative transformation of Western culture.

In *The Well of Loneliness*, Sodom is a reproach to society, a locus of pitiable and needless suffering; in *Virgile, Non*, Hell is the heteropatriarchy, a place of female torment. The desert in *Desert of the Heart* is a more complex and ambiguous image. Evelyn subscribes to a nominal Christianity, but there is little sense of Hell in the traditional theological sense, as a condition of being cut off from God. God is never a presence; Evelyn's church associations, which are only vaguely alluded to, seem little more than the pieties of a willed conformity in a culture still marginally Christian. At the start of the book, she fears the desert because it brings her sharply in touch with the desolation she has begun to recognise in herself as her marriage has come to an end: 'the desert of the heart', a state of being not only loveless but without value or purpose – a reflection, in fact, of the despair that has gripped her husband. The marital relationship, the terrain prescribed for them by social convention and conventional morality, has proved to be a ground where neither of them can flourish. But divorce, however necessary, remains, as the book's first paragraph describes it, a 'voluntary exile', a movement into unknown territory.[15]

Ann, the 'change-apron', in the androgynous style of clothing prescribed as a staff uniform by the casino where she works, strikes Evelyn as altogether exotic. For a moment, the novel seems about to take up and transpose the middle-class male homosexual fantasy – so prevalent in the later years of the last century and the early years of this one – of the young manual worker as idealised sex object, the working class as a wild terrain of sexual freedom and spontaneous feeling.[16] Very soon, though, the 'change-apron' is revealed as only a masking identity; Ann, it transpires, is a cartoonist, gifted and successful, and the fantasy modulates into the myth of the artist as bohemian and free spirit. To Ann, 'allergic' to faithfulness, lover of women and men, committed to a dead-end job in a vast institution dedicated exclusively to processing naked greed, the desert is her home. She loves it, both for its beauty, its subtle planes and colours, and because her cartoonist's allegorising imagination finds in it imagery to suit her bleak vision of human society. The gambling town in the barren wilderness is for her 'the simple truth about the world. . . . We can't have what we need, but we can take what we want.'[17] Those of us who survive are all living at the expense of others, a disturbing perception, but undeniable.

For Ann, her apparently aimless life in Reno is a positive choice: to work for a morally compromised organisation like Frank's Club is simply to accept the human condition. The very ordinary people she watches every night as, in their feverish pursuit of a lucky win, they neglect even the most insistent of human ties – children, newly wedded bridegroom – may be monstrous, but they are also representative members of the human race. Ann, the cartoonist, the artist, witnesses, judges and loves them, and sets down on paper the grotesque truths they inadvertently show her. But to Evelyn, the good woman, the overcontrolled scholar, who has fought so hard within her failing marriage to be right, to be 'saved', Ann's world – a world, as she sees it, 'without guilt or goodness' – is threatening.[18] Drawn to Ann in tenderness, in desire, she fears that if she rejects conventional moral positions on sexuality, she will lose her sense of any limits and therefore any meaning to her actions. She will find herself confirmed in the hell she has feared since leaving her marriage – a hell of alienation, anomie, a barren, isolated existence in a pathless wilderness. Rule is here reinterpreting Hell through the familiar territory of the Outsider, that continually reimagined, much-debated figure of the fifties and sixties, with his (seldom her) vertiginous perception of the meaninglessness of socially constructed reality.[19]

But Evelyn is troubled by more than the desert landscape, the hells of theology or alienation. She and Ann share a close physical resemblance, which both find perplexing. Each of them haunts the other with an image of herself, a double, doppelgänger, mirror. Once again, Rule is deliberately invoking both an influential strain in the literary imagery of lesbianism and a major discourse, this time the discourse of psychoanalytic theory. The idea that a woman who loves another woman is merely loving herself in a mirror has been part of received masculine wisdom for centuries. In 'Sappho to Philaenis', a wittily erotic self-consciously daring verse epistle, first published in 1633 as the work of John Donne and either by him or after his style, Sappho is made to proclaim to her female lover, 'Me, in my glass, I call thee'.[20] 'Lesbos', one of the poems censored in 1857 from Charles Baudelaire's collection *Les Fleurs du Mal*, says of the inhabitants of that notorious island that they 'engage only with their mirrors' ['*Qui font qu'à leurs miroirs*'].[21] In the early years of the twentieth century Sigmund Freud, so much of whose work is a systematisation and refinement of folk belief, designated self-love 'narcissism', following the legend of the Greek youth Narcissus, who fell in love with his reflection in a pool and was drowned while trying to reach it. In the course of evolving his complex theory of narcissism – which identifies it, among other things, as characteristic of an early stage in the progress towards personal maturity – Freud lent his immense prestige to the notion that a love-object of the same sex is always a manifestation of narcissism in a marked degree. From this

it was only a short step to characterising homosexuals as generally possessing narcissistic – that is, cold and self-regarding – personalities.[22]

The construction of same-sex love as a disguise for loving the self is
potentially even more of a chill to the affections, a threat to the lover's
sense of self-worth, than the categorisation of sodomy as a sin. After all,
according to orthodox theology, everyone is in some degree a sinner. But
love of all kinds – parental, comradely, romantic – has been traditionally
judged and justified by the quality of its attention to the Other, its
readiness to regard the Other's needs. The imagery of mirrors – and still
more the theory of homosexual narcissism, at least in the form in which
this has passed into the common understanding – neatly brackets lesbian
or homosexual love well outside the possibility of any such justification.
Moreover, the mystifications of popularised psychoanalytic theory are
powerfully effective in denying any appeal. In the twentieth century, it
has become harder for the layperson to argue with proclaimed science
than with revealed religion, and it is difficult in any case to debate the
existence or presence of formations and compulsions that are defined from
the beginning as beyond the reach of the conscious mind.

In *The Well of Loneliness*, Radclyffe Hall tackles the accusation – for such
it is – of narcissism through two main strategies. One is to make her
heroine, Stephen, almost insanely altruistic and self-sacrificing in her
treatment of Mary, her lover, to the final point where she manipulates her,
quite deliberately, into turning towards the man who wants to marry her,
because he can offer her a 'better' – that is, socially accepted – way of life.
The other is the use of theories of 'congenital inversion' in characterising
Stephen as a woman who should have been born a man – who, apart
from the possession of a penis, is defined as masculine in every detail
that physiology or convention might demand. To complement her, she
is given a lover who is a parody of conformity to stereotypes of female passivity and dependence: clinging, childlike, without any kind of
personal resource. This extreme polarisation banishes the image of
Narcissus, but only at the expense of articulating a vision of all sexual
relationships, whether lesbian or heterosexual, as trapped in the requirements of a given masculinity and femininity, conceived in nearly the most
mutually oppressive terms.

Rule's approach is very much bolder. Instead of exaggerated difference,
the two women whose relationship is at the centre of her book are marked
by an emphasised similarity. Evelyn looks at Ann and sees her younger
self; Ann is mistaken for Evelyn's daughter. Evelyn is only too aware
that a woman who feels tenderness towards her own likeness is 'at
least narcissistic'. Other items of popularised psychoanalytic doctrine are
brought into the picture. Evelyn had wanted a child; had conceived with

great difficulty, and miscarried. She acknowledges a maternal element in her feeling for Ann. Ann's mother had left her when she was small; in case it has never struck her that she is looking for a 'mother figure', her friend Silver is keen to point this out.[23]

One may guess, though there is no certain evidence, that one of the texts behind *Desert of the Heart* is the chapter on 'The Lesbian' in Simone de Beauvoir's massive critique of womanhood, *Le Deuxième Sexe* (1949). Here, most of the popular stereotypes of lesbianism jostle shoulders: the woman whose childhood was lacking in maternal affection, the maternal woman without a child, the woman disappointed in relationships with men, the strong, intelligent woman unable to subordinate herself to the male. De Beauvoir is often uncritical in her use of material from other writers; in her attitude towards lesbianism she is alternately defensive, condescending, celebratory and hostile. However, at the centre of her account are some important ideas: that aetiology is not the crucial question; that lesbianism, like heterosexuality, takes many different forms; that it is neither a willed perversion nor an arbitrary curse but a choice, a particular way of solving the problems presented by the condition of being a woman; and that it is not lesbianism in itself that ought to be placed at issue, but 'its manner of expression in actual living'.[24]

Both Rule and de Beauvoir make their own uses of the image of the mirror. De Beauvoir is the more traditional: for her, lesbian love-making is 'the miracle of the mirror', a way of re-creating the self through the other, envisaged in opposition to the love-making of woman and man, in which, as she argues, self is lost, where each becomes the other.[25] But when Ann makes love with Bill, the man who loves her, whom she loves but will not marry, they find themselves, in a borrowed room full of mirrors, looking not at each other, but 'at the images of each other they found most exciting'. A woman and a man may miss each other entirely, fail to see past each other's image, to engage or communicate, and in the process, like Evelyn and her husband, risk losing their sense of who they are. But if a woman sees herself mirrored in another woman, that, too, is a false image; it is necessary to look through it. When Ann looks at the mirror ceiling in the casino where she works, she sees herself but knows that on the other side, invisible, a security man may well be looking back. The image in the mirror may look like you, but what lies behind it is someone else entirely. After Ann has kissed Evelyn, a kiss to which Evelyn refuses to respond, Evelyn begins to look at her in a new way: 'What she saw was no longer an imperfect reflection of herself but an alien otherness she was drawn to and could not understand'.[26] Narcissism has been invoked, only to be banished; whatever its role in the initial at-traction, in interaction with the Other, under pressure from her own desires and perceptions, it has speedily dissolved, to be replaced by an acute awareness of her separate identity.

But in any case, likeness may disturb and repel as well as excite or reassure; and to see one's own face on another woman may easily be imagined to be intensely threatening. Encountering Evelyn, finding herself attracted, Ann calls to mind the traditional belief that the meeting with the double is an omen of death. More than anything else, Ann wants to be free. She does not want to be mirrored by anyone. What she fears is a loss of self, a kind of death, being caught in an image of herself that freezes her in a single form. Until she meets Evelyn, having sex with women has been a way of detaching herself from them, distancing herself: not re-creating her image of herself, but shattering her idealised image of them, to escape the risk of love, of personal commitment. The challenge she confronts in Evelyn is the image of herself as a lover; just as the mirror that Evelyn sees in Ann reflects the disquieting spectacle of herself as a lesbian.[27]

Still fighting her growing desire and plagued by guilt, Evelyn falls back, not for the first time, on a quasi-theological vocabulary: 'Surely she could not be judged for a nature her will had never consented to', and again: 'For the rest, the moments of unacknowledged tenderness and vague desire, the unconsenting will must surely ransome [sic] nature.'[28] This is New Testament language, the language especially of the epistles of St Paul. But in Evelyn's internal debate, it floats oddly free of connections. Whose judgement does Evelyn fear? Hardly God's. Her own judgement, presumably. But by whose laws? From what does she seek to be ransomed? Hell? But even at the start of the book, Evelyn doesn't believe in the literal Hell of traditional Christianity. Meanwhile, in moral and social terms, she has willed all her life so far to avoid 'damnation', to make the 'right' choices: and she has found herself in the limbo of divorce, with a hell of aimlessness looming all around her.

As for 'nature': the use of this term in the writings of St Paul is far from consistent. I have already referred to the well-known passage in which he expresses his disapproval of homosexual acts by describing them as 'against nature'.[29] It is clear from the context that at this point 'nature' carries the sense of an innate pattern or order in the way things are: behaviour that is 'against nature' goes against what is right, fitting, in accordance with how human beings, properly constituted, are and ought to be. However, there are several places in St Paul's epistles where the idea of 'nature' means something very different. In these passages it is bound up with his doctrine of Original Sin, which states that ever since the 'Fall', the primal sin of Adam and Eve, all human beings have been born into the world fatally compromised by hereditary guilt and an innate disposition towards wickedness. In this context the state of 'nature' is the state of being 'fallen'.[30] But if St Paul is erratic, Evelyn's reflections suggest that she is thoroughly muddled, at least in terms of orthodox Christian theology. For this teaches that it is precisely because its 'nature' is 'fallen', corrupted by Original Sin, that humanity is liable to judgement, while no one can be 'ransomed' by the 'will', which is itself only a part of 'fallen nature'.

At the start of her agonised debate with herself, Evelyn seems to be eliding a vague notion of human nature as 'fallen', warped by Original Sin, with a concept of her own nature in particular as inclining towards an innate disposition to be attracted to women. At the same time, by setting up an opposition between 'nature' and 'will', she tempers the tendency towards an essentialist view of lesbianism with the implication of choice. Her notion of will raises the question of identity: she begins to question whether the self may be equated with a governing will, which constructs an identity from out of the genetic inheritance in accordance with the dictates of social convention. Evelyn's sense of who she is has finally fallen apart, shattered in the conflict between her desire and the will that persists in denying it.[31] For a moment, the central issue presents itself as a question of whether she can make a deliberate choice to take on a new, lesbian identity.

In the end, though, Evelyn slides out of her dilemma without ever acknowledging that she has failed to find a proper resolution of it. Her main escape route is 'nature', that exceptionally slippery term: 'perhaps the most complex word in the language', according to Raymond Williams.[32] From identifying her desire for Ann as springing from a nature that is implicitly, but not quite expressly, constructed as flawed, it is a small step in language to constructing her desire as 'natural' – but a very large, sideways step in semantics. This gambit has already been foreshadowed in the book's imagery, in the storm that breaks over the desert after the first time Ann has kissed her. Metonymically, as Evelyn drives through the storm, the exercise of rigid concentration, as she controls the skidding car, is both representative of and instrumental in the process of controlling her feelings; metaphorically, the storm is an image of the sexual passion that Ann has stirred up, to which Evelyn, at that point, is determined not to yield. Once the two have become lovers, the language of 'nature' becomes pervasive, a vocabulary that seeps into Ann's discourse, too: 'wild, natural, insistent poetry', 'an animal freedom', 'animal desire', 'like the cry of some mythical water bird'. Evelyn's final position is summed up in her reflection: 'Nothing else I've ever known has been as right and as natural as loving you'.[33]

This, of course, is a direct challenge to Dante, and behind him to St

Paul. The shades of those lost sodomites, wandering through their barren, terrifying landscape, are exorcised in a formula that, while rejecting Dante's verdict, remains in some important respects firmly locked into the same terminology and intellectual traditions. To join Plato and St Paul in condemning lesbian and homosexual behaviour as unnatural is to suggest that it goes monstrously against all instinct, or sense of what is orderly and right; a sense that is constructed as inborn and identified as an index of fundamental moral values, or 'natural law'. In very similar fashion, to describe lesbian love as 'natural' is to characterise it as compelling, irresistible – like a storm: but also to appeal to that compulsive, or instinctive, quality for vindication in constructing it, as Evelyn does explicitly, as 'right', as fulfilling the 'natural law'. By such a manoeuvre, human law and social convention are overruled; guilt is absolved; questions of choice become irrelevant; theories of aetiology are rendered quite beside the point; and the whole matter is placed in an essential realm of uncontestable meaning, beyond the reach of scrutiny and challenge.

To use the terms that de Beauvoir would have applied, the language of Sartrean existentialism, at the point when she invokes 'nature' to justify her actions, Evelyn makes a classic gesture of *mauvaise foi*, bad faith, an evasion of responsibility.[34] To put the issue in terms that I myself prefer: although the tactic may have turned out to be sufficient to appease her guilt and fear, it does not solve any of her problems, moral, social, or intellectual. Morally, the appeal to 'nature' is really a disguised appeal to strong feeling; an obvious difficulty here is that a rapist may justify his action in just the same terms, and many rapists do. Intellectually, it ignores the fact that lesbianism is itself a social convention, a construct; different from marriage, certainly, proscribed, concealed, much less rich in buttressing images, narratives and rituals, but correspondingly less rigid: more open to the risks of alienation, but equally – or so one may hope – to the possibilities of creative reconstruction. Finally, in social terms, to refer lesbian desire and sexuality to the realm of 'nature' cannot help in defining a context for a lesbian relationship within society. About that project the book is explicitly pessimistic. Evelyn believes that 'no intellectual campaign' can defeat the power of 'that old dictum: marriage is the best life for a woman'. Time is beginning to prove her wrong; but in 1964 she could, I think, be excused the mild melodrama of the words with which she finally capitulates to her love and Ann's: 'It's a terrible risk, Ann'.[35]

Desert of the Heart is an ambitious novel, at once a polemical challenge to received wisdom, a reformed primer of lesbian images, an effort at a paradigmatic encoding of lesbian experience. Even the names gesture towards archetype: Ann and Evelyn, Adam and Eve.[36] In this context, when Jane Rule locates her lesbians in a version of Hell, it is because so long as she confined her imagination strictly within Western literary tradition, there was virtually no alternative: from Dante, through Baudelaire, to Sartre in his play *Huis-clos* (1944), all the most prestigious authors insist on Hell as the place where lesbians are to be found. Even Radclyffe Hall's heroine Stephen, in *The Well of Loneliness*, though too fastidious and courageous to despair, is driven by social hostility to take refuge in a bar culture depicted as an anteroom of Hell. Only the classical writers know nothing at all of Sodom; and their testimony – when it isn't, with Juvenal and Martial, ribald and belittling – is available only from tantalising remnants: the surviving fragments of Sappho, Nossis, Erinna.

In *Desert of the Heart*, the barren sodomites' Hell so powerfully depicted by Dante is reconstructed with irony and grace as the scene of a romance, a place for the flowering of love. Region of a fading cultural empire, the Hell of traditional Christianity is open to conquest and colonisation: but to recognise and reject the dogmatism of organised religion, the constricting artificialities of social convention, is to venture into an unmapped wilderness, to risk the hell of continually receding meanings, the terrors of the perpetual fall through the pit. *Desert of the Heart* makes a move towards that territory, but then retreats into a dead end. By referring the source of meaning, of value, to a given realm of 'nature', it evades the more disturbing implications of acknowledging the extent to which meaning is socially constructed; but it also restricts the scope within which it may be scrutinised and made over – no less drastically, indeed, than by referring it to the dictates of a divine revelation.

Nevertheless, *Desert of the Heart* remains a book to celebrate. First, for the integrity and courage of its author who, by refusing the protection of a concealing nom de plume, put at risk her job as a university teacher, and nearly lost it.[37] Second, for the unequivocally affirmative treatment of the sexual relationship between the two women. It is hard to remember, now, how unusual this was even as recently as the middle of the seventies. In the early sixties, when the book was published, it was almost as rare as a comet. Finally, for the boldness with which it appropriates and transforms its two central images. In the middle of the desert storm, Evelyn and Ann encounter a valley full of light, a dazzling vision: sunlight, rainbows and lightning in simultaneous play, the transfigured counterpart to Dante's flakes of fire.[38] This is the grace – call it love – in the depths of the wilderness. To those with the courage to take up its challenge, the mirror, too, holds out its promise of reward. The narrative closes on a view of Ann and Evelyn, side by side, advancing towards their reflection in the glass doors of the courtroom where Evelyn is to collect her decree of divorce: two strong, creative women, confronting and acknowledging in each other 'their own image', as lesbians, as lovers.[39]

Notes

1. Jane Rule, *Lesbian Images* (1975), published in Britain by Peter Davies, London, 1976, pp. 180, 182.
2. To signpost even a part of the work so loosely summarised here would be an essay in itself. My own approach owes a good deal to the lucid and coherent position outlined by Catherine Belsey in *Critical Practice* (London: Methuen, 1980), but I cannot accept the full rigour of her views on the determining role of language. Deborah Cameron (*Feminism and Linguistic Theory*, London: Macmillan, 1985) offers a useful critical analysis of current ideas on language, and a challenge to extreme determinist positions.
3. Belsey, *Critical Practice*, p. 5.
4. Diane Hamer, '"I Am a Woman": Ann Bannon and the writings of lesbian identity in the 1950s', in Mark Lilly, ed., *Lesbian and Gay Writing*, London: Macmillan, 1990, p. 51; Carolyn Brown, 'Feminist literary strategies in the postmodern condition', in Helen Carr, ed., *From My Guy to Sci-Fi: Genre and women's writing in the postmodern world*, London: Pandora, 1989, p. 115.
5. *I Know My Own Heart. The Diaries of Anne Lister (1791–1840)*, ed. Helena Whitbread, London: Virago, 1988, p. 268; see Juvenal, Satire VI, ll. 306–26.
6. Jane Rule, *Desert of the Heart*, London: Pandora, 1986, pp. 2, 16, 43.
7. *Ibid.*, p. 116, and see pp. 122–3; Dante Alighieri, *Inferno*, Canto XIV; quotation on l. 74. See Jane Rule, *Outlander. Stories and Essays*, Tallahassee, FL: Naiad Press, 1981, pp. 152–3.
8. *Inferno*, Canto XI, ll. 46–51, 94–111.
9. Romans 1: 26–7.
10. Plato, *The Laws*, 636b–c.
11. For a fuller account of traditional Christian teaching on usury, see R. H. Tawney's excellent introduction to Thomas Wilson, *A Discourse Upon Usury*, London, 1925.
12. Genesis 18: 16–19: 29.
13. Radclyffe Hall, *The Well of Loneliness*, London: Virago, 1982, pp. 393, 446.
14. Monique Wittig, *Virgile, Non*, published as *Across the Acheron*, transl. David Le Vay and Margaret Crosland, London: The Women's Press, 1989.
15. *Desert of the Heart*, pp. 118, 1.
16. Cf. Jeffrey Weeks, 'Inverts, perverts, and Mary-Annes: Male prostitution and the regulation of homosexuality in England in the nineteenth and early twentieth centuries', in Martin Bauml Duberman, Martha Vicinus and George Chauncey, Jr, eds, *Hidden From History: Reclaiming the gay and lesbian past*, London: Penguin, 1991, pp. 203–4.
17. *Desert of the Heart*, pp. 175–6, 112.
18. *Ibid.*, p. 117.
19. Colin Wilson, *The Outsider* (London: Gollancz 1956) is a popularising and conspicuously tendentious but comprehensive examination of the seminal texts, which had an immense influence on its own account.
20. John Donne, *The Complete English Poems*, ed. A. J. Smith, Harmondsworth: Penguin, 1971, pp. 128, 452.
21. Charles Baudelaire, *Les Fleurs du Mal*, ed. Ad. Van Bever, Paris, 1925, p. 254.
22. See, for example, Sigmund Freud, *Standard Edition of the Complete Psychological Works*, ed.

James Strachey, London: Hogarth, vol. VII (1953), pp. 144–6; vol. XIV (1957), pp. 73, 88; vol. XVI (1961), pp., 426–7; D. J. West, *Homosexuality*, 2nd rev edn, Harmondsworth: Penguin, 1968, pp. 195–6.

23. *Desert of the Heart*, pp. 14, 72, 118, 85.
24. Simone de Beauvoir, *The Second Sex*, tranl. H. M. Parshley, London: Jonathan Cape, 1953, reprinted 1972, p. 413.
25. *Ibid.*, p. 406.
26. *Desert of the Heart*, pp. 38, 27, 128.
27. *Ibid.*, pp. 39, 41, 244, 135–6, 128.
28. *Ibid.*, pp. 123, 127.
29. See Note 9 above.
30. See especially I Corinthians 15: 21–2; Ephesians 2: 3, and cf. (Authorised or King James Version only) I Corinthians 2: 14; 15: 44, 46.
31. *Desert of the Heart*, p. 128.
32. Raymond Williams, *Keywords: A vocabulary of culture and society*, revised and expanded, London: Fontana, 1988, p. 219.
33. *Desert of the Heart*, pp. 120, 163, 185, 237.
34. Cf. Arthur C. Danto, *Sartre*, Glasgow: Fontana/Collins, 1975, p. 33.
35. *Desert of the Heart*, pp. 234, 244.
36. If this interpretation seems strained, compare *Desert of the Heart*, p. 136: 'like . . . a rib', with Genesis 2: 20–24.
37. *Lesbian Images*, p. 1.
38. *Desert of the Heart*, p. 120.
39. *Ibid.*, p. 244.

THE POLITICS OF SEPARATISM AND LESBIAN UTOPIAN FICTION

/Sonya/Andermahr/

In the early 1980s I came across an article by the Leeds Revolutionary Feminist Group entitled 'Political lesbianism: The case against heterosexuality'.[1] Although I identified as a feminist, I had never read anything like it before and found myself shocked and excited. Political lesbianism seemed more radical than anything else that was on offer then, which for me meant student politics or the local Labour Party. Neither of these came near to confronting the issues of sexual identity at the heart of political lesbianism, or dared to pass political judgement on sexual acts. Although I found its equation of heterosexuality and rape unacceptable, political lesbianism appealed to me because it was provocative and out-rageous at a time when feminism on the whole wasn't.

For women who, like myself, had been too young to take part in the Women's Liberation Movement, revolutionary feminism, 1980s style, offered a way of living out the feminist slogan 'The personal is political' by politicising the most intimate of relationships: that between lovers. It presented the opportunity to re-create in our private lives the sense of revolutionary possibility represented by the feminist politics of the early 1970s.

The politicisation of lesbianism coincided with the emergence of feminist separatism, the doctrine of withdrawal from men and male culture, which evolved in the Women's Liberation Movement in the early 1970s. Before the 1970s the close connection between lesbian sexuality and feminist activism was never openly acknowledged; for many women in the 1970s they came to be seen as inseparable, and the words of an earlier lesbian-feminist, Charlotte Wolff, became something of a truism: 'The lesbian woman is a feminist by nature because she is free from emotional dependence on the male.'[2]

By the late seventies the case for the inseparability of lesbianism and feminism had been made powerfully many times, and heterosexual feminists and other dissenting voices found it increasingly difficult to counter. Like some magic act, two more or less distinct entities went into the hat and one apparently seamless object came out of it: if lesbians were 'naturally' feminists, then feminists were 'naturally' lesbians. It was no good arguing that all lesbians were not in fact feminists; 'false consciousness' theories which condemned 'heterosexual role-playing' were offered, quite successfully, to explain this anomaly:

> To us, lesbianism and feminism were synonymous, either one without the other was untenable. A non-feminist lesbian was just a failed heterosexual. A non-lesbian feminist was just a male-apologist.[3]

Separatism takes various forms and can be absolute or strategic; most feminisms have recognised the desirability of women-only spaces such as refuges, retreats, bars and conferences. Similarly, lesbian separatism is not a homogeneous discourse; separatists differ in their conceptions of sexual identity and sexual politics, and draw on different, sometimes conflicting, epistemological and ontological frameworks. However, two more or less distinct positions have emerged, which I shall call the 'political' model and the 'utopian' model. The 'political' model, characteristic of political lesbianism and revolutionary feminism, sees separatism primarily as a means of undermining male power. It argues that if women cease to co-operate with men on a daily basis, the system of male power which oppresses women will no longer be able to sustain itself. Separatism is therefore primarily a tactical weapon, a means to an end. The emphasis is on political struggle in the here and now:

> [L]esbians, by loving women and not men, pose a direct threat to the very basis of male supremacy. From this analysis, we conclude that lesbians have the ability and commitment to women that will be necessary to overthrow male supremacy and its attendant forms of oppression . . .[4]

The second form of separatism, the 'utopian' model, characteristic of cultural feminism and the radical feminism of the 1970s, sees separatism not only as a strategy but as a final solution to the problem of women's oppression in male-dominated society. The emphasis is not so much on overthrowing the male system as on withdrawing from it for good. Having disengaged from male society, women will create an all-female world based on the 'female' values of co-operation, non-violence, community, nurturance, motherhood and ecological coexistence:

[We see]. . . lesbian separatism as . . . a viable, permanent alternative, which will prepare us for the time when we will be able to reinstate new forms of old matriarchal societies and when, once again, the Female Principle will have jurisdiction over the earth.[5]

This model is based on an ultimately essentialist notion of female nature, positing women as biologically and morally superior to men. The political model, on the whole, rejects the idea of a fixed female nature or sexuality, and tends to see sexuality as subject to conscious control rather than innate. However, central to both these conceptions is a belief in the fundamentally oppressive nature of heterosexuality. Heterosexuality, whether it is defined as an institution, a philosophical system, a biological impulse, or any sexual act between women and men, is seen as antithetical to women's liberation. In many separatisms there is a slippage between these designations, making it difficult to distinguish between them and so negotiate the various different aspects of heterosexuality. While all feminisms problematise heterosexuality to some extent, here heterosexuality simply *is* oppression:

We see heterosexuality as an institution of male domination. . . . Penetration is an act of great symbolic significance by which the oppressor enters the body of the oppressed. . . . Every act of penetration for a woman is an invasion which undermines her confidence and saps her strength.[6]

Here, 'heterosexuality' is not so much a social institution as a biologically determined act of male aggression. Political lesbians, unlike cultural feminists, make no claims about women's 'innate' sexuality and, indeed, stress women's ability to choose their sexual orientation, as the slogan 'Any woman can be a lesbian' demonstrates.[7] Sexuality therefore becomes a voluntaristic act of sexual reorientation, rather than the more positivist form it assumes in cultural feminist discourse, as expressive of female desire. It is a sexuality without any ontological basis, defined in opposition to 'male' sexuality. Heterosexual women, in particular, are denied any stake in their own sexuality:

We defined a political lesbian as a woman-identified woman who did not fuck men . . . it's rubbish to say that women fuck men; what happens is that men fuck women, or women get fucked by men.[8]

Men's sexuality, on the other hand, is endowed with immanence; it appears fixed and inevitably destructive. Biological models of sexuality, fiercely rejected regarding women, are reinstated to construct men's sexuality.

The French feminist Monique Wittig has rejected what she sees as the 'biologising interpretation of history' common to both these forms of separatism:

> For me this could never constitute a lesbian approach to women's oppression, since it assumes that the basis of society . . . lies in heterosexuality. . . . Furthermore, not only is this conception still imprisoned in the categories of sex (woman and man), but it holds onto the idea that the capacity to give birth (biology) is what defines a woman.[9]

Wittig therefore rejects the notions that women and men constitute different species and that male violence is a biological inevitability. Here her social-constructionist perspective allows her to locate women's oppression in an institutional or ideological heterosexuality, rather than in biological dimorphism.[10] This, she argues, is crucial if we are to have any *politics* of women's oppression and any hope of change:

> . . . by admitting there is a 'natural' division between women and men, we naturalize history, we assume that men and women have always existed and will always exist. Not only do we naturalize history, but also consequently we naturalize the social phenomena which express our oppression, making change impossible.[11]

This, I believe, is a more fruitful ground for a politics of lesbianism. However, in her article 'One is not born a woman' she goes to the other extreme and defines 'lesbian' *oppositionally* to 'woman'. 'Woman' has been thoroughly colonised by man; lesbian, as the silent, taboo, or 'outsider' identity, is the only viable identity for the feminist subject:

> Lesbian is the only concept that I know of which is beyond the categories of sex (man and woman), because the designated subject (lesbian) is not a woman, either economically, or politically, or ideologically.[12]

Wittig argues that lesbian societies are not based on women's oppression; while this may be so, they certainly don't exist outside it. Isn't Wittig, here, in danger of setting lesbianism outside history? Instead of the biologically based lesbian subject, she produces the transcendent political lesbian subject who is somehow entirely (and always?) outside the designation 'woman' and, by implication, outside the categories of race and class as well.

The different conceptions of these forms of separatism engender different conceptions of the lesbian subject. The utopian model posits a lesbian subject whose identification with other women is total and exclusive. All women are part of a universal sisterhood, 'journeying' towards self-realisation in and through the Lesbian Nation in solidarity and love. The figure of the lesbian 'everywoman' and the idea of 'lesbian journeying' are central to utopian separatist discourse. The political model, on the other hand, envisages the lesbian subject as a warrior figure, or 'guerrilla', perpetually fighting male power. Alongside the political separatist scenario of continual battle against the forces of male supremacy is the utopian, wish-fulfilment, fantasy of sisterhood and mutual love. If the utopian model is about women's community, the political model is about conflict.

In the early 1970s four women, Alice, Gordon, Debbie and Mary, using the political model, defined lesbian separatism as a new ideology which alone was capable of speaking to the needs of all women and destroying patriarchy and male supremacy.[13] Yet women's actual experiences of separatism have been far more disparate and contradictory than this account hoped for, and its ability to meet the needs 'of all women' has hardly been borne out. In particular, issues of classism and racism in the women's movement as well as in the wider society have precluded an overarching, unified response to patriarchy. Janet Dixon, in her fascinating article about her experience of separatism and its ideological effect on her life, highlighted the sacrifices demanded of its practitioners whom she compared to religious ascetics:

> Separatism is to feminism what fundamentalism is to Christianity. It is the centre, the beating heart, the essence. The dogma is of absolutes, the lifestyle is of attempted purity and the zealot subject to continuous derision . . .[14]

Central to Dixon's account of political separatism is the notion of renunciation, be it of male lovers, friends, children, man-made produce and technology, so-called masculine pursuits, practices, roles – of anything that isn't 'female' in origin or character: 'male culture in all its manifestations is shunned'.[15] The stress here is all on political imperative, on what women *must* do in order to overturn male supremacy; women's particular emotional, sexual, psychological needs and desires are not addressed. By contrast, the utopian model does engage with women's perceived needs, addressing the lesbian subject as an emotional as well as a political entity. Radicalesbians, for example, speak of lesbianism in liberal individualist terms as a journey towards 'the liberation of self, inner peace, real love of self and of all women'.[16] This seems to suggest that the achievement of individual 'selfhood' is as important as the overthrow of male supremacy.

Far more common in utopian separatist discourse, however, is the construction of the lesbian subject as a member of the collective rather than as an individual seeking self-identity. Women's needs are perceived in terms of the need for nurturance and interrelatedness and, frequently, in terms of the desire for the pre-Oedipal relation to the mother.[17] The goal of feminism is not the individuation of women's identities but their merger in a common female identity. As Radicalesbians put it: 'To confront another woman is finally to confront oneself'.[18] Many utopian separatist writings speak in mythical terms about female identity, invoking myths of rebirth and mutual self-creation. In an article which envisages women's separation from men, Julia Penelope addresses 'the women who created me in love and in life, in our lives, of whom I am and will be in this life'.[19] Her own identity becomes merged with that of her reader/s on a continuum of women loving and creating each other. Penelope utilises a discourse of mutual empowerment; her separatist world gives women the freedom to express their love for one another and to rediscover suppressed forms of female bonding, which men have inhibited by monopolising female nurturance. For Janet Dixon, however, the essentialist myth of female community at the heart of utopian separatism is politically unacceptable:

> In defining the source of women's oppression being pro-male sexism rather than capitalism, separatism shifted the emphasis of the whole of feminism. But, having done this, separatism went on to offer only one solution, an *all-women world*. Here, separatism dissolves, at best, into romantic/cosmic/ evolutionary answers, or at worst into violence and male genocide.[20] (emphasis added)

While the attempt to realise the utopian solution of the 'Lesbian Nation', or the self-sufficient lesbian community, has undoubtedly failed the Lesbian Nation has had a powerful ideological effect on the women's movement. In 1970, in *The Dialectic of Sex*, Shulamith Firestone lamented that 'We haven't even a literary image of this future society; there is not even a utopian feminist literature yet in existence.'[21] The next ten years saw the emergence both of a separatist utopian literature giving fictional realisation to an all-female world, and of lesbian reading communities in the United States and Europe. A close and dynamic relationship existed between radical feminist theory and practice, between feminist writers and readers. Firestone's text, for instance, was itself the inspiration for Marge Piercy's novel *Woman on the Edge of Time*. Katherine V. Forrest's *Daughters of a Coral Dawn*; Sally Miller Gearhart's *The Wanderground*; Joanna Russ's *The Female Man*; Rochelle Singer's *The Demeter Flower*; Monique Wittig's *Les Guérillères* and Donna Young's *Retreat* portray all-female societies which are explicitly lesbian, and start from the premiss that separatism is a prerequisite for social change.[22]

Sally Miller Gearhart's separatist utopia *The Wanderground: Stories of the hill women* was published in 1978 and quickly became a feminist bestseller. Unlike other texts in the utopian tradition, such as Charlotte Perkins Gilman's *Herland*, Gearhart's novel does not attempt to realise another world through exact descriptions of the socioeconomic and political new order. Rather, *The Wanderground* presents a romantic vision of a group of women living in harmony with each other and their natural surroundings. It functions not as a blueprint for a better society but as a myth of female community, expressing an emotional and physical experience. This mythic quality is reflected not only in the rendering of archetypal female experience and character, but also in the narrative structure. There is no linear narrative; *The Wanderground* comprises a series of loosely linked short stories or episodes, each focusing on different members of a community of hill women and on different aspects of their common experience.

Critical appraisal of the novel has also stressed its mythic quality. Sandy Boucher describes it as presenting 'a world we know in our hearts must surely exist somewhere'.[23] Similarly, Elizabeth A. Lynn comments: 'We need such visions. Many women, reading them, will find their own dreams reflected.'[24] Both these comments suggest that the novel's 'vision' corresponds to a register of women's shared psychic experience. The use of maternal and pre-Oedipal archetypes allows the novel to address women's emotional needs in a way unavailable to political lesbian discourse, which tends to reject myth as inimical to political praxis. Where the latter stresses opposition to masculinity, *The Wanderground*'s cultural feminism celebrates the mothering aspects of femininity. The hill women share in an economy of female desire based on mother-love and maternal creation, as the scene in the 'cella', the womblike caves where conception takes place, demonstrates:

> Fora imagined herself marching in the cavalcade of her own sowing and implantment. A long line of women surging down the path, their arms and voices linked to each other . . . rank on rank, body on body, voice on voice. Entwined by her own arms were Tolatilita and Phtha, two of her seven sisters, and behind them Yva marched, carrying in her cradled hand the precious egg-laden liquid. . . . Fora reached out in her mind to touch each one. Brightly they all swung down the curling passage, to the center of the Kochlias, to the narrow low place at the bottom of the world.[25]

The Wanderground represents a fictional and literal realisation of the separatist concept of 'lesbian journeying'. In each episode a woman makes a journey which enriches her in some way, and brings her a stronger sense of female interdependence. Fora travels to the cella 'womb' and comes into contact with Mother Earth; Alaka returns from the city to the peace and harmony of the Wanderground; Clana journeys telepathically through women's collective history of oppression in the remember rooms; and Evona relearns the journeying power of windriding. Although each woman and each episode possesses individual characteristics and demonstrates a different aspect of female experience, in effect they work interchangeably, as parables. Each mirrors and reinforces the others, underscoring not difference but commonality and homogeneity.[26] More fundamental differences between women, such as race and class, are also seen to dissolve in the text. Skin colour becomes a feature of each woman's physical appearance rather than a marker of a cultural identity which may be shared with some men. While the achievment of racial harmony is part of the wish-fulfilment function of the utopia, it also mirrors the radical feminist stress on the primacy of sexual oppression over other oppressions in contemporary societies.

Interwoven into *The Wanderground*'s evocation of female community is a more explicit engagement with contemporary feminist politics, specifically the issue of separatism versus coexisting with men. On this level the novel is in my view disappointingly conservative, espousing a belief in biologically determined sexual difference and thereby undercutting the possibility for a sexual *politics*. The novel, at times, is aware that maleness is not undifferentiated brutality and cannot be equated with one oppressive form of masculinity. This is recognised early on by Jacqua, who 'dutifully recites' the hill women's creed: 'It is too simple to condemn them all or to praise all of us.'[27]

Theoretically the hill women accept the untenability of a belief in absolute, biologically determined difference, but they argue, for practical reasons and 'for the sake of earth and all she holds, that simplicity must be our creed'.[28] Therefore they *act* as if men's and women's differences are irreconcilable, and as if there is no possibility of men changing. The distinction made by the hill women between theory and practice is in one view sensible politics; in another, it effectively elides the theory. The apparent justification for this distinction lies in their continued survival. For women to trust men and admit them to closer community, the text implies, would be to threaten this hard-won survival.

However, by the text's own demonstration, all men are not the same. *The Wanderground* creates a group of men, the Gentles, who have thrown off oppressive attitudes and behaviour and who, out of respect for the women's autonomy, have voluntarily withdrawn from their society:

'In the beginning we kept ourselves from you in spite of our needs, out of respect for your wishes. And because we knew that women and men can do nothing but violence to one another.'[29]

To some extent the Gentles correspond to the contemporary gay male community: men who do not see women as sex objects and who have an understanding of sexual oppression. But the Gentles are more properly political celibates; they don't actively love men; rather, they withdraw from women 'out of respect'. While refusing to allow the Gentles to relate to women, the novel does not depict them as having warm relationships with one another; homoeroticism between men is completely absent from the text. As Diana Fuss has argued, gay men represent the 'invisibilised other' of lesbian feminist texts, whereby same-sex love is conceived of in purely female terms.[30] When male homosexuality is represented, as in Adrienne Rich's article 'Compulsory heterosexuality', it is seen as motivated by a misogynistic impulse to reject women and femininity and occupy a macho male haven.[31] This representation reflects the suspicion with which many radical and revolutionary feminists of the 1970s and early 1980s viewed gay male culture, whose values they saw as consumerist and inimical to women's political interests.

At one point, in the story 'The Remember Rooms', an older woman, Alaka, assures the girl-child Clana that, in the past, 'some physical expression between women and men might have been good'.[32] Clana, however, is sceptical – and with good reason, for all the memories relived in the remember rooms have been of unmitigated suffering and pain at the hands of men. The hill women's retelling of history corresponds to separatist political discourse, and is informed by the same pessimism about the capacity of women and men to find ways of loving in the face of sexism. Clana is shown pornography to exemplify male attitudes to women and, in the absence of more positive and varied representations, she is understandably confused: 'How could you let someone enter your body that way and not be a victim?'[33] Since Clana has been taught to equate penetration with rape, the guides' careful disclaimers are lost on her. The ideological message echoes revolutionary feminism's insistence, in the early 1980s, that penetration was fundamentally phallocentric. Are we also to assume that penetration is not part of the hill women's own sexual repertoire, and that vaginal 'enfolding' of any part of the body is therefore out of bounds?[34]

In another story, 'A Man in the City', the hill woman Betha meets Aaron, a Gentle, and ponders the important question 'What makes him a man?':

About most men here she could give a quick easy answer. About the Gentles she could not; her absolutes began to get fuzzy . . .[35]

This insight works to challenge the biological essentialism of the hill women's political philosophy. But no sooner has Betha made the valuable discovery that masculinity is not monolithic, that men can change and have changed, than her insight is undermined by the very biological essentialism it challenged:

> He was not a woman, after all, and there seemed only the thinnest possibility of mindstretch between them. Somehow men – even Gentles – found it difficult or impossible really to share power.[36]

In the end the Gentles represent the acceptable face of manhood not because they are good, loving and kind, but because they have accepted the hill women's belief in irreducible gender difference – a difference which, ultimately, boils down to anatomy. Moreover, Betha has to 'act' in a comradely way towards Aaron; it does not come naturally to her. Whereas women's relations with each other are presented as natural and authentic despite differences, women's and men's are somehow inevitably forced and inauthentic.

This inauthenticity is also represented at the level of language. For instance, the novel employs a different linguistic register in conveying the encounter between the hill women and the Gentles. Their thoughts do not travel back and forth harmoniously; instead words are exchanged combatively. Meaning lies not in the saying, as it does in woman-centred language, but in what is said. The text makes clear that this shift is a result of 'the cock-centred energy' of the city and that there, it is more appropriate to speak of a 'woman-fucker' than of a sexual 'enfoldment'.

The equation of masculinity and femininity with particular linguistic modes has become commonplace in both feminist theory and literary practice. In *Woman on the Edge of Time* Marge Piercy elaborates a woman-centred language system which privileges the present continuous tense and verbalises nouns, making states dynamic rather than passive propositions.[37] These systems share an assumption that verbs, especially perfect-tense or transitive ones, are somehow masculine, and nouns and states of being are somehow feminine. In privileging the latter, female experience is validated. While acknowledging the importance of such linguistic interventions, especially the coining of new, non-gender-specific terms in the public world such as 'chairperson', 'firefighter' and 'police officer', I am troubled by the similarities between some feminist language systems and what many feminists have identified as phallogocentrism. For instance, Hélène Cixous has demonstrated the ways in which patriarchal binary thought works to subordinate the 'feminine' through an equation with the 'negative' pole:

Activity/Passivity
Sun/Moon
Culture/Nature
Father/Mother
Head/Emotions
Intelligible/Sensitive
Logos/Pathos[38]

Simply inverting this opposition in order to privilege the feminine merely reinforces the binary principle and fails to challenge the hierarchical, sex-based ordering of knowledge. *The Wanderground* never seriously seeks to undermine binarism – in fact, the philosophy and politics it propounds are based on it. For this reason no amount of Gentle self-sacrifice and sensitivity will redeem masculinity; firmly welded to biological maleness, it has already been judged irredeemable.

The most extreme demonstration of the Gentles' inability to change for the better is provided by the episode in which they demonstrate their newly discovered telepathic powers to the hill women. The episode is used to demonstrate not the creative potential of men but their propensity to appropriate women's gifts and discoveries. Moreover, the Gentles' power is different in kind to that of the hill women, being 'like a bridge, not a circle. . . . We think it is a different form altogether . . . a form unique to men.'[39] In order to exercise this power the Gentles have to line up, as if for a conga; thereby underlining, as it were, the essentially linear nature of male energy. Although, as Tony points out, a bridge is a potentially positive image, representing a link between people, Evona rejects this interpretation, preferring the phallic image of a sword as a fitting analogue. Old habits die hard, I suppose. Andros is understandably indignant at Evona's self-righteous attitude:

'Does it ever occur to you that we might have some humanity too? That as a special breed of men we may be on the brink of discovering our own non-violent psychic powers?'[40]

The answer from Evona is an emphatic 'no':

'Nonviolent? Never. You know what will happen. You'll use your new power all right. You'll use it, perfect it, manufacture it, package it, sell it, and tell the world that it's clean and new because it comes from a different breed of men. But it's just another fancy prick to invade the world with. And you'll use it because you can't really communicate, you can't really love! Of course it's not an enfoldment. You couldn't enfold an ant if it crept into the middle of your hand!'[41]

Such sentiments reflect the 1970s cultural feminist equation of masculinity and military aggression, and feminist pessimism about men's ability to change. The growth in this period of women's retreats and camps was a response to the diagnosis that men were not ready or able to give up their 'fancy pricks'. In England in the 1980s the Greenham Common Peace Camp drew successfully and spectacularly on the identification of women as peacemakers and guardians of the life of the planet.

If *The Wanderground* is deeply sceptical of men's ability to change for the good, it must surely allow for women's change in consciousness, the precondition of women's liberation and affirmative action. Or does it? In fact, the hill women change themselves and their environment very little. The means of their liberation is not so much their own political action, in the form of separatism, but a *deus ex machina*, an external metaphysical event – the 'Revolt of the Mother', whereby nature, or Nature, herself rejects and disables male power. As a fantasy or mythic resolution, Gearhart's solution is a stroke of genius; as practical politics, with which the novel does engage, it is a non-starter. Men are oppressors, women are their victims, and you can't do much about it. Once the text is engaged with on this level it becomes a very depressing read; as June Howard comments in her reading of the novel: 'Women are essentially powerless on any terrain which resembles the present.'[42] Likewise, Sylvia Bovenschen picks up on this implicit defeatism, arguing for the necessity of distinguishing between myth and reality, and for the recognition that 'the moment of resistance is contemporary and political'.[43] While I would agree with this, I would also not wish to underestimate the power of fantasy. As Rosemary Jackson has argued, fantasy does serve a political purpose:

> The modern fantastic . . . is a subversive literature. It exists alongside the 'real' . . . as a muted presence, a silenced imaginary other. . . . [It] aims at dissolution of an order experienced as oppressive and insufficient.[44]

Imaginative extrapolation, by virtue of being oppositional or because it envisions an alternative, serves to denaturalise the status quo and to interrogate the nature of the 'real'. Yet although I acknowledge the empowering aspects of the Wanderground myth, I am not convinced that *The Wanderground* demonstrates the negating activity characteristic of fantasy. It seems to me that rather than transgressing the 'real' and exploring the limits of what Jackson calls 'our culture's epistemological and ontological frame', the novel shores up some of the most oppressive aspects of patriarchal culture, not least gender binarism.

* * *

Joanna Russ's *The Female Man* represents a radically different utopian discourse to that of *The Wanderground* and the utopian model of separatism. Russ's novel, first published in 1976, is both a deconstruction of the utopian myth which informs these discourses, and a reconstruction of 'utopia' to include political praxis and change. *The Female Man* seeks to define a politics of the possible, rather than create an impossible pre-Oedipal dream-world. The female utopian community, Whileaway, and the worlds of sexual conflict in the novel are shown to be linked, both through the characters of the four *J*s (Joanna, Jeannine, Jael and Janet) and through praxis, or conscious political action. Moreover, there is no single and totally oppressive society which is juxtaposed to the utopia; Russ provides three other, discernibly different, societies, in different stages of patriarchal rule and feminist struggle, against which we apprehend Whileaway. Where Gearhart's novel is sublime, celebratory and mythical, Russ's is ironical, iconoclastic and satirical. *The Female Man* seeks to challenge the kind of uncritical myth-making which permeates *The Wanderground*, and is critical of the cultural feminist celebration of 'female' virtues, clearly locating them as part of patriarchy's myth of feminity:

> Woman is purity; woman is carnality . . . woman is the life-force.
> 'I am the gateway to another world' (said I, looking in the mirror) . . . 'I am the life-force, I am selfless love.' (Somehow it sounds different in the first person, doesn't it?)[45]

While *The Wanderground* deconstructs some aspects of the feminine myth – namely, woman-as-thing-for-man – it fails to confront fully the cultural construction of femininity. This is precisely Russ's project in *The Female Man*. Her intention is signified by the title of the novel, which alerts the reader to its central problematic: What is meant by the signifiers of gender difference, and how does this relate to the way we experience ourselves as gendered beings? *The Female Man* undermines fixed gender roles and implies that they are just that – roles that we acquire, rather than expressions of our inner nature. When Jeannine insists 'I enjoy being a girl', Joanna's ironic reply demonstrates how ridiculous the statement is: 'Has anyone proposed the choice to you lately?'[46] The idea put forward in *The Wanderground* – that femaleness is an essential property – is rejected in *The Female Man* as part of the feminine myth. This novel insists that women are not repositories of virtue; women can be stupid (Janet), murderous (Jael) and fallible. Moreover, they have a right to be; the novel implies that the compulsory superiority of Gearhart's hill women is just as oppressive as enforced housewifery. Whereas *The Wanderground* approaches the question of gender difference by affirming traditionally feminine qualities, *The Female Man* interrogates the categories themselves, even to the point of asking whether 'women' can be said to exist, much as Wittig does. If women are as men define them, then perhaps it is better, as Joanna concludes, not to be one and to become a female man instead.

In *The Female Man* a positive female identity is not the result of a reassertion of existing feminine qualities but the redefinition and reconstruction of the category 'woman'. Part of this redefinition involves a reappraisal, and sometimes a rejection, of heterosexuality. Joanna and Laura become lesbians in the course of the novel, Janet has always been lesbian, Jael fights for women against men, and Jeannine learns a sense of sisterhood. Lesbian identity in *The Female Man* is not a manifestation of a natural female nature, as it is in *The Wanderground*, but, in Joanna's case, part of a process of negotiating and resisting gender difference.

The novel provides a variety of socially situated lesbian identifications. Janet represents the lesbian utopian hero; she comes from the all-female world of Whileaway – 'a name for Earth ten centuries from now, but not *our* Earth . . . Whileaway, you may gather, is in the future. But not *our* future.'[47] The fact that there is no historical continuity between Joanna's world and Whileaway has the effect of relativising their respective realities and forms of lesbian identification. Heterosexuality and sexual binarism are not part of Janet's reality; lesbianism consequently carries a different signification. Lesbian existence is the norm, not the silenced 'other', and homophobia and heterosexism are unknown in Whileaway. As a result Janet is confused by the dynamics of sexual power relations and gender roles operating in Joanna's world. The clash between different conceptions of lesbianism is made the basis of much of the novel's humour, as in the episode between Janet and Joanna in which the latter, with devastating consequences, misreads Janet's actions:

> She smiled. She put her arm around me.
> Oh, I couldn't!
> ?
> That's different
> (You'll hear a lot of those two sentences in life, if you listen for them . . .)
> She bent down to kiss me, looking kind, looking perplexed, and I kicked her.
> That's when she put her fist through the wall.[48]

Janet's lesbian identity, the text makes clear, is not (yet) available to the contemporary lesbian reader. It is a product of a utopian society in which heterosexuality is a distant memory. Janet is self-consciously inscribed as a fantasy of lesbian universality; the reader is invited to believe in her at the same time as her existence is denied:

> Goodbye to Janet, whom we don't believe in . . . but who is in secret our saviour from utter despair, who appears Heaven-high in our dreams with a mountain under each arm and the ocean in her pocket. . . . Radiant as the day, the Might-be of our dreams, living as she does in a blessedness none of us will ever know, she is nonetheless Everywoman.[49]

One criticism that could be levelled at the text is that in constructing the Everywoman figure and the four *J*s as white, it presents white experience as exemplary. But I would argue that, far from eliding racial difference, the text is very aware of how race operates as a power relation which cuts across gender oppression. The novel goes beyond *The Wanderground*'s critique of male domination in connecting sexual oppression to Western imperialism, fascism and racism. Jael's remark – 'We're all white-skinned, eh? I bet two of you didn't think of that' – can be read as a comment on the colour blindness of white readers as well as that of the other characters.[50]

Through Jael, the novel presents another version of Everywoman. Jael comes from a radically sex-polarised society in which men and women are involved in a struggle to the death. The war between 'Us and Them', in the name of the binary oppositions outlined by Cixous, represents a 'worst-case scenario', in which the struggle for privileged status has become an armed struggle. Jael is a lesbian warrior figure, a 'rosy, wholesome, single-minded assassin', akin to Wittig's 'guerrilla'.[51] She articulates a 'political' separatist analysis and her identity is shaped by political imperative, rather than by sexual preference (she doesn't seem to have time for love affairs, although she does make love to a male robot called Davy). She is dedicated to 'The Cause'; her mission is to kill Manlanders: men who have become so debased by violence that they are no longer human. Far from feeling guilty about killing men, Jael is strengthened by each murder:

> Anybody who believes I feel guilty for the murders I did is a Damned Fool . . . I am not guilty because I murdered.
> *I murdered because I was guilty.*
> Murder is my one way out.
> For every drop of blood there is restitution made; with every truthful reflection in the eyes of a dying man I get back a little of my soul; with every gasp of horrified comprehension I come a little more into the light. See? It's *me!*[52]

This an absolutist world in which men and women are no longer of the same species and there is no hope of reconciliation. In this 'Us' and 'Them' world, biology once more becomes the mark of difference, except this time femaleness functions as the central signifier. For Jael, femininity is not so much acquired as 'in the blood', yet even this absolutism is undercut as she ironically adds: 'But whose?' She is the definitive separatist freedom fighter: courageous, militant, independent. Of all the *J*s, Joanna admires her the most:

> . . . twisted as she is on the rack of her own hard logic, triumphant in her extremity, the hateful hero with the broken heart.[53]

While Gearhart's journeying hill women represent the 'utopian' model of lesbian subjectivity, Russ's Jael character brilliantly conveys the anger, self-righteousness and single-mindedness of political separatist psychology. The novel's portrait of Jael has much in common with Janet Dixon's description of her experience of separatism, especially when she comments, 'The rage and sense of injustice, for a separatist, is not powerfully enough voiced anywhere else.'[54] The difference is that whereas anger eventually became self-destructive and regressive for Janet Dixon, Jael, the ultimate revenge-fantasy figure, continues to thrive on and draw sustenance from hers.

The Jael sections perform a function important to the politics of *The Female Man* as a whole: they serve to debunk Janet's organic myth of the origins of Whileaway. According to Janet her world came into being when a plague killed all the men. Like the 'Revolt of the Mother' in *The Wanderground*, the plague is a natural expedient for dispensing with men, and is more palatable than genocide. But, says Jael:

> 'That "plague" you talk of is a lie. I know. . . . It is I who gave you your "plague", my dear . . . I, I, I, I am the plague . . . I and the war I fight have built your world for you.'[55]

In other words, 'utopia' is struggled for, it does not miraculously appear. People, motivated by utopian impulses rather than God or Nature, are the only real agents of change. *The Female Man* seeks to represent history as a process of change, initiated by political action. Utopia is not a static future but more a 'coming into being' through radical action. For all Gearhart's stress on the present participle, it is actually Russ's text, not Gearhart's, which privileges 'becoming' over 'being', process over state. In Gearhart's world you are what you are; in Russ's you are what you do to change your world for the better.

The Female Man, actually written in 1969, is one of the earliest novels both to affirm lesbianism and to insist on its multiple forms. It argues that there is no one way to be a lesbian, that lesbianism is not *the* solution, although it can be part of the liberation process. This kind of fictional representation is fundamentally different to both the 'political' and 'utopian' types of separatist discourse which each sets up a single, monolithic model of lesbian identity; the one defined by opposition to heterosexuality, the other rooted in an essentialist concept of femininity as motherhood. *The Female Man* makes space not only for political action and mothering but also for sexual relations between women, an element which is largely lacking in separatist discourse. There is no contradiction in the novel between articulating a critique of male power *and* depicting sex between women. The absence of sexual images of women in lesbian feminist texts of the 1970s, including *The Wanderground*, is, I think, due to the influence and dominance of lesbian feminisms which define relations between women in terms of either female bonding or political solidarity. *The Female Man* is rare in managing to articulate sexual desire and political critique together without subordinating one to the other.

The discourses of 'utopian' and 'political' separatism were products of two moments of Women's Liberation: the cultural feminism of the late 1970s and the political lesbianism of the early 1980s. Both had a powerful capacity for motivating and organising the desires of women who, like myself, came to feminism and lesbianism in this period. Of the two, political lesbianism has been more important in the formation of my own sexual and political identity. It provided a way of relating my disaffection with heterosexuality to a more public politics against sexism. Now, however, I feel much more resistant to its analysis and to the forms its politics took in the 1980s. While I agree that the sexual is political, I don't think that the two can be collapsed in the way it suggests. This elision of sexuality and politics had the negative effect in the 1980s of creating a new sexual orthodoxy for lesbians: a set of correct behaviours which effectively policed 'deviant' lesbian sexualities.[56] At times lesbian politics of the 1980s seemed like a battle between competing definitions of lesbianism to occupy the moral high ground. Because part of lesbianism's attraction for me was its transgression of heterosexual orthodoxy, I find this development disturbing. The 1970s utopian dream of a community of all women gave way to a bitter row over who would have access to lesbian spaces, such as the London Lesbian and Gay Centre, over which books and films are suitable for us to look at, and over who would be allowed to march at Pride.[57] Moreover, some of the most effective political action in the 1980s, around the issues of Section 28 and AIDS, was not a separatist initiative in the name of 'lesbian' or 'woman', but was taken by a coalition of lesbians and gay men across – albeit uneasily – all their various sexual and political differences.

Notes

1. Leeds Revolutionary Feminist Group, 'The case against heterosexuality', in M. Evans, ed., *The Woman Question*, London: Fontana, 1982.
2. Charlotte Wolff, quoted in Bonnie S. Anderson and Judith P. Zinsser, eds, *A History of Their Own*, Harmondsworth: Penguin, 1988, vol. 2, p. 426.
3. Janet Dixon, 'Separatism', *Spare Rib*, **192**, 1988, p. 9.
4. Alice, Gordon, Debbie and Mary, 'Separatism', in Sarah Lucia Hoagland and Julia Penelope, eds, *For Lesbians Only: A separatist anthology*, London: Onlywomen Press, 1988, pp. 31–40.
5. *Ibid.*, p. 32.
6. Leeds Revolutionary Feminist Group, 'The case against heterosexuality', p. 65.
7. Attributed to Alix Dobkin in *For Lesbians Only*, p. 11.
8. Leeds Revolutionary Feminist Group, 'The case against heterosexuality', p. 71.
9. Monique Wittig, 'One is not born a woman', in *For Lesbians Only*, p. 440.
10. Although, as Diana Fuss shows in *Essentially Speaking* (New York: Routledge, 1989), Wittig's perspective is not consistently social-constructionist; at certain moments her discourse reinstates an essential lesbian subject.
11. Wittig, 'One is not born a woman'.
12. *Ibid.*, pp. 446–7.
13. Alice *et al.*, 'Separatism', p. 31.
14. Janet Dixon, 'Separatism', p. 6.
15. *Ibid.*, p. 9.
16. Radicalesbians, 'The woman-identified woman', in *For Lesbians Only*, p. 17.
17. See Nancy Chodorow, *The Reproduction of Mothering* (Berkeley: University of California, 1978) for an account of the pre-Oedipal relation to the mother and its significance for women. Chodorow argues that girls identify with their mothers more than boys because of their shared sex, and hence have more difficulty separating from them and forming an 'independent' identity. Moreover, because it is women rather than men who perform the nurturing role, women's emotional needs go largely unmet by men. Joanna Ryan, in her essay 'Psychoanalysis and women loving women', in J. Ryan and S. Cartledge, eds, *Sex and Love* (London: The Women's Press, 1983, pp. 196–209), suggests that lesbianism represents a means for women to receive and give maternal nurturance.
18. Radicalesbians, 'The woman-identified woman', p. 21.
19. Julia Penelope, 'A cursory and precursory history of language, and the telling of it', in *For Lesbians Only*, p. 55.
20. Dixon, 'Separatism', p. 11.
21. Shulamith Firestone, *The Dialectic of Sex: The case for feminist revolution*, New York: Morrow, 1970.
22. Marge Piercy, *Woman on the Edge of Time*, London: The Women's Press, 1979; Katherine V. Forrest, *Daughters of a Coral Dawn*, Tallahassee, FL: Naiad Press, 1984; Sally Miller Gearhart, *The Wanderground*, Watertown, MA: Persephone, 1978; Joanna Russ, *The*

Female Man, London: The Women's Press, 1976; Rochelle Singer, *The Demeter Flower*, New York: St Martin's Press, 1980; Monique Wittig, *Les Guérillères*, London: The Women's Press, 1979; Donna J. Young, *Retreat! As It Was*, Tallahassee, FL: Naiad Press, 1979.
23. Sandy Boucher, dust jacket, *The Wanderground*.
24. Elizabeth A. Lynn, dust jacket, *The Wanderground*.
25. Sally Gearhart, *The Wanderground*, p. 46.
26. See Sheila Jeffreys's *Anticlimax* (London: The Women's Press, 1990), which emphasises the eroticisation of sameness, rather than difference.
27. Gearhart, *The Wanderground*, p. 2.
28. *Ibid*.
29. *Ibid* p. 172.
30. Fuss, *Essentially Speaking*.
31. Adrienne Rich, 'Compulsory heterosexuality and lesbian existence', *Signs*, **5**, 1980.
32. *Ibid.*, p. 158.
33. *Ibid*.
34. See Andrea Dworkin's *Intercourse* (London: Secker & Warburg, 1987), which argues that the distinction between consensual penetration and rape is consistently blurred, suggesting that penetration is a fundamentally hostile act.
35. Gearhart, *The Wanderground*, p. 115.
36. *Ibid*.
37. Marge Piercy, *Woman on the Edge of Time*. See also Suzette Haden Elgin's *Native Tongue* (London: The Women's Press, 1985), which takes as its theme the notion of a gendered language system.
38. Hélène Cixous, quoted in Toril Moi, *Sexual/Textual Politics*, London: Methuen, 1985, p. 104.
39. Gearhart, *The Wanderground*, p. 178.
40. *Ibid.*, p. 179.
41. *Ibid*.
42. June Howard, 'Widening the dialogue on feminist SF' in G. Wolfe, ed., *Science Fiction Dialogues*, Chicago, 1982.
43. Sylvia Bovenschen, quoted in *ibid.*, p. 159.
44. Rosemary Jackson, *Fantasy, The Literature of Subversion*, London: Methuen, 1981, p. 180.
45. Joanna Russ, *The Female Man*, London: The Women's Press, 1985, p. 205.
46. *Ibid.*, p. 86.
47. *Ibid.*, p. 7.
48. *Ibid.*, p. 33.
49. *Ibid.*, p. 213.
50. *Ibid.*, p. 161.
51. *Ibid.*, p. 187.
52. *Ibid.*, p. 195.
53. *Ibid.*, p. 212.
54. Dixon, 'Separatism', p. 11.
55. Russ, *The Female Man*, p. 211.
56. For example, 'deviant' lesbian sexualities include butch/femme and s/m, but certain practices such as penetration, the use of sex toys, and 'rough' sex are also defined as unfeminist by some lesbian feminists. The 'debate' over access to the LLGC took place in London in 1985. Initially 'Lesbians Against s/m' succeeded in getting s/m lesbians excluded from the Centre, but after a second general meeting another group, 'Lesbians for the Centre', managed to get the decision overturned. For a fuller account, see Susan

Ardill and Sue O'Sullivan, 'Upsetting an applecart: Difference, desire and lesbian sadomasochism', *Feminist Review*, **23**, 1986, pp. 31–58.
57. Some feminist bookshops have refused to stock the magazines *On Our Backs* and *Quim*. A group of lesbian feminists attempted to prevent the screening of Sheila McClaughlin's film, *She Must Be Seeing Things*, in 1988 in London and in 1989 in Manchester, where the Cornerhouse cinema received bombing threats. At the 1990 Pride some lesbians objected to the presence on the march of members of an s/m club.

ORANGES ARE NOT THE ONLY FRUIT
Reaching Audiences Other Lesbian Texts Cannot Reach

/Hilary/Hinds/

Jeanette Winterson's first novel, *Oranges Are Not the Only Fruit*, is one of those success stories of which feminists feel proud. From its small-scale beginnings as a risky undertaking by the newly formed Pandora Press in 1985, through the winning of the Whitbread Prize for a first novel later the same year, to its much-lauded adaptation for BBC television by Winterson herself in January 1990, the work's reputation, like that of its author, has grown and prospered. Winterson herself is now unquestionably treated as a 'serious' author, highly praised by other 'serious' authors such as Gore Vidal and Muriel Spark; yet she is also a popular success, appearing on Clive James's television chat show and being sympathetically profiled in the popular press. The 'serious' side of the success story, her qualification as a representative of high culture, is largely dependent on her literary output: *Oranges* and, more especially, her third novel, *The Passion*; her popular success and high media exposure can be dated to the television adaptation of *Oranges*. That an author who is a lesbian and a feminist should be so successful in such contrasting contexts is seen by other lesbians and feminists as something to celebrate. Whatever misgivings may be felt about the traps and pitfalls of the mainstream, the sight of 'one of us' being given so much approval by the pillars of the establishment, whence usually comes opprobrium, is a source of enormous pleasure.

This essay examines the meanings of the ambiguous cultural status of *Oranges*, a text which cut across the high/popular culture divide with its success as a BBC2 'quality' drama, and its acclaim from the popular press, lesbian audiences and serious critics alike. Through an analysis of its reception, I shall examine what it meant for an avowedly lesbian novel to be fêted by the mainstream media and press as well as being so successful within a subcultural context. Did the reviewers in the lesbian, feminist and radical press read it differently from those in the mainstream? Was the text's 'literariness', its high-cultural status, apparent from the outset, and how important was this to the acceptability of its unambiguous affirmation of lesbianism?

'First Fruit':[1] *Oranges* the novel

Oranges Are Not the Only Fruit was published in Britain on 21 March 1985 by Pandora Press, the feminist imprint of Routledge & Kegan Paul. Usually described by reviewers as a 'semi-autobiographical novel', it focuses on the childhood and adolescence of 'Jeanette', and her relationship with her Evangelical-Christian mother. Her mother's plans for Jeanette to become a missionary are thwarted when she discovers that she is having a sexual relationship with her best friend, Melanie; the rest of the narrative is concerned with Jeanette's resolution of the divergent pulls of Church and sexuality on her life. Interspersing this narrative are short fables or fairy tales, commenting on the principal action, and direct interventions by an authorial voice.

Most reviewers agreed that *Oranges* was a notable first novel. In the mainstream and alternative presses, words like 'brilliant', 'beautifully written', 'decidedly imposing in [its] originality', and 'moving' recur. Critics delighted in its humour, decided it was 'quirky' and 'eccentric', and proclaimed Winterson a 'talent to watch'. A few reviewers, admittedly, were not unequivocal in their praise, complaining of 'utterly routine moments', that the novel became 'shrill', had 'the superficially modern pace of a pop video', or veered 'dangerously close to indulgent high-school diary entries'.[2] First impressions, however, were generally extremely positive.

There was general agreement, too, about the source of this novel's distinction: its decidedly 'literary' quality. *Time Out* identified 'an encyclopaedic depth of knowledge [which] will appeal to literary magpies, with strange facts and unusual references popped in here and there' (March 1985). Others adopted the tone of the professional literary critic. John Clute in *New Statesman* wrote of:

> the dense, polychromatic clarity of its rendering of the circumstances in which the protagonist and her mother pass their days, pixillated, obsessed with a revivalist God and His fallible Pastors, insanely blinkered but joyful.
> (*New Statesman*, 12 April 1985)

Marsha Rowe suggested that 'a narrative stance of bravado and sharp style plays with the idea that history is only storytelling' (?1);[3] Zoë Fairbairns discussed the functions of the three different viewpoints in the novel (*Spare Rib*, July 1985); *Ms* magazine compared Winterson with the established authors Flannery O'Connor and Rita Mae Brown, and *New Statesman* compared the novel with a painting by L. S. Lowry. This initial acclamation of *Oranges* as a 'literary' text by the radical press was later taken up by the mainstream reviewers, particularly once the novel had won the Whitbread Prize. The prize became an increasingly important part of Winterson's pedigree, particularly once she adapted the novel for television. This combined with the notion of *Oranges* as a 'quality' text, and both became central to how the television adaptation was previewed and reviewed. 'Quality' is a key word to which I shall return later, but it is important to note that this concept was in play from the outset, not resulting from the Whitbread but certainly greatly augmented by it.

The consensus amongst the different presses as to the 'brilliance' of the book, however, was not straightforwardly extended to their assessments of its themes. They generally agreed that the novel was 'about a Lancashire girl growing up on the Evangelist lunatic fringe' (*Time Out*, March 1985), or concerned the:

> Early life and times of our heroine with her adopted mum, self-styled Missionary on the Home Front among north country heathen. Bible quizzes, distributing tracts and laying out the dead are all normal routine until adolescence sows the seeds of temptation. A delightfully quirky and original first novel. (*Sunday Times*, 1 December 1985)

Characteristically, a light-hearted, even flippant, tone was adopted; at times the reviewers even seemed to be trying to mimic the novel's narrative tone. Humour, then, and a childhood within the context of an Evangelical sect, were seen as being at the heart of *Oranges*.

What marks out the 'mainstream' critics, however, is their contentment with this highly individualised account of the novel, its meaning discussed in the classic literary terms of character, narrative and authorial expertise. Critics who assessed it on grounds other than these were to be found within the 'alternative' presses. Zoë Fairbairns located *Oranges* specifically in relation to feminism and religious ideologies: it showed 'the flourishing and development of some religious women's strength in spite of a patriarchal concept of god' (*Spare Rib*, July 1985). Few other reviews saw feminism as of any significance, *Time Out* even taking pleasure in distancing Winterson from the whole idea: 'Jeanette describes herself as a "post-feminist" and refuses to be allied to the oppressed women faction'

(*Time Out*, March 1985). Most interesting, perhaps, is Liz Barker's review in the *Liberator*, which took the political significance of the novel for granted in a way few of the others had:

> The first [major point of interest] is in watching the power of institution unleashed when a challenge is presented. In this case it's the author's homosexuality which the church views as the work of a demon. . . . The second is that . . . the writer goes through the process of feeling rejected by the church but manages to leave behind the intolerance and illiberalism of it. (*Liberator*, date unknown)

This assumption that *Oranges* had a political dimension, and could be read as a case-study of the power of institutions (the Church and the family), rather than simply being about a girl growing up with an Evangelical mother, was exceptional, and did not recur in subsequent reviews of the novel or television adaptation.

Most interesting, perhaps, in the light of critical developments in relation to the television adaptation, were the assessments made of the theme of lesbianism in the novel. Most reviews, both mainstream and alternative, mentioned it; they saw it, however, more as an element of the 'quirkiness' and humour than anything else: 'Jeanette, out shopping with Mother, discovers lesbianism while watching Melanie boning kippers on her fish-stall' (*Observer*, 22 December 1985). Lesbianism was thus constructed as one more comic device, useful in moving on the action, marking the shift from childhood to adolescence, and effecting the break from the domestic status quo that the narrative demands. Other critics seemed to regret the lesbian theme as an untimely intervention into an otherwise 'highly enjoyable first novel': 'with the daughter's discovery that she loves other women . . . the novel shifts in tone – becoming more serious, but also more shrill and less self-assured' (*Publishers Weekly*, 12 April 1985). Few, other than the *Liberator* reviewer quoted above, saw the lesbianism as symptomatic of anything other than the next stage in this *Bildungsroman*. It was not until later, when Winterson herself had come to be treated more as an 'author', that lesbianism became the subject of prurience and intrigue; then, much more familiar stereotypes began to appear:

> The Winterson legends which float around literary London would make a Bournemouth colonel gasp and stretch his eyes. Lock up your wives and daughters – rumour has it that many a well-heeled lady cared no more for the marital goosefeather bed when this gipsy came to her door. (*Evening Standard*, 7 September 1989)

The text alone had not seemed to offer the possibility of sexual intrigue and titillation to reviewers. It was only once it became identified with its author that the potential for 'lesbianism' to equal 'scandal' began to be realised.

By the mainstream press particularly, then, *Oranges* was not seen principally as a lesbian text: Jeanette's lesbianism was seen merely as a suitable foil to her mother's Evangelicalism, its significance assessed in terms of humour, narrative and 'character'. Far from confirming Winterson's own assertion that lesbianism is at the centre of the story, on the basis of the reviews one would think it were, as one reviewer put it, one of 'countless novels on the stands about families, separation, and the emotional spaces people create or don't create for one another' (*Ms*, October 1985). By suggesting that Jeanette is a character with whom we can all sympathise, because lesbianism is just another human experience, these critics aspire to a universal reading. Whilst this liberal humanist reading has the advantage of being accepting and inclusive of lesbian experience, it does deny all sense of the novel having any *specificity*, whether to lesbian experience or to Northern working-class experience. Lesbian oppression, whether in the form of violence, repression, stereotyping or denial, has no part in such a depoliticised reading, and thus remains unacknowledged.

'The Year of the Fruit': the television adaptation in context

At the end of December 1989, the television and newspapers were suddenly full of a forthcoming serial, Winterson's adaptation of her novel *Oranges Are Not the Only Fruit*, to be shown in January 1990. A good deal of media publicity and excitement, in the form of extracts, previews and interviews with Winterson herself, heralded the first episode. However, the screening of *Oranges* was also subject to a degree of pre-broadcast nervousness: what would a television audience make of the uncompromising lesbianism of the text? The BBC took precautions, many of the previews making clear that there would be scenes of an 'explicitly' lesbian nature. Despite the producer, director and writer predicting that controversy 'was as likely to result from the satirical treatment of evangelical religion as the sexual content' (*Guardian*, 3 January 1990), the newspapers focused unerringly on the 'explicit nude lesbianism' (*Today*, 10 January 1990) in their build-up to the screening. Its lesbianism was seen to be the text's defining characteristic, and was the prime focus of the pre-broadcast press excitement.

Elsewhere, however, Winterson also suggested that the lesbianism would indeed be the focus for any controversy generated amongst viewers, because of the way the protagonist, Jess (Jeanette in the novel), was represented:

> What will make people most angry is a feeling that they have been manip-
> ulated because it is very difficult *not* to be sympathetic with Jess. You want
> her to win out and it is very difficult to sympathise with the other side which
> is where most people would normally place themselves. . . . Finding
> themselves in complete sympathy with Jess (rather than family or church) is
> what some will find most difficult. (*Lancashire Evening Telegraph*, 9 January
> 1990)

Being 'manipulated' into identifying with a lesbian character, she predicts, will be the source of this hostility. But it did not work out this way; instead, reviewers in tabloids and broadsheets alike applauded long and loud.

What happened, then, to this expected rumpus, the outrage at 'explicit' lesbian sex scenes? In order to investigage this question, two factors contributing to the context in which the text was produced are worth exploring further, before turning to the press responses: first, the speci-fically historical and political context of the production; second, the context formed by the history of television drama itself.

Particularly significant for the reception of *Oranges* were the repercus-sions from the arguments that had circulated in relation to two events of 1988 and 1989 respectively: the passing of Section 28 of the Local Government Act, which aimed to ban the 'promotion of homosexuality' by any bodies funded by local authorities, and the death threat made against Salman Rushdie on the publication of his novel *The Satanic Verses*. These two events had elements in common, most significantly in the responses and opposition they elicited: the liberal arts establishment saw each as undermining the principle of free speech. One of the most successful counter-arguments made in opposition to Section 28 was that posed by the arts lobby, who saw 'great works', either by lesbian and gay writers or concerning lesbian and gay issues, as being under threat from this legislation.[4] This argument carried the implication that lesbianism and homosexuality were to be understood differently in this context: they necessitated a response in keeping with their status as art, rather than in relation to their sexual/political status. Concerning Rushdie, the argu-ments were similar: the novel might be offensive to Islam; nevertheless the artist should not be silenced, but allowed to function free from outside political or religious constraints. In both instances, then, the issue of 'art' was seen to be paramount: a text's status as art should protect it from the crudities of political critique. Thus *Oranges* was read in a cultural context where high-cultural 'art' had been established as having a meaning separable from questions of politics, sexual or otherwise.

Significant, too, in relation to Rushdie and to *Oranges*, is the way religious fundamentalism was represented in the media: freedom of speech was being threatened by religious extremists, who were characterised as repressive, violent and alien to the liberal traditions of their 'host' country. Although this related specifically to the Muslim faith, it fed into and fortified a pre-existing climate of opinion regarding so-called fundament-alism, fuelled by news stories from the USA exposing financial corrup-tion and sexual intrigues within the ranks of high-profile Evangelical groups. 'Fundamentalism', then, came to be characterised as both a violent threat (viz. Rushdie) and an object for our superior laughter, as its essential hyprocisy was exposed (viz. US groups).[5] Both these elements can be seen to have played their part in the television representation and media reception of the Evangelical group so central to Jess's childhood in *Oranges*.

Also important for the reception of *Oranges* was the specifically tele-visual context: the traditions of drama and literary adaptations which have formed such a significant part of (particularly) the BBC's output. One line of the heritage can be traced from the Wednesday Play in the 1960s, through Play for Today to the current Wednesday night positioning, dubbed by the press 'The Controversy Slot'; these all have a reputation of presenting high-quality work, although the subjects they treat and their modes of visual representation have also earned them the reputation of being 'difficult' or controversial. The other line of the heritage is traceable through the long tradition of literary adaptations on television, initially of nineteenth-century 'classics' by Dickens, Austen, Trollope, and so on; and latterly of more contemporary novels such as *Brideshead Revisited* and *Jewel in the Crown*, until, as with the instances of David Lodge's *Nice Work* and Winterson herself, adaptations followed very swiftly on the publica-tion of the novel. *Oranges* was able to draw on these two traditions, the drama and the literary adaptation, for it both occupied a drama slot – associated with such prestigious writers as Dennis Potter, whose *The Singing Detective* is still used as a benchmark of 'quality' television drama – yet was also a literary adaptation and thus took advantage of the pre-existing status of the novel and the author.[6] *Oranges*, then, was able to benefit from the institutional significance of the television drama and the literary adaptation even before the first episode was screened.

'High Quality Drama to Silence the Prudes': lesbianism
and art television

The traditions of television drama and the literary adaptation, then, have
strong associations of 'quality' and 'high culture', and are traditions on
which, by virtue of its scheduling and publicity, *Oranges* was able to draw.
'Quality' was a watchword from the start, both for author – 'whatever else
Oranges is, it is very high quality television' (Winterson in *Spare Rib*,
February 1990) – and for the previewers and reviewers: 'We *are* discussing
art in the case of *Oranges Are Not the Only Fruit*' (*Sunday Times*, 21 January
1990). One of the ways it was identified as 'art' was to mark it out as
different from the everyday output of television:

> This series may not be the 'safe' kind which automatically delivers huge
> audiences, but it undeniably provides some of the most moving and humor-
> ous scenes seen on television for a long time. (*Television Today*, 18 January
> 1990)

The programme's quality was widely expected to result in formal recognition through television awards: many joined with Tom Bussmann in
predicting that 'there's a whiff of BAFTA in the air' (*Guardian*, 11 January
1990) and suggested that this was the natural sequel to the novel having
won the Whitbread. Only Louise Chunn, writing in the *Guardian*,
wondered if Winterson was not straying away from the pinnacles of high
culture in adapting her work for the small screen:

> But this is the woman Gore Vidal called 'the most interesting young writer I
> have read in 20 years', she's a Whitbread prize winner, a *serious* writer. Surely
> she's a novelist above all else? (*Guardian*, 3 January 1990)

Although Chunn wondered if Winterson's literary credentials were not
being compromised by this dallying with a mass medium, and thus with
popular culture, other reviewers were more confident that she was simply
translating her talents from one area of high culture into another: from
'Literature' into a television equivalent of 'art cinema': namely, 'art television'.[7] *Oranges*, placed as it was in the 'serious' Wednesday night slot, can
be seen to share a number of characteristics with what film critics have
identified as 'art cinema'. With its high-cultural overtones of European
seriousness and the avant-garde, 'art cinema' has come to hold an almost
revered place in some circles, in contrast to other more popular cultural
forms such as Hollywood cinema or television. Thus *Oranges* was able to

retain its high-cultural status despite its translation into television, usually ascribed as a low-cultural form. However, the question remains as to how a *lesbian* text was able to occupy this high-cultural space so successfully.

Mandy Merck, in her article '*Lianna* and the lesbians of art cinema', has suggested that there is a particular relationship between art cinema and the representation of lesbianism: as she aphoristically puts it, 'if lesbianism hadn't existed, art cinema might have invented it' (Merck, 1986, p. 166). By this she means that the representation of lesbianism in art cinema is sufficiently 'different' from dominant (more popular) cinematic representations of sex and sexuality to be seen as courageous and challenging, yet at the same time it simply offers more of the same: that is, it works with the familiar equation 'woman = sexuality'. Merck concludes that 'it is the legitimisation of the female spectacle which makes lesbianism such a gift to art cinema' (p. 173). Thus what is at stake is not only *what* is represented, but *where* it is represented: the underlying equation of women with sexuality may be the same in all kinds of representation, but none the less lesbianism is read as 'meaning' something different in art cinema as opposed to other contexts; similarly, it was read as meaning something different in 'art television', the context in which *Oranges* was read, as opposed to elsewhere on television.

The 'controversy slot'

As with other 'quality' dramas, the controversy of *Oranges* was seen to arise primarily from the explicit representation of sex. Certain of these productions acted as sexual reference points for *Oranges*.

> A lesbian love scene between two adolescent girls on BBC2 next week could mark a new stage in the passage of television from the kitchen sink to the boudoir.
> This new challenge to viewers comes after the explicit straight sex of David Lodge's *Nice Work* and Dennis Potter's *Blackeyes*. (*Sunday Times*, 7 January 1990)

The representation of sex in *Oranges*, then, was seen as an advance on the work of Potter and Lodge in two ways: first, it showed lesbian rather than 'straight sex', which of necessity represented something more challenging, risky and 'adult'. This seems to confirm that for 'art television', as for art cinema, there is a strong association with and expectation of 'adult' and 'realistic' representations of sex. The sexualised context of this position in the schedule was of significance for the serial's reception: the representation of sex in *Oranges* could be seen as risky and challenging, rather than merely titillating. Secondly, the 'quality' of Winterson's drama was better: *Blackeyes* was repeatedly berated as 'that over-publicised, overrated Dennis Potter effort' (*Lancashire Evening Telegraph*, 9 January 1990) or as 'exploitative nonsense' (*Today*, 10 January 1990). Its 'quality' was a guard against 'those dreary public outbursts of British prudishness' (*Birmingham Post*, 18 January 1990). Together, then, these two elements worked to produce a context in which lesbianism could be read as something positive.

De-centring lesbianism

A second possible reason for the acceptability of the lesbianism in *Oranges* follows from Merck's claim that another feature of art cinema is that it 'characteristically solicits essential humanist readings' (1986, p. 170). If this were also the case in relating to *Oranges*, then, it would imply that the adaptation's success rested on the critics' ability to read it as being *really* about something other than its lesbianism. If this were so, then it would confound Winterson's own stated hopes, for she asserted quite clearly that she framed the whole text as a challenge:

> I know that *Oranges* challenges the virtues of the home, the power of the church and the supposed normality of heterosexuality. I was always clear that it would do. I would rather not have embarked on the project than see it toned down in any way. That all this should be the case and that it should still have been so overwhelmingly well received cheers me up. (Winterson, 1990, p. xvii)

The critics, in the mainstream press at least, signally failed to pick up the gauntlet that Winterson had thrown down. As with the novel, the lesbianism is de-centred and the critics present us with a drama 'about' all sorts of other things. The three-part series, we are told, 'is fundamentally about a young person looking for love' (*Today*, 10 January 1990); it is 'a wonderfully witty, bitter-sweet celebration of the miracle that more children do not murder their parents' (*Observer*, 14 January 1990); it 'follows Jess in a voyage of self-discovery from her intense religious background, via a friendship with another girl' (*Todmorden News*, 18 August 1989); it is 'a vengeful satire on Protestant fundamentalism' (*Listener*, 18 January 1990). Although *Time Out* complains about 'the author's own use of that hoary liberal cop out about *Oranges* being about "two people in love" – who wants to see that tedious story again?' (18 January 1990), most critics welcome the opportunity to read *Oranges* as essentially about *all* human relationships, rather than specifically about lesbianism.

As with the novel, the de-centring of the lesbianism does not involve its denial: in most accounts of the story line it is mentioned, but nearly always in relation to something else, generally the ensuing rejection and exorcism of Jess by members of the Evangelical group. In this context, lesbianism is seen either as a comic comeuppance for her mother's repressive childbearing methods – 'Warned off boys by this hell-fire freak, Jess turns instead to girls' (*Financial Times*, 10 January 1990) – or as a source of pathos: 'a bittersweet tragedy, the tale of how a young woman tries and fails to reconcile her religion with her lesbianism' (11 January 1990). Lesbianism, then, is always seen in relation to other issues, be they religion, the family, or simply 'growing up'.

'Unsafe sects'

However, this humanist perspective on the text is only one element in this de-centring of lesbianism; another is the emphasis that is placed on the representation of religion. This is important not only as an example of this de-centring but also because, contrary to what most previewers predicted, it was this that became the focus for viewers' and reviewers' anger, rather than the representation of lesbianism itself. So, as well as the Evangelical group being seen as one of the main sources of the humour of the series, its members are also written about as ridiculous ('prattling, eye-rolling, God-fearing women' [*Daily Express*, 11 January 1990]) and as a potentially violent threat ('each and every one . . . looked as though she could kill with a blow of her nose' [*Times*, 11 January 1990]). Class stereotypes of small-minded working-class women here reinforce the ridiculousness of the Evangelicals. Furthermore, their Christian fundamentalism is explicitly linked to Muslim fundamentalism, by now associated with repression and violence in the press reviews: Jess is brought up 'in a provincial family whose fundamental religious beliefs make the Ayatollah Khomeini, by contrast, seem a model of polite tolerance' (*Evening Standard*, 22 January 1990). This association of the two fundamentalisms, Christian and Muslim, with repression is further strengthened when *Television Today* expresses the hope that the 'small, if vocal, number of objectors' to the serial will not 'turn writer Jeanette Winterson into the nineties Salman Rushdie' (*Television Today*, 18 January 1990).

Subject to the most anger, however, was the exorcism of Jess carried out by the pastor and assorted members of the congregation when her sexual relationship with Melanie is discovered. Critics commented on the 'brutal' nature of this scene, noted that it is 'sexually-charged', and Steve Clarke suggested that:

> if anybody was disturbed by the scene in which the pastor – armed with rope, gag and pulsating neck – straddled the young Jess to exorcise the demon of illicit love, then so they should have been. (*Sunday Times*, 21 January 1990)

Hilary Kingsley in the *Mirror* concurred: the headline announced that the scene was 'Brutal, Shocking, Horrifying. But You Mustn't Miss It' (*Daily Mirror*, 15 January 1990). Anger and disgust were not only legitimate – they were to be actively sought as the 'correct' response; thus emotions that many expected to be directed towards the lesbian scenes were actually located instead with the representation of this repressive religious group. Perhaps it was possible for so much sympathy to be shown to the plight of Jess and Melanie not only because of the way their relationship was interpreted, but also because of the brutality of the punishment they underwent. Their persecutors had already been established as outmoded, repressive and anti-sex, and it was a small step to add violence to this list by drawing on pre-existing connotations of fundamentalism:

> Jess . . . is promptly subjected by her mother's fundamentalist sect to the sort of persecution and torture so dear to the hearts of religious fanatics throughout the ages. (*Financial Times*, 10 January 1990)

This clearly suggests that the punishment tells us more about religious fundamentalists than it does about the status of lesbianism in our society. The liberal viewer can feel distanced from the punishment meted out to Jess because these people, after all, are not 'normal' members of our society. This sympathy, then, can be seen to rest on two mutually reinforcing bases: first, it is a response to the punitive, anti-sex attitudes of the Evangelical group – and even gay and lesbian sexual rights had increasingly become the objects of liberal championing since the passing of Section 28; secondly, it is responding to the representation of fundamentalism, which had become a prominent target in the wake of the Rushdie affair. Thus, it appears that the yoking of the lesbianism with the fundamentalism was itself crucial for the favourable mainstream liberal response: lesbianism became an otherness preferable to the unacceptable otherness of fundamentalism.

'Unnatural passions': the role of the sex scene

If the representation of the Evangelical group is a crucial factor in determining critical response to the series, this raises the question of what place was ascribed to lesbian sexuality by the reviewers. In relation to art cinema, Merck suggests that the lesbian love scene carries a particularly heavy burden of meaning: because of the tendency to allegorise these films, to read them as essentially about something other than the overt narrative, these scenes have taken on a particular symbolic function, namely 'the ability to represent "lesbian experience"' (1986, p. 169), to encapsulate the entire range of meanings of lesbianism, whether sexual, social or political. What meanings, then, were ascribed to *Oranges*' long-awaited sex scene, 'arguably the most explicit female love scene yet broadcast on British television' (*Sunday Times*, 7 January 1990)?

The makers of the series declared that their intention with this scene was 'to avoid the kind of romantic idealism with which lesbian scenes were portrayed in the 1988 BBC production of D. H. Lawrence's *The Rainbow*' (*Sunday Times*, 7 January 1990). The producer, Phillippa Giles, told the *Daily Mirror*: 'We decided to make it obvious that the girls were having a sexual relationship, not a wishy-washy thing. . . . We wanted to face the question everyone asks – *What do lesbians DO?*' (*Daily Mirror*, 15 January 1990). Most reviewers, however, read it with the kind of romantic idealism the makers were trying to eschew. 'It is romantic, innocent and beautiful', wrote Christopher Dunkley (*Financial Times*, 10 January 1990); the erotic relationship is portrayed in a way 'which maintains its essential innocence' (*7 Days*, 11 January 1990). Steve Clarke, in the *Sunday Times*, surpassed the others in his breathless enthusiasm for the scene: 'the two girls' tentative exploration of each other's bodies was almost Disneyesque in its innocent wonderment' (*Sunday Times*, 21 January 1990); anybody who objected to these scenes would simply be 'dreary' (*Today*, 10 January 1990). There is scant evidence, then, that these reviewers were shocked by this representation of lesbianism. Not only did the manifest youth of Jess and Melanie allow them to define and praise the relationship in terms of its tenderness and innocence, it also implicitly allowed the lesbianism to be understood as an adolescent phase, a naive exploration that would be outgrown. Moreover, the fact that the critics ignored any other scenes that might modify, or even contradict, this reading of tenderness and innocence meant that this characterisation of the sex scene alone was allowed to represent the text's 'lesbianism', avoiding any broader or more challenging meaning of this concept.

Significantly few of the mainstream reviewers commented on *Oranges* as in any way erotic. Whilst most talked only of Jess's first relationship, with Melanie, in the 'quality' press only Mark Steyn allowed Jess's relationship with Katy, her second lover, to contribute to this assessment of the text:

> More shocking than any nudity was the parallel between religious salvation and sexual discovery, subtly drawn in scenes which were nevertheless masterpieces of suppressed eroticism. 'You were going to tell me about Jesus,' said Katy. 'Well, what is it you wanted to *know*?' asked Jess. 'Why don't you tell me,' Katy replied, lolling against the caravan, '*gradually*'. (*Independent*, 25 January 1990)

Steyn alone showed a willingness to go beyond the feeling that for lesbianism to be acceptable it had to be tender, innocent, essentially asexual.

Critics elsewhere, however, were more willing to contemplate an active erotic reading of the text. In the alternative publications, on the one hand, and in some of the tabloids, on the other, there is a marked contrast to this predominantly liberal mainstream interpretation of the sexuality in *Oranges*. Some of the tabloids, for example, made a concerted effort to construct a pornographic reading of the text. They anticipated the 'fruitiest lesbian love scenes ever on British TV' (?4, 11 January 1990), employing words like 'steamy' or 'torrid', and concentrated on the actresses' feelings about the sex scene to try and enhance this sense of the illicit and risky. Most notable of these attempts was one that appeared in *Today*:

> According to a male friend, the lesbian love scenes in this drama are not nearly fruity enough. In order to fully fulfil the 'ultimate male fantasy' he says the actresses should have had bigger breasts.
>
> What we need, he adds, is a lot more tits. Samantha Fox and Maria Whitaker would be ideal.
>
> Had this transpired, I would have had to suggest a slightly different title for this excellent serial: Melons Are Not The Only Fruit . . . (*Today*, 25 January 1990)

By referring to perhaps the two most famous 'Page 3' models as potential participants in this drama, there is a clear – perhaps even rather desperate – attempt to recruit what had looked as if it was going to be 'the ultimate male fantasy' for that function. The serial had evidently fallen short of what might be expected of something that included 'explicit nude lesbianism'. Since it was not close enough to the ethos of 'Page 3', it was necessary both to force this reading on to the text by means of such epithets as 'torrid' and 'steamy', and to reconstruct it as a tabloid ideal by recasting and renaming it, both of which would emphasise more strongly its pornographic possibilities. Whilst, then, the 'eroticism' of the text was acknowledged as central here, this review makes it clear that the text did not lend itself easily to the expected and desired pornographic understanding of lesbianism: it was seen as having a meaning independent of, or separate from, dominant male fantasy, and was thus in need of reworking in line with such conventions.

In the alternative presses, by contrast, this separateness both from male fantasy and from 'Disneyesque' tenderness was seen as one of the serial's strengths: Jonathan Sanders in *Gay Times* noted that 'Jess and Melanie's fireside coupling steered a fine course between eroticism and the straight male prurience consideration' (*Gay Times*, March 1990). Cherry Smyth's assessment of the sex scene in *Spare Rib* identified it as 'radical' and different from more usual representations of lesbianism on television:

> Although a little pre-Raphaelite in style, the scene is uncomplicated and unapologetic. Their refreshing lack of embarrassment and shame is a breakthrough for a mainstream TV drama slot. Is BBC2 stealing the radical remit from Channel 4? Jess is too knowing and sure of her desire for the scene to collapse into pre-pubescent coyness and 'innocent' caressing. (*Spare Rib*, February 1990)

The very quality of innocence which the mainstream reviewers identified is denied here, and is instead replaced by its opposite: the assertion that Jess is 'knowing' and 'sure of her desire'. Sanders, similarly, had found 'heartening' the 'uniform moral ease and technical skill with which the teenage lesbians expressed their desires' (*Gay Times*, March 1990). Although Rosalind Brunt identified one of the main themes of *Oranges* as 'passionate erotic friendship between young women' (*New Statesman and Society*, 12 January 1990), it was only the lesbian and gay critics who situated the text firmly within a discourse of desire. Not only was 'innocence' countered in these reviews, but also – in *Spare Rib* in particular – there was an emphasis on the subtlety of the sexual references employed: 'Jess introduces Melanie to church and leads the congregation in "When I was sleeping, somebody touched me", a delightful innuendo that prefigures the scene where the young women make love' (*Spare Rib*, February 1990). This interpretation and emphasis from Smyth suggest that perhaps the text operated rather differently for lesbian and gay audiences: used to relying on the subtleties of innuendo and veiled meanings, they read the text through a specific set of codes apparently undiscerned by other audiences.[8]

The politics of the lesbian text

As well as discussing the sex scene, Smyth also broadened out the political focus of her review by stressing the radical possibilities of the representation of lesbianism in *Oranges*: 'At the point where the fate of many a dramatic lesbian character is firmly sealed, Jess continues to convert young women to her way of loving'; Jess thus retains her position as agent and heroine throughout. This review is notable, too, for referring outside the series, to a 'lived experience' of lesbianism, in order to measure the 'quality' of the drama.

> The awkward milkshakes and doorways she shares with Katy, her young Asian lover, convey the desperately unhappy courtship of adolescents who haven't 'somewhere proper to go'. (*Spare Rib*, February 1990)

It was not only the alternative publications that hinted at the political significance of the drama. Kate Battersby, in *Today*, hinted at a feminist reading of the text when she suggested that 'many women will identify with the adolescent Jess's bid for freedom and self-expression' (10 January 1990). Another very favourable piece – also by a woman, Hilary Kingsley – says that *Oranges* is:

> an important milestone for women.
>   Male homosexuality has been represented in television drama frequently over the years.
>   But to television, as to Queen Victoria, lesbians do not exist – except in an Australian jail.
>   No wonder the late night soap *Prisoner: Cell Block H* has a high following among gay women. (*Daily Mirror*, 15 January 1990)

Despite historical inaccuracies (lesbianism clearly *had* been represented on television before[9]), Kingsley was identifying something important by suggesting that *Oranges* was an exceptional text in making lesbianism its central concern.

Lesbian viewers seemed to agree that *Oranges* was a milestone, staying at home in droves on Wednesday nights to watch it. This enthusiasm was in part, no doubt, because it made lesbianism a visible presence on television, where – with the exceptions of *Prisoner*, 'Out On Tuesday', and some documentaries and films – it was usually invisible. Moreover, it became visible in a mainstream slot, rather than in the furtive late-night positions of most representations of lesbian and gay issues on television.

The way the lesbianism was represented was also unusual: rather than becoming either villain or victim, the lesbian protagonist remained a heroine throughout. The screening of *Oranges* on BBC2 also represented the infiltration of that bastion of television high-cultural respectability by a programme directed and produced by women, scripted by a lesbian, and one whose main theme was lesbianism; this, too, added a certain edge to the pleasure of *Oranges* for a lesbian audience. Furthermore, whatever debates may rage about the dangers or desirability of being accepted by dominant culture, here, at last, was a programme about lesbianism that, far from being run down or ignored by the reviewers, was praised to the skies. From many perspectives, then, *Oranges* signified something pleasurable and exceptional for lesbian viewers.

Conclusion: *Oranges* to everyone's taste

> BBC2's *Oranges Are Not the Only Fruit* . . . had the capacity to make us laugh and cry, to shock us with its brutal exorcism scene, to move us with its compassion for youthful lesbian love and to leave us – as at the end of a good book – silently grieving the loss of a friend.
>
> *Oranges* is a book, of course. And how delighted author Jeanette Winterson must have been. Seldom can a fine novel have been transported with such skill and with such little disruption to the small screen. (*Daily Express*, 25 January 1990)

In many ways Peter Tory's review summarises some of the complexities of what *Oranges* represented for viewers, as well as suggesting some of the reasons why it met with such success. To begin with, it confirms the text as an example of high-status 'art': the prestige lent to the whole enterprise by the presence of the original novel; the 'faithfulness' of the adaptation, avoiding what Mark Steyn had called 'the coarsening effects' of translation into a mass medium (*Independent*, 25 January 1990); the text's capacity to appeal to our common humanity and provoke the great and enduring human emotions and responses of joy, sadness, anger and compassion – all these confirm the text's relationship to high culture.

Yet this review did not appear in a 'quality' newspaper, where we might expect to find support for such a cultural product, but in the popular press, endorsing a serial whose precursors, such as Potter's *Blackeyes*, had often been roundly condemned as pretentious nonsense. Moreover, it appeared in the *Daily Express*, a newspaper not usually noted for its sympathy for 'do-gooding' liberal causes. Tory's 'compassion for youthful lesbian love' may not be the response which many lesbians would seek, but it is none the less an unequivocally and uncharacteristically welcoming reading of the production's representation of lesbianism.

These complexities and ambiguities demonstrate the need to consider the validity of the terms of the high/popular culture divide, for *Oranges*, as a complete cultural product – author, novel, television drama – seems consistently to elude and collapse these categories. Central to this elusiveness seems to be the text's lesbianism. Although it may be true to say that the lesbianism is defused by the text's associations with high culture and its consequent openness to a liberal interpretation, it is also true that *Oranges* has retained, and increased, its lesbian audience and its subcultural consumption, and has also been praised by a tabloid press usually hostile to lesbian and gay issues.

Not all lesbian texts, of course, operate as *Oranges* does. However, the remarkable – if rather confusing – popularity of this text highlights some of the general complexities that emerge when one introduces the category of the 'lesbian text' into cultural analysis. Whilst it is possible to think of several lesbian texts that come within the category of high culture, such as those of Gertrude Stein or Radclyffe Hall, and others, such as those by Sarah Dreher and Ann Bannon, that would be considered lesbian pulp fiction, many lesbian texts defy such categorisations. Indeed, even the examples mentioned above pose problems: some critics happily claim *The Well of Loneliness* for the canon whilst still conceding that it is 'bad writing'. Moreover, the readership of much recent lesbian pulp fiction is arguably more diverse than its heterosexual equivalent. Precisely because of the lack of representations of lesbianism within mainstream culture, lesbian texts which are available take on a particular significance. Lesbian readers and viewers do not divide neatly into consumers of high or popular culture, since their prime interest here is often the representation of a lifestyle, an identity or a sexuality which is marked by its absence elsewhere within the media or literature. This, then, raises the question of whether the introduction of the lesbianism issue confounds many of the assumptions about texts and readers which have informed debates about high and popular culture in much criticism in recent years.

And what, finally, of *Oranges* itself? Having asserted its fluidity, its ability to cut across so many critical and cultural categories and positions, its refusal to be pigeonholed as one sort of text or another, its appeal for a diversity of audiences, it is impossible to arrive at a conclusive statement about it. Perhaps it is enough to suggest that any text that can transgress so many barriers deserves all the critical attention – from whatever source and from whatever perspective – it can get.

I would like to thank the following people for their help, and for their perceptive and encouraging comments on earlier drafts of this article: Richard Dyer, Lynne Pearce, Martin Pumphrey, Margaret Reynolds, Fiona Terry and, especially, Jackie Stacey.

Notes

1. Subtitles appearing in inverted commas are borrowed from newspaper reviews of *Oranges*.
2. These comments are drawn from reviews of *Oranges* published in, amongst others, *New Statesman*, *Publishers Weekly*, *Everywoman*, *Times Literary Supplement*, *Sunday Times*, *Ms*, *Observer*, and *Time Out*.
3. Extracts that are referenced ?1, ?4, and so on are from uncredited reviews kindly sent to me by Pandora Press.
4. For further exploration of the terms of the challenges presented to Section 28, see Jackie Stacey, 'Promoting normality: Section 28 and the regulation of sexuality', in Sarah Franklin, Celia Lury and Jackie Stacey, eds, *Off Centre, Feminism and cultural studies*, London: HarperCollins Academic, 1991.
5. For a discussion of Western characterisations of Islam, see Edward Said, *Orientalism*, London: Routledge & Kegan Paul, 1978. For a discussion of the impact of the Gulf War on such notions, see Kevin Robbins, 'The mirror of unreason', *Marxism Today*, March 1991, pp. 42–4.
6. For discussions of the notion of 'quality' television, see Paul Kerr, 'Classic serials – to be continued', *Screen*, **23**, 1, 1982, pp. 6–19; and Charlotte Brunsdon, 'Problems with quality', *Screen*, **31**, 1, 1990, pp. 67–90.
7. 'Art television' remains a rather tentative concept within critical work; John Caughie, however, provides a useful discussion of it in 'Rhetoric, pleasure and "art television" – dreams of leaving', *Screen*, **22**, 4, 1981, pp. 9–31.
8. For examples of studies which have moved away from textual analysis and investigated audiences and readers of popular texts, see Ien Ang, *Watching Dallas: Soap opera and the melodramatic imagination*, London: Methuen, 1985; and Janice A. Radway, *Reading the Romance: Women, patriarchy and popular literature*, Chapel Hill: University of North Carolina Press, 1984.
9. Previous representations of lesbianism on television are few and far between. They include isolated episodes in serials and soap operas such as *Brookside*, *Eastenders*, *St Elsewhere*, *The Golden Girls* and the 1988 dramatisation of D. H. Lawrence's *The Rainbow*; or, more unusually, TV movies such as *The Ice Palace* and *A Question of Love*, which dealt more centrally with lesbianism.

Works Cited

Brunsdon, Charlotte (1990), 'Problems with quality.' *Screen*, **31**, 1, pp. 67–90.

Caughie, John (1981), 'Rhetoric, pleasure and "art television" – Dreams of leaving.' *Screen*, **22**, 4, pp. 9–31.

Caughie, John (1984), 'Television criticism: "A discourse in search of an object".' *Screen*, **25**, 4–5, pp. 109–20.

Caughie, John (1986), 'Popular culture? Notes and revisions', in Colin McCabe, ed., *High Theory/Low Culture: Analysing popular television and film*. Manchester: Manchester University Press, pp. 156–71.

Kerr, Paul (1982), 'Classic serials – To be continued.' *Screen*, **23**, 1, pp. 6–19.

McCabe, Colin (1986) 'Defining popular culture', in McCabe, ed., *High Theory/Low Culture: Analysing popular television and film*, pp. 1–10.

Merck, Mandy (1986) '*Lianna* and the lesbians of art cinema', in Charlotte Brunsdon, ed., *Films for Women*. London: BFI Publishing, pp. 166–75.

Modleski, Tania (1982), *Loving with a Vengeance: Mass-produced fantasies for women*. London: Methuen.

Myers, Katy (1984), 'Television previewers: No critical comment', in Len Masterman, ed. *Television Mythologies: Stars, shows and signs*. London: Comedia, pp. 132–8.

Pearce, Lynne (1990), 'Jane Eyre eat your heart out: Jeanette Winterson's re-reading of romantic love in *Oranges Are Not the Only Fruit*'. Unpublished paper given to Northern Network, 1990.

Poole, Mike (1984), 'The cult of the generalist: British television criticism 1936–1983'. *Screen*, **25**, 2, pp. 41–61.

Winterson, Jeanette (1985), *Oranges Are Not the Only Fruit*. London: Pandora.

Winterson, Jeanette (1990), *Oranges Are Not the Only Fruit – The script*. London: Pandora.

LESBIAN PORNOGRAPHY
Cultural Transgression and Sexual Demystification

/Lisa/Henderson/

Introduction

This essay comes from an uncertain position in what feminists and observers have called the 'sex debates' or sometimes the 'porn wars', a long international series of analyses, counter-analyses, direct-action campaigns, legislative initiatives, testimonies, disavowals, revocations and regroupings, all around the nature of gendered sexual experience and explicit sexual representation. For close to fifteen years these debates have raised critical questions about the relationship between sexual imagery and female sexual identity and autonomy. They have also polarised anti-pornography and *anti*-anti-porn feminist camps.[1] Why this division emerged or expanded when it did is not certain, though as Alice Echols points out, 'it seemed in part a reaction to the sexual revolution [of the 1960s], which increased women's sense of sexual vulnerability by acknowledging their right to sexual pleasure while ignoring the risks associated with [women's] sexual exploration' (1991, p. 289).

The complex analyses put forward by both feminist groups cannot be adequately reviewed here, though it is important to understand that for anti-porn feminists, female subordination in patriarchy is both cause and effect of female degradation in pornography. Among anti-anti-porn feminists, on the other hand, suppressing pornography inevitably becomes part and parcel of a long history of female *sexual* suppression, 'closing the avenues of sexual speech at a time when women are only beginning to participate in hitherto male-dominated conversations' (Ellis, O'Dair and Tallmer, 1986, p. 6).

My position in these debates is 'uncertain' – not because I can't decide who to march with; since the mid-1980s I have talked, taught and marched with the feminist anti-anti-porn contingent. Uncertain, instead, because I believe that inclusiveness is essential for sexual critique and transformation, and is undermined by a pre-emptive certainty about 'good' and 'bad' desire, including a feminist certainty in which some women seek to save others from themselves and their dubious sexualities, and to strip still others of their claim to feminism. To say this is not to deny sexual fear and anxiety, nor rightful anger at coercion and brutality. It is to take stock of women's sexual variability and empower sexual outsiders (especially lesbian and gay people) in a selectively anti-sexual public sphere.

This essay also comes from a poststructuralist perspective in communications and cultural studies. From this perspective, the salvation motive in anti-pornography politics is reminiscent of the mass-culture critiques of the 1940s and 1950s, which claimed mass culture's damaging effects on users and on 'legitimate' culture at large. As Andrew Ross points out, though the anti-porn critique proposes to reorganise cultural conflict along gender (instead of strictly class) lines, it often 'reproduces the same languages of mass manipulation, systematic domination, and victimization which had been the trademark of the Cold War liberal critique of mass culture' (1989, p. 176). Women, like other helpless groups, need protection from pornography and its users. Women who use pornography need protection from themselves, from a critical inability to pierce their (presumed) patriarchal false consciousness.

Recent studies of media and culture have contested the model of wholesale domination, in part by looking at the reception of mass culture among different audiences or interpretative communities (e.g. Radway, 1984; Ang, 1985; Morley, 1980). Those audiences' variable uses and interpretations challenge the image of monolithic and direct effects, not just because people do different things with the media (as liberal-pluralism might propose) but because the nature of meaning is interactive rather than determined by producer and text. Readers too create meanings, and in the process they may rework a text's dominant messages. In other words, meaning is not hermetically sealed by the text, and interpretation can become the site of cultural resistance or opposition (though it does not necessarily do so). The privileged approach to studying cultural reception in this alternative model is ethnography – engaging with a community through close participation and conversation and constructing theoretically informed narratives of their social and symbolic practices, including their accounts of themselves.

These stances – an uncertain sexual politics, a cultural analysis still interested in the relationship between determination and resistance, and ethnography as a fraught but fruitful research position – underwrite the study of pornography I think is needed in ongoing feminist discussions.

Though this essay is not yet a properly ethnographic account, I use these perspectives in an analysis of lesbian pornography and lesbian reading. My purposes in focusing on lesbian material are to introduce it as a symbolic domain virtually overlooked in contemporary debates, even where lesbian sexuality (in some versions) has been foregrounded, and to locate it at the sexual and political nexus of women's liberation and lesbian and gay liberation.

But what is 'lesbian porn'?

Defining pornography is tricky political business, Potter Stewart's confidence notwithstanding. (Stewart, a US Supreme Court Justice, made the legal definition airtight by claiming that he couldn't say what it was but he knew it when he saw it.) For my purposes, pornography is any symbolic expression which 'seeks to arouse or which represents arousal' (Smyth, 1990, p. 153). What, then, is lesbian pornography? Depictions of women together in sexual scenarios?

This definition would include those 'lesbian' scenes which occur as conventional preambles to otherwise heterosexual narratives. Such scenes raise questions of authenticity in a community whose members are wary of images – particularly sexual ones – that somehow refer to us but which we perceive to be unintended for our pleasure, unmarked by other signifiers of lesbian identity (perhaps short fingernails and haircuts, or women's communities). That does not mean such images are not pleasurable to some lesbians on some occasions. If we can read 'Cagney and Lacey' as a lesbian narrative (and we do), we can also make something sexual for ourselves out of 'lesbian' scenes in straight porn (cf. Williams, 1989, p. 274). Lesbian 'reader address' – textual elements which suggest lesbians as the intended audience – may connote authenticity and heighten the pleasure for those who want to identify as lesbians with porn models, characters and scenarios.[2] Lesbian pleasure is not restricted to such 'authentic' representations, however, nor are the pleasures they offer restricted to lesbians.

Such definitional problems acknowledged, this analysis begins with texts that seem conspicuously 'lesbian', those which directly address lesbian readers and solicit lesbian identifications. The first is a sex magazine called *On Our Backs*, independently produced in San Francisco since 1984, by and for lesbians.[3] With few exceptions, *On Our Backs* publishes women-only fiction, poetry, drawings and photographs. It also features sexual advice columns, editorials on lesbian sexual culture and sexual politics, book, film and video reviews, display advertising for sexual and non-sexual services and supplies, letters to the editor, reports from lesbian events, occasional readership surveys, safer-sex guidelines, and classified personal ads and announcements, among other attractions.

The second text is *Macho Sluts* (1988), Pat Califia's debut collection of erotic short fiction, most (though not all) in the leather or sadomasochistic vein. Califia is also a novelist, an occasional contributor to *On Our Backs* and a regular sex columnist for *The Advocate*, a US national gay and lesbian weekly.

Despite differences in genre and form, *On Our Backs* and *Macho Sluts* accomplish some of the same ends. They challenge received sexual ideologies, and self-consciously position their words and images on the terrain of lesbian sexual politics. As I argue, they are also 'culturally transgressive' and 'sexually demystifying'.

On Our Backs and cultural transgression

In *The Politics and Poetics of Transgression* (1986), Peter Stallybrass and Allon White debunk the notion that the transcendent and the grotesque – the 'high' and the 'low' – are independent in the cultural history of the European bourgeoisie. On the contrary, high and low are radically *inter*dependent, the genteel bourgeois subject officially identifying itself by reviling the 'low' – the crass, the dirty, the contaminating – but constituting itself through that very process of revulsion (p. 193): 'This', it proclaims, 'is what we are not.'

The dynamic between high and low is part of the attraction and fascination of pornography, particularly of marginal varieties. It unabashedly objectifies, while proper society dictates that subjectivity is the means to civilisation. It invokes what consciousness represses. It foregrounds a demonised body at the expense of an idealised mind. In Stallybrass and White's captivating phrase, it poses a scandal to the dignity of hegemony (p. 25).

The visual and verbal images in *On Our Backs* connote many transgressive qualities of the 'low', particularly in the political context in which the magazine was established. Here was a text subtitled 'entertainment for the adventurous lesbian', a coy appropriation of the *Playboy* tag which (unlike *Playboy*) positioned lesbians as sexual objects *and* sexual subjects, directed lesbian images squarely at a lesbian readership, and opposed the stereotype of asexual, lesbian high-mindedness. Indeed, where the subtitle parodied *Playboy*, the magazine title itself was an irreverent gesture to the sexually conservative feminist publication *off our backs*. So, in 1984 – at the height of both Reaganism and the feminist sex debates in the USA[4] – a group of uppity women with few resources devote what they have to launching a declaration of sexual independence, appropriating, in the process, sexual stances and strategies rooted in San Francisco's gay men's community (cf. Echols, 1991, p. 52). By anti-porn feminist standards, a retrograde moment; by the heterosexist standards of a sexually retrenching society, downright *sub*cultural.

On Our Backs came out celebrating a range of lesbian sexual roles, practices and fantasies, among them romance, mysticism, penetration, sadomasochism, dominance–submission, sweet-touching, butch–femme, humping, cruising, leather, bestiality, bondage, cunnilingus, lace, pyrotechnics, cross-generational seduction, public sex, exhibitionism, anal fucking, biking, group sex, masturbation, courting and fisting. Some images subvert a variety of public sexual standards (at least in my academic judgement). Some are more explicit than others in denoting women's bodies and expressing sexual responses through gestures or words. Many portray temptation, seduction, charged and spontaneous scenarios in public and private places, rather than bodily friction; but all are sexually direct.

In the stories, women characters come – some of them frequently, all of them refusing to accept the notion of orgasm as peculiarly and oppressively male, ambitiously (and thus masculinely) 'goal-directed'. The visual images feature stylised physique poses of women body-builders, close-up photographs of open mouths and tangled tongues, multiple-frame pictorials of indoor and outdoor seduction, women on the verge of penetration by fingers, hands and dildos, frenzied, arched bodies intertwined, bare-breasted, leather-jacketed dykes astride motorbikes, pierced clitorises and nipples, lace lingerie falling from muscular shoulders, studded leather against skin, latex-sheathed hands in the throes of safe (or is it fetishistic?) fucking. Models and characters are mostly white, though also Asian, African-American, Latina and Native American;[5] mostly thin or fleshy, though also heavy; mostly young, though also old; mostly able-bodied, though sometimes with disabilities. All connote 'dyke', partly through the details of style and dialogue but also because they are, sublimely, with other women.

So here is an inventory of anti-repressive lesbian sexual portrayals, which is not to say 'doing what comes naturally' so much as 'doing what comes pleasurably'.[6] Envisioning a deeply sexual world among women, these images trade at once on liberatory imagination and subcultural cachet. Lesbians may not consciously experience their sexuality as transgressive, even as they know it to be institutionally reviled. But such fixed, public representations of lesbian sex in a declaratively lesbian context like *On Our Backs* are a potentially transgressive and transformative site. What is socially marginal becomes symbolically central (Stallybrass and White, 1986, p. 23) through a politicised appropriation of sexual taboo, a threat (in the service of lesbian desire) to the sexual codes of both straight society and anti-porn feminist orthodoxy.

Demystifying desire

At the same time, though, the liberatory spirit is sexually demystifying in both the fictional and non-fictional contents of *On Our Backs*. In other words, the magazine brings lesbian desire above ground, affirming its legitimacy and encouraging lesbian women to find and embrace what pleases them sexually. For example, in a lesbian sex advice column perkily named 'Toys for us', editor Susie Bright (under the byline 'Susie Sexpert') introduces practices which, she suggests, may be arousing but also unnerving for many lesbians. Responding to one reader anxious about 'residual heterosexuality' in her attraction (and her lover's) to vaginal penetration, Susie writes:

> Ladies, the discreet, complete and definitive information on dildos is this: penetration is as heterosexual as kissing! Now the truth can be known! Fucking knows no gender. Not only that, but penises can only be compared to dildos in the sense that they take up space. Aside from difference in shape and feel, the most glaring contrast is that the dildo is at your service; it knows no desire other than your own or your partner's. Too many lesbians try on a dildo and harness in the Good Vibrations dressing room and expect the device to just take off with a life of its own. That might be exciting for a couple of sessions, but the truth is that it is much more satisfying to take the time, trial and pleasant error to find out how to maneuver your own dildo for optimal pleasure. Pretty soon you'll find yourself with a whole darling collection of dongs, and will be reduced to giving them pet names: 'Where is Henri?' 'Has Boom-Boom been cleaned yet' and 'how could you lend out Amelia?' (1984, p. 13)[7]

Here, Bright's persona is reassuringly forthright, a 1950s-style sexual naturalism transposed to *women's* sexuality,[8] a lesbian Dr Ruth whose mission is not only to approve lesbian sexual variability and sexual practices repudiated elsewhere, but to assure her readers of the stability of their lesbian identity in the process. 'You want it?' she asks. 'Try it, you'll still be a lesbian in the morning.'[9] She closes her opinion of penetration with an appeal to the traditionally feminine approach of 'taking your time' in sexual explorations, and a domesticated, pop-cultural invocation of all things French as sexual – 'Where', she asks, 'is Henri?'

Elsewhere in the magazine, anti-porn feminism's disavowal of *On Our Backs*'s erotic stances is dismissively pre-empted. In a recent issue, the 'Sextracts' department (which reports goings-on of relevance to lesbian sexual politics) observes that in an interview in *off our backs*, anti-pornography feminist Andrea Dworkin had 'targeted *On Our Backs* as a prime offender' in perpetuating sexist and patriarchal sex. 'Intercourse has nothing to do with lesbians or lesbian sexuality,' Dworkin is quoted as saying. 'Ask Good Vibrations about their dildo sales sometime, Andrea,' responds Greta Christina, the Sextracts columnist, who continues:

> Frankly, Ms. Dworkin, we find your attitudes about lesbian sex restrictive, oppressive, and yes, patriarchal. . . . But thank you for sharing (1990, p. 12)

Some readers I have encountered complain that *On Our Backs* simply doesn't have enough sex. Others are perhaps indifferent to its 'non-pornographic' content (like the Sextracts column) but satisfied by the porn. Still others, though, may be reassured by the framing of lesbian pornography amid commentary which reconciles sexual exploration and lesbian empowerment; to partake is not to abandon but to heighten your hard-won consciousness. Again, the message here is the power not of transgression but of sexual revelation – discovering what pleases you. To quote Scott Tucker, 'it is not true that forbidden fruit is sweet simply because it is forbidden. It is sweet because it is sweet . . .' (1991, p. 19).

The tempering effect of demystification also occurs in *On Our Backs*'s fiction, through what Sara Dunn calls a 'political anxiety' circumscribing lesbian pornography (1990, p. 164). Dunn describes this anxiety as too great a concern for the politics of sexual oppression in a form whose motive is – or should be – sexual fantasy. Lesbian porn writers, she says, are so concerned about preserving 'good' politics that they often come between their readers and their characters – for example, inserting the phrase 'But Dana did not feel degraded' just before a submissive Dana is laid on her back to take the powerful woman in her mouth. To Dunn, it is not clear that readers want to be reassured at that moment of Dana's self-esteem, whether or not they identify with Dana.

A similar quality consistently appears in *On Our Backs*'s fiction. For example, a softball player (and first-person narrator) who finds herself roughly seduced in the locker room by an opposing outfielder declares:

> I was reduced to helpless writhing. Even if Jamey hadn't been holding my wrists, I probably wouldn't have fought her off (Dellatte, 1990, p. 42).

The player is rescued from a dubious image of coercion by acknowledging her own desire to be 'handled'. Her acknowledgement, like the rest of the narration, comes in interior monologue, a voice which connotes subjectivity in her desire for sexual objectification at that moment. At the same time, though, it is a wary voice, speaking words like 'helpless' and making the consent ambiguous with qualifiers like 'probably'. The ambiguity incorporates a range of reader responses. 'Ah,' says the aficionado of rough sexual fantasy, 'she "really" is being taken.' 'Interesting,' responds the tentative reader, 'she wants it but she thinks it's tricky.'

Another example which recovers an image of sexual danger, this time through a dominant narrator, comes from a story called 'The Phoenix Chair' by Susan M. (1986). It is a pyrotechnic scenario, where a woman is blindfolded and bound to a chair by her lover, who contrives to douse her in gasoline then, placing a lighter in her hand, solicits her trust by asking her to roll the tumbler. The bound woman does so, and screams wildly as she senses a fiery flash igniting before her. The dominant woman is moved by the other's trust and explains, as she holds her, how the scenario had been created – with water and just a whiff of gas, and flash paper to simulate the explosion. Considerable space is devoted to this de-briefing, to describing the scene as trustworthy theatre.

This story was in the first issue of *On Our Backs* I purchased, and I read it nervously (though still I read it). Without the de-briefing (or the frequent references to 'safe words', which the bound woman could speak to stop or change the scene) I might not have looked at another issue, unable to reconcile myself to such an intense image of sexual danger, though it was indeed that: an image. Perhaps anticipating that response, perhaps reiterating s/m practice as theatre and play, risk though not coercion, the story had ended with an account of the fabrication. In this example, like the softball scenario, the transgressive representation of pleasure in danger is explicated, demystified and at least partly recovered, for readers like me.

The dialectic of transgression and demystification comes through in other readers' experiences with lesbian pornography – for example, the following comment from writer and activist Joan Nestle (1990), who makes and uses lesbian porn:

> I'll tell you the one story that transformed things for me. . . . You know, written erotica, it gives permissions, for explorations. Some people say that's terrible, I think it's wonderful. There was a very important story for me in *On Our Backs*, a story with three women together, two of them butches, wearing dildos. For the first time, the first time I'd read, a woman called her dildo a cock, and another woman went down on her. All my gay life, I wanted to use my mouth. When I read it, first I was confused. I had to reread it, thinking,

'but this is three women.' Since then I've enjoyed doing both. Later I wrote a story about it. That's what that story enabled. What the words did was make me face a desire and see what the taboo was about it, that desire.

Earlier in our conversation, Nestle had described the legacy of sexual shame attached to coming out as a queer in New York during the mid-1950s. For her (like others), butch and femme are roles to be reclaimed as part of lesbian history and contemporary lesbian identity, not repudiated as a pathetic or falsely conscious mockery of patriarchal gender distinctions. The pornographic image exposed, affirmed – 'demystified' – her desire to go down on that cock, a desire which had troubled her as taboo: transgressive, and contemptibly so.

What aroused Nestle about this and other stories was the image of sexual tension – in her words 'the manipulation of desire by three powerful people, negotiating differences in language, physical or verbal, in expressing their desires, challenging their sexual fear' (1990). Unlike Susie Sexpert's perky reassurances about the benign dildo in 'Toys for us', Nestle was moved by how dildos *could* be used in the story to connote subversions of conventional gender identity and the tense (if consensual) play of sexual power between or among women partners.[10]

Nestle's comment about sexual discovery reminded me of other lesbians who, they told me, had literally 'come out' through pornography, affirming their sexual attraction to women before ever having the pleasure of a woman lover. In one case, *On Our Backs*'s explicit imagery had been the source, enabling a woman in her late twenties to construct for herself an image of lesbian desire and her place within it, despite her 'embarrassment at buying and owning a lesbian porn rag'. Here again, the dynamic was less about transgression as an end in itself than about demystification and sweet reasurance, in a sexually hostile world which volunteers few happy occasions or means for newly experiencing one's sexuality as a lesbian.

Macho Sluts

In Pat Califia's sexual storytelling, gone are *On Our Backs*'s often idyllic daytime reveries of lesbian narrators who exhibit themselves and their arousal to handsome telephone linewomen just outside the bedroom window. Califia's dominance–submission scenarios in *Macho Sluts* are high-contact, otherworldly, and often deeply romantic (if never pastel). As sexual fantasies they are sequestered in cars, hotel rooms or erotic chambers, but their characters are very much connected to lesbian and gay communities. The stories are not tentative but nor, as I shall describe, are they indifferent to sexual coercion and brutality.

In Sara Dunn's reading, Califia is among the few lesbian porn writers who 'moves beyond the need to apologize', whose stories exploit rather than 'coyly forgive' politically troublesome sexual images and the 'disparity between private pleasures and public faces' (Dunn, 1990, pp. 167–8). Indeed, in her introduction to *Macho Sluts*, Califia calls the book a 'recruitment poster, as flashy and fast and seductively intimidating as I could make it' (p. 10). Here and throughout the collection, she takes on the lesbian and gay movement's nervous resistance to moral-majority demonising about homosexual conscription. 'Gays can't reproduce, so they *recruit*,' opined Anita Bryant in her successful 1977 campaign to repeal a gay rights ordinance in Dade County, Florida. In the oppressive company of homophobes, overturning stereotypes of predatory perverts seducing young innocents is important political work. But in the long struggle for the rights of lesbian and gay people, this has come at the expense of sexual cultures within the movement (especially leatherfolk and cross-dressers), who are often repuditated by others fearful of being identified with or through them. The same is true in anti-porn feminist circles, where lesbian sadomasochists have become the fetishised 'Other' of anti-porn sexual politics.

Califia will have none of it – neither from the religious Right or Women Against Pornography nor from anti-*censorship* feminists or the American Civil Liberties Union. Her reasons are not meekly libertarian, and her utopia is explicitly and richly sexual, among other qualities:

> Sex may seem like a trivial part of a radical, futuristic vision, but if we are not safe to indulge in this playful, vulnerable and necessary activity, pleasure ourselves and the others who fascinate us, how safe can a society be for women? A world that guaranteed food, shelter, medical care, full employment, literacy, day care, civil rights and democracy, but denied us sexual license, would make us nothing but well-fed domestic animals with suffrage. (1988, p. 14)

Despite Califia's refusal to retreat, the eight stories in *Macho Sluts* (including one 'vanilla', or non-s/m) are introduced by a substantial pro-sex critique which, assuming one reads it, positions the porn in explicitly political terms. In other words, this too is transgressive-sex-plus-consciousness. Unlike 'Toys for us', there is nothing perky about Califia's introduction, though it, like the stories, is often funny. But much like the magazine commentaries, it offers readers a new understanding, an intellectual and emotional filter for separating guilt from desire.

While Califia describes the book as her own sexual chronicle, written for those who 'understand what I need and value what I see' (p. 10), she is no s/m supremacist. She acknowledges that lesbian sexual tastes vary. Her characters begrudgingly concede the legitimacy of 'vanilla' sex: 'Look, they have a right to their own version of a good time,' says the manager of a women's sex emporium about the club's non-s/m crowd (p. 106). Califia also knows that the scenes she offers are rightly subject to readers' imaginations. Resisting the assumption that lesbians want only female characters in erotic fiction, she includes two stories which prominently feature gay men. 'But,' she says, 'if fantasies about men aren't erotic at all for you, you might want to skip these stories or mentally change the male characters into women wearing strap-ons' (p. 17). Though she is seriously critical of 'hackneyed' commercial porn and lobbies for 'well-written obscenity', here as elsewhere Califia does not claim an artist's privilege of suggesting that the truth or worth of a piece lies in its author's literary intention. Throughout *Macho Sluts*, readers (novice and expert) are fondly implicated.

By the public standards of official culture, the book's sexual episodes are deeply transgressive. Among Califia's characters are an aloof and hard-edged bass player in a women's rock band called The Bitch, a name which taunts feminist protest against the Rolling Stones; the club proprietor, a six-foot, stiletto-heeled topwoman with knee-length white hair who, for a fee, orchestrates a gang scene for another topwoman; and three leather-clad policemen who 'abduct' a leatherwoman to dominate her sexually. In ritually propped and costumed scenarios, these characters fetishise the infliction and endurance of pain, whether by hand, cane, clamp or other device. They encounter and sometimes push the limits of their own sexual experience and consciousness. For them, sadism and masochism are disciplined transformations, evocations of the body's 'stamina and grace' (p. 25).

Readers who inhabit some version of *Macho Sluts*'s sexual environments may find the stories a welcome affirmation, a rare instance of a self-identified s/m dyke writing and publishing her pieces. But as Califia makes clear throughout the book, it would be a mistake to describe as 'insiders' only those who do the kinds of things her characters do. Indeed, there is an organised (and controlled) community of s/m practitioners, and Califia moves among them. But pornographic *fantasies* are just that:

> a realm in which we can embrace pleasures that we may have very good reasons to deny ourselves in real life (like the fact that something might not be nearly as much fun to do as it is to think about). (Califa, 1988, p. 16)

Accepting the stories *as* fantasies, where are we to draw the line between 'insider' and 'outsider'? Where stands the lesbian who never wears more leather than a softball glove or a pair of sensible pumps, yet in reading

Califia recognises her own desire to be sexually taken, to have her nipples pinched, if not clamped (by something as unambiguous and thus threatening as a sexual gadget); her arms pinned by another's hands, if not locked in cuffs? To know the intimacy of offering up her sentient, vulnerable body to someone who will respect her safety *and* her desire? And where is the woman who, in bed, wants nothing more of *Macho Sluts* than the book? Is she in or out of Califia's transgressive universe?

Califia herself poses this question. In the introduction, she reminds the audience that 'reading this won't make you an outlaw (it's not that easy, sweetheart)' (p. 21). Here she guards hardboiled distinctions between sexual 'radicals' (those who publicly position themselves on or outside the margins of sexual legitimacy) and mere consumers, and addresses the latter among her readers. In the same sentence, however, she suggests that those who enjoy the book might 'think about why the law is trying to get between you and your prurient interests' (*ibid.*). In this shift of focus – from social participation in 'deviant' subcultures to challenging legal restrictions on obscene writing – Califia recognises continuities in lesbian sexual desire and reminds the vanilla not to be smug: you too are deviants, she cautions, and ought to choose your allies carefully.

Macho Sluts and sexual consent

Macho Sluts also addresses a range of readers through its demystifications of s/m practice, particularly around images of consent. Indeed, in her introduction Califia challenges critics who would argue that amid the sexual coercions of patriarchal society, women cannot truly consent to sadomasochism:

> If you don't believe we choose to do s/m, you aren't using the term 'consent' in any meaningful way, but rather as a synonym for 'mature,' 'socially acceptable,' and 'politically correct.' (p. 26)

Notwithstanding an important final chapter on lesbians, AIDS and safer sex, *Macho Sluts* is not presented as a guide to sexual practice (though Califia has published two such guides, one called *Sapphistry*, the other *The Lesbian S/M Safety Manual*). Virtually all the stories, however, make pointed distinctions between sadomasochism and sexual coercion. For example, in 'Jessie', about the seduction of The Bitch's bass player, a reporter for the local feminist press interviews band members about a fight that broke out between two women at one of the band's concerts. The members are contrite, agreeing that the fight was an unfortunate moment for the women's community. Only Jessie, the bassist, dissents:

She scowled and announced that it was time for women to reclaim their violence. 'I just wish the stupid cunts would cut up some rapist instead of each other.' Then she offered the interviewer a line of coke.

The journalist, Amazon Birdsong, was not mollified. She could afford to buy her own coke (pharmaceutical, an ounce at a time). She had wealthy parents who love TeKanawa, had never heard of Chuck Berry, collected first editions of D. H. Lawrence, but never went near an adult bookstore. After the stinging review she published ('Pornographic Attitudes Infiltrate Wimmin's Music'), The Bitch didn't get any gigs for six months. They were rescued by a women's karate school on the brink of bankruptcy. The benefit concert they did there salvaged their foundering reputation and gave the bar owners an excuse to start booking them again. (pp. 32–3)

Invoking feminist taboos against drug use, women's violence and sexual name-calling, this passage opposes 'politically correct' identifications with Jessie. It also provides a terse and witty caricature of a lesbian community divided by social class (the taste for pharmaceutical versus street coke, TeKanawa versus Chuck Berry, and D. H. Lawrence versus smut), where some use traditional capitalist sanctions against a women's rock band and the band is revived, ironically, by members of the feminist anti-violence movement. Amid this ambivalent characterisation of women's communities and Jessie's identity as an s/m dyke, the dialogue is also clear about what Jessie won't stand for: rape. Here, the story presents an unambiguous distinction between rape, as sexual violence, and dominance and submission, as consensual sexual forms.

Califia makes a similar distinction in 'The Surprise Party', though the story heightens the image of sexual danger by withholding implied consent until the end. A topwoman is stopped on the street by three male police officers and taken to a hotel room for a long night of sexual submission. Throughout the encounter, the woman's reflections shift between fury at her captors and desire for the glossy, musucular and leather-bound cops.

What are we to think as we read? Has the woman been abducted? Is she being raped? The title ('Surprise Party') suggests that things may not be as they seem, and this is finally confirmed when the ringleader 'cop' gives the woman a ride home, where she discovers a note from her lover on the kitchen table:

'Honey, I let myself in. Don called last night and said he and a couple of his friends were taking you to a surprise party for your birthday, so I'm not surprised to find you gone. I just climbed into your bed to wait for you. Come join me and tell me about it. I brought homemade blintzes for breakfast. I love you slavishly. Fran.'

> What a lucky dyke I am, she thought. First I get to star in the most scary porn movie in the world, now I come home and find that my best darling girl is waiting for me . . . (p. 242)

Though the woman did not expect the encounter, through the denoue-ment we understand her trust in the men and thus can imagine her willing participation in the scene. The story recovers her from the corrupt image of the 'rape victim who wanted it', though not without playing that image as sexual fantasy. *As* fantasy, the story's portrayal of submissive desire is not simply an articulation of the passive feminine position conventionally inscribed in gender relations. Instead, it becomes the object (or focus) of sexual agency: unlike rape, the woman character (and the reader who identifies with her) controls the fantasy.

A final example of sexual consent, complicated further still, comes from 'The Calyx of Isis'. The Calyx is a lesbian sexual utopia, a com-mercial centre where 'maybe for the first time in history, lesbians have the choice to be really promiscuous, if that's what they want to do' (p. 94). In the club are bars, baths, dance floors, restaurants and massage rooms patronised by women of all persuasions. Says Tyre, the manager:

> We get couples looking for a threesome, single women looking for Ms. Right or Ms. Wrong or Ms. Right Away, black and white and Hispanic and Asian women who are bisexuals, transsexuals, homosexuals, heterosexuals and try-sexuals, as in 'I'll try anything.' Witches and bikers and herbalists and cops and chiropractors and truck drivers and real-estate agents and drug dealers and lobbyists and martial-arts instructors and female bankers and mechanics and dentists and housepainters. (*ibid.*)

The Calyx is ensconced in feminist communities and sensibilities, providing grants to childcare centres, setting up weekday clinics for cervical smears and STD tests, and responding to curious inquiries from nearby anthropologists about the chance to do participant observation. 'Only if they'll take their clothes off and stay in the maze,' says Tyre. A popular place, the club protects its clientele from gaybashers who cruise the neighbourhood looking for someone to hurt. Well-equipped bouncers guard the nightly queue, dealing personally with threatening passers-by and taking licence plate numbers to track down harassing drivers. At The Calyx, the staff are serious about women's safety.

The club also caters to 'specialty' scenarios – indeed, the story unfolds around an extended group scene commissioned by a topwoman to witness her lover's strength and devotion. One after the other, Roxanne (the lover) wears out eight dominant women in the basement chambers. Throughout the scene the narration returns to Roxanne, whose fear and desire are elaborately voiced in the third person. The tops change, but Roxanne remains at centre stage.

In so consistently voicing Roxanne's consciousness, in describing the scene as 'hers', and through frequent references to 'safe words', Califia implies consent in dramatic acts of submission and the fetishising of pain and trust. Late in 'The Calyx of Isis', however, she uses the rule of consent to intensify the story's transgressions. When one of the topwomen bad-mouths another, the offending woman's lover is infuriated and rushes at her, *rescinding* her safe word and (with the others) subjecting her to sexual domination. 'This is not consensual' screams the first, a line which took me by surprise. Am I to read this, too, as a staged part of the scenario? In the ritualised codes of sadomasochism, are safe words ever rescinded? I find myself appealing for reassurance to the world beyond the book. The story has abandoned the denotation of consent and relies on the nature of representation itself to distinguish between sexual coercion and sexual fantasy. My anxiety as a reader is visceral, but emotional realism needn't reify the image as sexual coercion. It is a character, not a woman, who is seemingly rushed against her will.

Conclusion

Appeals to representation, however, will satisfy neither my critics nor Califia's, and in many ways that is as it should be. Images and the practices they signify are different but not unrelated. Some critics and activists refuse the difference and argue that pornography *is* violence against women. Others say it cultivates callousness towards the sexual brutality many women suffer. Few consider the women (and men) for whom sexual imagery is one link in a social and cultural lifeline, a link emblematic of their refusal to accept established sexual hierarchies and their will to make their own place. In *On Our Backs* and *Macho Sluts*, the refusal is drama-tically public. While their images transgress anti-porn feminist orthodoxy and the heterosexual mainstream, they also expose, demystify and affirm precisely that part of lesbianism that is so threatening: we take our place among women through sexual and political desire, and in the process declare some resistance to heterosexist and patriarchal cultural scripts. That is not to say, however, that thus declared we are unencumbered. Resistance is resistance, not freedom – to wit, a concluding retrospection:

Some years ago, at the meetings of an academic association, I took a taxi from the conference hotel to a lesbian bar, to attend a get-together hosted by the association's lesbian and gay caucus. A friendly and easy-going driver in his early sixties greeted me as the tourist I obviously was and asked me where to. In my caution and self-consciousness, I named the intersection rather than the lesbian establishment.

'You going to the bar?' he inquired as we pulled away from the kerb. 'Yeah,' I told him, smiling at the irony. The driver asked what brought me to town and I described the conference. Was I a professor? I said I was. He looked over his shoulder and shook his head, smiling an easy smile.

'You don't need anybody, do you?' he said, half asking, half stating. I laughed out loud. 'I need a lot of folks' was my response, but I knew what he meant. We reached the bar, like so many others a friendly, shabby place in a treacherous and isolated part of town. The driver told me he would wait until I got inside, and gave me the taxi company's card so I could call when I was ready to leave.

'Don't wait on the street for your cab back,' he cautioned, 'the driver'll come in and get you.' I thanked him for his hospitality.

Inside the bar, I thought for a moment about our exchange. Here I was (as the driver could tell) looking neither for men's companionship nor for economic security, yet vulnerable in this spot at this moment, a lesbian open to dykebashing by her presence in the very place that promised some retreat. The driver had been struck by her independence, but seeing she was alone, he offered his protection. A paternal gesture? Perhaps, but also a respectful one: the danger was real and she deserved his concern.

I close with this account because it speaks to both distance and proximity between dominant and resistant cultures. The driver, a working person, was not the ruling class, but our encounter and his insight deeply and clearly reflected the structural position of women in patriarchy: even in sexual resistance, we define ourselves (and are partly defined) in relation to dominant gender and sexual orders.

As resistant texts, *On Our Backs* and *Macho Sluts* embody this contradiction. Lesbian pornography does not exist beyond sex–gender and other forms of oppression, but nor does it simply reproduce them. My anxious response to 'The Phoenix Chair' or 'The Calyx of Isis' comes, perhaps, from a sexual fear many women know, but it is not the same fear that keeps me off some streets at night, nor does it negate the spirit or the image of lesbian sexual self-recognition and celebration, both there for the interpreting through the lens of sexual political struggle. *On Our Backs* and *Macho Sluts* are not for everyone, but they happily imagine a world in which sexual violence and coercion are separated from the power of female sexuality, and neither poses a singular or proscriptive equation for lesbian desire.

On Our Backs and *Macho Sluts* are also commodity forms (though their modest profits are more equitably created and distributed among a different group of cultural producers). While it is compelling to imagine desire released from commodification as well as fear, it is not clear that certain sexual practices will disappear if and when their commodification does. Sex is embedded in capitalism, but sex and capitalism are not the same. Nor is resistance necessarily doomed to 'licensed release', a ritual contestation which ultimately consolidates the established order (cf. Stallybrass and White, 1986, p. 13). While social structures are always at work in private experience, such a rigidly deterministic view misses the survival value and the political momentum of small and great subversions, refusals, irreverences, new imaginings – particularly those made in the name and experience of pleasure. Their power is often to make and keep the struggle – for self-determination – possible.

With thanks to the Lesbian Herstory Archives in New York City for their pornography files. The Archives is an extraordinary place to work and to keep one's faith in resistance as an essential part of culture, politics, scholarship and everyday life. Thanks as well to LHA co-founder Joan Nestle for her time and insight, and to Kathryn Furano, Larry Gross, Bette Kauffman, Sally Munt, Scott Tucker and Angharad Valdivia for their critical and editorial assistance.

Notes

1. Some of the pivotal texts in feminist anti-pornography writing include Dworkin (1981), Barry (1979, esp. Ch. 9), Lederer (1980), Cole (1989), Jeffreys (1985, 1986) and Leidholdt and Raymond (1990). For the anti-anti-porn position, see, e.g., Vance (1984), Snitow, Stansell and Thompson (1983), Burstyn (1987) and *Feminist Review* (1990).
2. The question of what media images women identify with remains open for many mainstream forms as well as for pornography. For further discussion, see Schwichten-berg, 1990. On pornography, see 'When girls look at boys' (1989), a group interview (which appeared in *On Our Backs*) of lesbian women who use gay men's pornography.
3. *On Our Backs* is not alone in the production of lesbian-directed pornography. *Bad Attitude* started up in Boston in 1986, joined shortly thereafter by *Outrageous Women* and *Idos*.
4. Though I do not equate anti-pornography feminism and reactionary federal politics, I do think the anti-porn position was poised for appropriation by political opportunists whose motives were and are anything but feminist (in the USA, Edwin Meese, Jerry Falwell and Jesse Helms among them).
5. In a recent issue (Nov./Dec. 1990), a reader wrote in to protest that *On Our Backs* featured too few images of Black models or stories about Black lesbian characters. In response, editor Susie Bright agreed, saying that although the magazine does publish work by Black lesbians, they don't get as many submissions as they'd like. She went on to encourage women of colour, big women, older women, 'all kinds of women', to submit stories and photography. Bright's 'diversity program' makes sense in terms of the

reader's letter, but it doesn't address why the magazine receives so few submissions from women of colour, who may have a more complicated historical relationship than white lesbians to sexual objectification by outsiders, and to predominantly white lesbian and gay communities (including the producers of *On Our Backs*).

6. For a critique of 'naturalism' in the rhetoric of both anti-pornography feminism and sexual liberationism, see Weir and Casey (1984).
7. Good Vibrations is a sex shop in San Francisco catering predominantly for women.
8. On the ideology of sexual naturalism in the USA of the late 1950s, see Richard Dyer's chapter on Marilyn Monroe in *Heavenly Bodies* (1986). Dyer discusses the use of Monroe's image in a rhetoric rarely directed towards *women's* sexual liberation.
9. Here I am quoting from Bright's 1986 presentation at Giovanni's Room, a Philadelphia lesbian/gay/feminist bookstore.
10. A gay male friend tells me that lesbians are not the only ones who play with gender signifiers in sexual contexts. Some gay men do too, saying (for example) 'I want *his* pussy' or 'I want him in my pussy'.

Works Cited

Ang, Ien (1985) *Watching Dallas: Soap opera and the melodramatic imagination*. New York: Methuen (English transl.)

Barry, Kathleen (1979) *Female Sexual Slavery*. New York: New York University Press.

Bright, Susie (1984) 'Toys for us.' *On Our Backs*, **1**, 1, p. 13.

Burstyn, Varda, ed. (1987) *Women Against Censorship*. Vancouver: Douglas McIntyre.

Califia, Pat (1981) *Sapphistry*. Tallahassee, FL: Naiad Press.

Califia, Pat (1988) *Macho Sluts*. Boston, MA: Alyson.

Califia, Pat (1990) (ed.) *The Lesbian S/M Safety Manual*. Boston, MA: Alyson.

Christina, Greta (1990) 'Sextracts: Dworkin saves us from ourselves.' *On Our Backs*, **6**, 5, pp. 12–13.

Cole, Susan G. (1989) *Pornography and the Sex Crisis*. Toronto: Amanita.

Dellatte, Gina (1990) 'Low and inside.' *On Our Backs*, **6**, 5, pp. 28–9, 42–3.

Dunn, Sara (1990) 'Voyages of the valkyries: Recent lesbian pornographic writing.' *Feminist Review*, **34**, pp. 161–70.

Dworkin, Andrea (1981) *Pornography: Men possessing women*. New York: Perigree.

Dyer, Richard (1986) *Heavenly Bodies*. New York and London: St Martin's Press.

Echols, Alice (1989) *Daring to be Bad: Radical feminism in America, 1967–1975*. Minneapolis: University of Minnesota Press.

Echols, Alice (1991) 'Justifying our love? The evolution of lesbianism through feminism and gay male politics.' *The Advocate*, **573**, pp. 48–53.

Ellis, Kate, Barbara O'Dair and Abby Tallmer (1986) 'Introduction', in Kate Ellis, Nan D. Hunter, Beth Jaker, Barbara O'Dair and Abby Tallmer, eds, *Caught Looking: Feminism, pornography, and censorship*. New York: Caught Looking.

Feminist Review (1990) Perverse Politics: Lesbian issues. No. **34**.

Jeffreys, Sheila (1985) *The Spinster and her Enemies: Feminism and sexuality, 1880–1930*. London: Pandora.

Jeffreys, Sheila (1986) 'Sadomasochism: The erotic cult of fascism.' *Lesbian Ethics*, **2**, 1, pp. 65–82.

Lederer, Laura (ed.) (1980) *Take Back the Night: Women on pornography*. New York: Morrow.

Leidholt, Dorchen and Janice G. Raymond (1990) *The Sexual Liberals and the Attack on Feminism*. New York: Pergamon Press.

M., Susan (1986) 'The Phoenix Chair.' *On Our Backs*, **18–19**, p. 49.

Morley, David (1980) *The Nationwide Audience*. London: British Film Institute.

Nestle, Joan (1990) Personal interview. New York, 10 May, 1990.

Radway, Janice (1984) *Reading the Romance: Women, patriarchy and popular literature*. Chapel Hill: University of North Carolina Press.

Ross, Andrew (1989) 'The popularity of pornography', in Ross, *No Respect: Intellectuals and Popular Culture*. New York: Routledge.

Schwictenberg, Cathy (1990) 'Theorizing the feminist audience.' Paper presented to the meetings of the International Communications Association, Feminist Scholarship Interest Group, Dublin, June.

Smyth, Cherry (1990) 'The pleasure threshold: Looking at lesbian pornography on film.' *Feminist Review*, **34**, pp. 152–9.

Snitow, Ann, Christine Stansell and Sharon Thompson, eds (1983) *Powers of Desire: The politics of sexuality*. New York: New Feminist Library/Monthly Review Press.

Stallybrass, Peter and Allon White (1986) *The Politics and Poetics of Transgession*. Ithaca, NY: Cornell University Press.

Tucker, Scott (1991) 'Gender, fucking and utopia: An essay in response to John Stoltenberg's *Refusing to be a Man*.' *Social Text*, **27**, pp. 3–34.

Vance, Carole, ed. (1984) *Pleasure and Danger: Exploring female sexuality*. London: Routledge & Kegan Paul.

Weir, Lorna and Leo Casey (1984) 'Subverting power in sexuality.' *Socialist Review*, **14** 3–4, pp. 139–57.

'When girls look at boys'. (1989) Group interview. *On Our Backs*, **5**, pp. 28–31, 42–3.

Williams, Linda (1989) *Hard Core: Power, pleasure and the 'frenzy of the visible'*. Berkeley: University of California Press.

SUGGESTIONS FOR FURTHER READING

Abbot, Sidney and Barbara Love, *Sappho Was a Right-On Woman: A liberated view of lesbianism*. New York: Stein & Day, 1972.

Abraham, Julie, 'History as explanation: Writing about lesbian writing, or "Are girls necessary?"' in Lennard J. Davis and M. Bella Mirabella (eds) *Left Politics and the Literary Profession*. New York: Colombia University Press. 1990: 254–84.

Adams, Parveen, 'Of female bondage', in Teresa Brennan (ed.) *Between Feminism and Psychoanalysis*. London: Routledge, 1989: 247–65.

Alicen, Debbie, 'Intertextuality: The language of Lesbian Relationships'. *Trivia*, 3, 1983: 6–26.

Allen, Jeffner, *Lesbian Philosophy*. Pala Alto, CA: Institute of Lesbian Studies, 1986.

Allen, Jeffner (ed.) *Lesbian Philosophies and Cultures*. Albany, NY: SUNY Press, 1989.

Allen, Paula Gunn (ed.) *Studies in American Indian Literature: Critical essays and course designs*. New York: MLA, 1984.

Allen, Paula Gunn, *The Sacred Hoop: Recovering the feminine in American Indian traditions*. Boston, MA: Beacon Press, 1986.

Andreadis, Harriette, 'The Sapphic-Platonics of Katherine Philips, 1632–1664'. *Signs*, 15, 1, 1989: 34–60.

Anzaldúa, Gloria, *Borderslands/La Frontera*. San Francisco: Spinsters/Aunt Lute, 1987.

Ardill, Susan and Sue O'Sullivan, 'Upsetting an applecart: Difference, desire, and lesbian sadomasochism'. *Feminist Review*, 23, 1986: 31–58.

Ardill, Susan and Sue O'Sullivan, 'Sex in the summer of '88'. *Feminist Review*, 31, Spring 1989: 126–34.

Arnold, June and Bertha Harris, 'Lesbian fiction: A dialogue'. *Sinister Wisdom*, 1, 1, No. 2, 1976.

Ash, Juliet and Wilson, Elizabeth, *Chic Thrills: A fashion reader*. London: Pandora, 1991.

Asher, Carol, Louise De Salvo and Sara Ruddick (eds.) *Between Women: Biographers, novelists, critics, teachers and artists write about their work on Women*. Boston, MA: Beacon Press, 1984.

Bennett, Paula, *My Life a Loaded Gun: Female creativity and feminist poetics*. Boston, MA: Beacon Press, 1986.

Bennett, Paula, *Emily Dickinson*. Hemel Hempstead: Harvester Wheatsheaf, 1990.

Bens, Susanna, 'Sappho in soft cover: Notes on lesbian pulp', in Silvera Makeda (ed.) *Fireworks: The best of fireweed*. Toronto: The Women's Press, 1986.

Benstock, Shari, *Women of the Left Bank: Paris, 1900–1940*. Austin: University of Texas Press, 1986.

Benstock, Shari, 'Portrait of the artist's wife'. *Times Literary Supplement*, 30 September 1988: 1065.

Benstock, Shari, 'Paris lesbianism and the politics of reaction, 1900–1940', in Martin Bauml Duberman, Martha Vicinus and George Chauncey, Jr (eds) *Hidden from History: Reclaiming the Gay and Lesbian past*. New York: New American Library, 1989: 332–46.

Benstock, Shari, *Textualizing the Feminine: Essays on the limits of genre*. Norman: University of Oklahoma Press, 1990.

Bethel, Lorraine, 'What chou mean *we*, white girl? Or, the cullud lesbian feminist declaration of independence'. *Conditions Five*, Autumn 1979: 86–92.

Birkby, Phyllis *et al.* (eds) *Amazon Expedition: A lesbian feminist anthology*. Albion, CA: Times Change Press, 1973.

Bogus, SDiane, 'Notes on the Black lesbian aesthetic in literature'. *Mama Bear's News and Notes*, August/September, Berkeley, CA, 1986.

Bonnet, Marie-Jo, *Un Choix sans équivoque: recherches historiques sur les relations amoureuses entres les femmes XVIe–XXe siècle*. Paris: Denoël, 1981.

Boyers, Robert and George Steiner (eds) *Homosexuality: Sacrilege, vision, politics*. Saratoga Springs, NY: Skidmore College, 1983.

Brady, Maureen and Judith McDaniel, 'Lesbians in the mainstream: Images of lesbians in recent commercial fiction'. in *Conditions*, **2**, 2, 1980.

Bristow, Joe, 'Being gay: Politics, identity, pleasure'. *New Formations*, **9**, 1989: 61–82.

Brodzki, Bella and Celeste Schenck (eds) *Life/Lines: Theorizing women's biography*. Ithaca, NY and London: Cornell University Press, 1988.

Brossard, Nicole, *The Aerial Letter*, transl. Marlene Wilderman, Toronto: The Women's Press, 1988.

Bulkin, E. and J. Larkin, *Lesbian Poetry*. Watertown, MA: Persephone, 1981.

Bullough, Vern L., *Homosexuality: A history*. New York: New American Library, 1979.

Bunch, Charlotte, 'Not for lesbians only', in C. Bunch and G. Steinem (eds) *Building Feminist Theory: Essays from quest*. New York: Longman, 1987: 67–73.

Butler, Judith, *Gender Trouble. Feminism, and the subversion of identity* London: Routledge, 1990.

Cant, Bob and Susan Hemmings (eds) *Radical Records: Thirty years of lesbian & gay history*. London: Routledge, 1988.

Card, Claudia, 'Lesbian attitudes and *The Second Sex*'. *Women's Studies International Forum*, **8**, 1985: 209–14.

Carruthers, Mary, '"The re-vision of the muse": Adrienne Rich, Audre Lorde, Judy Grahn, Olga Broumas'. *Hudson Review*, **36**, 1983: 293–322.

Cartledge, Sue and Joanna Ryan (eds) *Sex and Love: New thoughts on old contradictions*. London: The Women's Press, 1983.

Case, Sue Ellen, 'Toward a butch/femme aesthetic', in Linda Hart (ed.) *Making A Spectacle: Feminist essays on contemporary women's theatre*. Michigan: Ann Arbor, 1988.

Causse, Michèle, 'L'Interloquée'. *Trivia*, **13**, 1988: 79–90.

Cavin, Susan, *Lesbian Origins*. San Francisco: ISM Press, 1985.

Chessman, Harriet Scott, *The Public is Invited to Dance: Representation, the body, and dialogue in Gertrude Stein*. Stanford, CA: Stanford University Press, 1989.

Christian, Barbara, *Black Feminist Criticism: Perspectives on Black women writers*. New York: Pergamon Press, 1985.

Christina, Greta, 'Sextracts: Dworkin saves us from ourselves.' *On Our Backs*, **6**, 5, 1990: 12–13.

Cixous, Hélène and Catherine Clement, *The Newly Born Woman*, transl. Betsy Wing. Minneapolis: University of Minnesota Press, 1986.

Clark, Wendy, 'The dyke, the feminist and the devil'. *Feminist Review*, **11**, 1982: 30–39.

Cook, Blanche Wiesen, '"Women alone stir my imagination": Lesbianism and the cultural tradition'. *Signs*, **4**, 1979: 718–39.

Cornwell, Anita, *Black Lesbian in White America*. Tallahassee, FL: Naiad Press, 1983.

Cruikshank, Margaret, (ed.) *Lesbian Studies: Present and future*. New York: Feminist Press, 1982.

Cruikshank, Margaret, 'Looking back on lesbian studies'. *Frontiers*, **8**, 3, 1986: 107–9.

Daly, Mary, *Beyond God the Father: Toward a philosophy of women's liberation*. Boston, MA: Beacon Press, 1973.

Daly, Mary, *Gyn/Ecology: The metaethics of radical feminism*. Boston, MA: Beacon Press, 1978.

Daly, Mary, *Pure Lust: Elemental feminist philosophy*. Boston, MA: Beacon Press, 1984.

Daly, Mary and Jane Caputi, *Webster's First New Intergalactic Wickedary of the English Language*. Boston, MA: Beacon Press, 1987.

Davy, Kate, 'Constructing the spectator: Reception, context, and address in lesbian performance'. *Performing Arts Journal*, **10**, 1986: 43–53.

DeKoven, Marianne, *A Different Language: Gertrude Stein's experimental language*. Madison: University of Wisconsin Press, 1983.

D'Emilio, John, *Sexual Politics, Sexual Communities: The making of a homosexual minority in the United States, 1940–1970*. Chicago and London: University of Chicago Press, 1983.

de Lauretis, Teresa, 'Sexual indifference and lesbian representation'. *Theatre Journal*, **40**, 1988: 155–77.

Derrida, Jacques, *Dissemination*, transl. Barbara Johnson. Chicago: University of Chicago Press, 1981.

Derrida, Jacques, *Margins of Philosophy*, transl. Alan Bass. Chicago: University of Chicago Press, 1982.

Dickson, Lovat, *Radclyffe Hall at the Well of Loneliness: A Sapphic chronicle*. New York: Scribners, 1952.

Dijkstra, Bram, *Idols of Perversity: Fantasies of feminine evil in fin-de-siècle culture*. New York and Oxford: Oxford University Press, 1986.

Dolan, Jill, 'Breaking the code: Musings on lesbian sexuality and the performer'. *Modern Drama*, **32**, Part 1, 1989: 146–58.

Douglas, Carol Anne, *Love and Politics: Radical feminist and lesbian theories*. San Francisco: ISM Press, 1990.

Dunker, Patricia, 'Writing lesbian', in *Papers of the Conference 'Homosexuality, Which Homosexuality?'* Amsterdam: Free University/Schorer Foundation, II, 1987: 32–46.

Dunn, Sara, 'Voyages of the valkyries: Recent lesbian pornographic writing'. *Feminist Review*, **34**, 1990: 161–70.

Dworkin, Andrea, *Woman Hating*. New York: Dutton, 1974.

Dyer, Richard, *Now You See It: Lesbian & gay film*. London: Routledge, 1990.

Echols, Alice, *Daring to Be Bad: Radical feminism in America, 1967–1975*. Minneapolis: University of Minnesota Press, 1989.

Echols, Alice, 'Justifying our love? The evolution of lesbianism through feminism and gay male politics'. *The Advocate*, **573**, 1991: 48–53.

Edelman, Lee, 'Homographesis'. *Yale Journal of Criticism*, **3**, 1, 1989: 189–208.

Elshstain, Jean Bethke, 'Homosexual politics: The paradox of gay liberation', in Boyers and Steiner, *Homosexuality*: 252–80.

Engelbrecht, Penelope J., '"Lifting belly is a language": The postmodern lesbian subject'. *Feminist Studies*, **16**, 1; 1990: 85–114.

Epstein, Steven, 'Gay politics, ethnic identity: The limits of social constructionism'. *Socialist Review*, **17**, 3/4, 1987: 9–54.

Evans, Martha Noel, *Masks of Tradition: Women and the politics of writing in twentieth-century France*. Ithaca, NY: Cornell University Press, 1987.

Faderman, Lillian, 'Emily Dickinson's homo-erotic poetry'. *Higginson Journal*, **18**, 1978: 19–27.

Faderman, Lillian, *Surpassing the Love of Men: Romantic friendship and love between women from the Renaissance to the present*. New York: Morrow, 1981.

Faderman, Lillian, *Scotch Verdict: Miss Pirie and Miss Woods v Dame Cumming Gordon*. New York: Quill, 1983.

Faderman, Lillian and Ann Williams, 'Radclyffe Hall and the lesbian image'. *Conditions*, **1**, April 1977.

Farwell, Marilyn R., 'Toward a definition of the lesbian literary imagination'. *Signs*, **14**, 1988: 100–18.

Feminist Review, Pornography Politics: Lesbian issues, *Feminist Review*, **34**, 1990

Ferguson, Ann, 'Lesbian identity: Beauvoir and history'. *Women's Studies International Forum*, **8**, 1985: 203–8.

Fetterley, Judith, *The Resisting Reader*. Bloomington: Indiana University Press, 1978.

Findlay, Heather, 'Is there a lesbian in this text? Derrida, Wittig and the politics of the three women', in Elizabeth Weed (ed.) *Coming to Terms*. London: Routledge, 1989.

Fletcher, John, 'Freud and his uses: Psychoanalysis and gay theory', in Simon Shepherd and Mick Wallis (eds) *Coming On Strong: Gay politics and culture*. London: Unwin Hyman, 1989: 90–118.

Foster, Jeanette H., *Sex Variant Women in Literature*. Tallahassee, FL: Naiad Press, 1985.

Freedman, Estelle B., Barbara C. Gelpi, Susan L. Johnson and Kathleen M. Weston (eds) *The Lesbian Issue: Essays from signs*. Chicago: University of Chicago Press, 1985.

Friedman, Susan Stanford, 'Women's autobiographical selves: Theory and practice', in Shari Benstock (ed.) *The Private Self*. Chapel Hill: University of North Carolina Press, 1988: 34–62.

Friedman, Susan Stanford and Rachel Blau DuPlessis, '"I had two loves separate": The sexualities of H. D.'s *Her*.' *Montemora*, **8**, 1981: 7–30.

Fuss, Diana, *Essentially Speaking: Feminism, nature and difference*. London: Routledge, 1990.

Gay Left Collective (eds) *Homosexuality: Power and politics*. London: Allison & Busby, 1980.

Gearhart, Sally, 'The future – if there is one – is female', in Pam McAllister (ed.) *Reweaving the Web of Life: Feminism and non-violence*. Philadelphia: New Society Publishers, 1982: 266–85.

Gilbert, Sandra M., *No Man's Land: The place of the woman writer in the twentieth century*. 2 vols. New Haven, CT: Yale University Press, 1988–9.

Gilbert, Sandra M. and Susan Gubar, *The Madwoman in the Attic: The woman writer and the nineteenth-century literary imagination*. New Haven, CT: Yale University Press, 1979.

Gilbert, Sandra M. and Susan Gubar, 'Tradition and female talent', in Nancy K. Miller (ed.) *The Poetics of Gender*. New York: Columbia University Press, 1986: 183–207.

Gilpi, Barbara Charlesworth, and Albert Gilpi (eds) 'When we dead awaken: Writing as revision', in *Adrienne Rich's Poetry*. New York: Norton, 1971: 90–8.

Gomez, Jewelle, 'A cultural legacy denied and discovered: Black lesbians in fiction by women', in Barbara Smith (ed.) *Home Girls: A Black feminist anthology*. New York: Kitchen Table Press, 1983: 110–23.

Gomez, Jewelle, 'Imagine a lesbian . . . a Black lesbian'. *Trivia*, **12**, 1988: 45–60.

Gossip: A Journal of Lesbian Feminist Ethics. Six issues, 1986–8, available from Onlywomen Press, 38 Mount Pleasant, London WC1X 0AP.

Grahn, Judy, *The Work of A Common Woman*. New York: St Martin's Press, 1978.

Grahn, Judy, *Another Mother Tongue: Gay words, gay worlds*. Boston, MA: Beacon Press, 1984.

Grahn, Judy, *The Highest Apple: Sappho and the lesbian poetic tradition*. San Francisco: Spinsters/Aunt Lute, 1985.

Grahn, Judy, *Really Reading Gertrude Stein*. Freedom, CA: Crossing Press, 1989.

Grier, Barbara (ed.) *Lesbiana: Book reviews from* The Ladder, *1966–1972*. Tallahassee, FL: Naiad Press, 1976.

Grier, Barbara (ed.) *The Lesbian in Literature*. Tallahassee, FL: Naiad Press, 1987.

Grier, Barbara and Coletta Reid (eds) *Lavender Herring: The lesbian essays from* The Ladder. Baltimore, MD: Diana Press, 1976.

Grosz, Elizabeth, 'Lesbian fetishism'. *Differences*, **6**, 2, Queer Theory Issue.

Gubar, Susan, 'Sapphistries'. *Signs*, **10**, 1984: 43–62.

Hallett, Judith P., 'Female homoeroticism and the denial of Roman reality in Latin literature'. *Yale Journal of Criticism*, **3**, 1, 1989: 209–27.

Halperin, David, 'One hundred years of homosexuality'. *Diacritics*, **16**, 2, 1986: 34–45.

Hanscombe, Gillian and Virginia L. Smyers, *Writing for Their Lives: The modernist women, 1910–1940*. Boston, MA: Northeastern University Press, 1987.

Harris, Bertha, 'What we mean to say: Notes toward defining the nature of lesbian literature'. *Heresies*, **3**, 1977: 5–8.

Hennigan, Alison, 'What lesbian novel'. *Women's Review*, **1**, 1985: 12.

Hennigan, Alison, 'Introduction' to *Girls Next Door: Lesbian feminist stories*. London: The Women's Press, 1985.

Hennigan, Alison, 'On becoming a lesbian reader', in Susannah Radstone (ed.) *Sweet Dreams: Sexuality, gender, and popular fiction*. London: Lawrence & Wishart, 1988: 165–90.

Hoagland, Sarah Lucia, *Lesbian Ethics: Toward new value*. Palo Alto, CA: Institute of Lesbian Studies, 1988.

Hoagland, Sarah Lucia and Julia Penelope (eds) *For Lesbians Only: A separatist anthology*. London: Onlywomen Press, 1988.

Hobby, Elaine and Chris White, *What Lesbians Do in Books*. London: The Women's Press, 1991.

Hokenson, Jan, 'The pronouns of Gomorrah: A lesbian prose tradition'. *Frontiers*, **10**, 1, 1988: 62–9.

Hollibaugh, Amber and Cherríe Moraga, 'What we're rollin around in bed with – sexual silences in feminism: A conversation towards ending them'. *Heresies*, **12**, 1981.

Homans, Margaret, '"Syllables of Velvet": Dickinson, Rossetti, and the rhetoric of sexuality'. *Feminist Studies*, **11**, 1985: 569–93.

hooks, bell, *Ain't I A Woman: Black women and feminism*. London: Pluto Press, 1990.

hooks, bell, *Yearning: Race, gender, and cultural politics*. London: Turnaround, 1991.

Irigaray, Luce, *Speculum of the Other Woman*, transl. Gillian C. Gill. Ithaca, NY: Cornell University Press, 1985.

Irigaray, Luce, *This Sex Which is Not One*, transl. Catherine Porter. Ithaca, NY: Cornell University Press, 1985.

Jardine, Alice A., *Gynesis: Configurations of woman and modernity*. Ithaca, NY: Cornell University Press, 1985.

Jay, Karla, *The Amazon and the Page: Natalie Clifford Barney and Renée Vivien*. Bloomington: Indiana University Press, 1988.

Jay, Karla and Joanne Glasgow (eds) *Lesbian Texts and Contexts: Radical revisions*. New York: New York University Press, 1990. London: Onlywomen Press, 1991.

Jay, Karla and Allen Young (eds) *Lavender Culture*. New York: Jove, 1978.

Jeffreys, Sheila, *The Spinster and Her Enemies: Feminism and sexaulity 1880–1930*. London: Pandora, 1985.

Jeffreys, Sheila, 'Sadomasochism: The erotic cult of fascism'. *Lesbian Ethics*, **2**, 1, 1986: 65–82.

Jin, M., 'Lesbian', in D. Choong, O. Cole Wilson, B. Evaristo and G. Pearse (eds) *Black Women Talk Poetry*. London: Black Womantalk, 1987.

Johnstone, Jill, *Lesbian Nation: The feminist solution*. New York: Simon, 1973.

Kannenstine, Louis F., *The Art of Djuna Barnes: Duality and damnation*. New York: New York University Press, 1971.

Katz, Jonathan, *Gay American History: Lesbians and gay men in the U.S.A.* New York: Thomas & Cromwell, 1976.

Kauffman, Linda, *Discourses of Desire: Gender, genre, and epistolary fictions*. Ithaca, NY: Cornell University Press, 1986.

Kehoe, Monika (ed.) *Historical, Literary, and Erotic Aspects of Lesbianism*. New York: Haworth, 1986.

Kennard, Jean E., *'Ourself behind Ourself*: A theory for lesbian readers'. *Signs*, **9**, 4, 1984. Reprinted in Elizabeth A. Flynn and Patrocinio P. Schweickert, *Gender and Reading*, Baltimore: Johns Hopkins University Press, 1986: 63–82.

King, Katie, 'The pleasure of repetition and the limits of identification in feminist science fiction: Reimaginations of the body after the cyborg', Pomona, CA: Paper given at the American Studies Association, 24 April 1984.

King, Katie, 'The situation of lesbianism as feminism's magical sign: Contests for meaning in the U.S. women's movement, 1968–72'. *Communication*, **9**, 1, 1985: 65–91.

King, Katie, 'Producing sex, theory and culture: Gay/straight remappings in contemporary feminism', in Marianne Hirsch and Evelyn Fox Keller (eds) *Conflicts in Feminism*. London and New York: Routledge, 1990: 82–101.

King, Katie, 'Lesbians in multinational reception: Global gay formations and local homosexualities', paper presented at the conference on *Feminist Theory: An international debate*, Glasgow: University of Glasgow, 12–15 July 1991.

Kitzinger, Celia, *The Social Construction of Lesbianism*. Newbury Park, CA: Sage Press, 1987.

Klaich, Dolores, *Woman Plus Woman: Attitudes toward lesbianism*. Tallahassee, FL: Naiad Press, 1989.

Knopp, Sherron E., '"If I saw you, would you kiss me?": Sapphism and the subversiveness of Virginia Woolf's *Orlando*'. Papers of the Modern Languages Association **103**, 1988: 24–34.

Koedt, Anne, Ellen Levine, and Anita Rapone (eds) *Radical Feminism*. New York: Quadrangle Books, 1973.

Lacan, Jacques, *Écrits: A selection*, transl. Alan Sheridan. New York: Norton, 1977.

Laity, Cassandra, 'H.D.'s romantic landscapes: The sexual politics of the garden'. SAGETRIEB, **6**, 1987: 57–75.

Leeds Revolutionary Feminist Group, 'The case against heterosexuality', in M. Evans (ed.) *The Woman Question*. London: Fontana, 1982.

Leidholdt, Dorchen and Janice G. Raymond, *The Sexual Liberals and the Attack on Feminism*. New York: Pergamon Press, 1990.

Lesbian History Group (eds) *Not a Passing Phase: Reclaiming lesbians in history*. London: The Women's Press, 1989.

Lesselier, Claudie, 'Social categorizations and construction of a lesbian subject'. *Feminist Issues*, Spring 1987: 89–94.

Lewis, Reina and Karen Adler, '"Come to me baby": Or what's wrong with lesbian SM', in Lon Flemming (ed.) *Sex and Violence*. London: forthcoming.

Licata, Salvatore and Robert Petersen (eds) *The Gay Past: A collection of historical essays*. Binghampton, NY: Harrington Park Press, 1985.

Lilly, Mark (ed.) *Lesbian and Gay Writing*. London: Macmillan, 1990.

Linden, Robin Ruth, Darlene R. Pagano, Diana E. H. Russel and Susan Leigh Starr (eds) *Against Sadomasochism: A radical feminist analysis*. Palo Alto, CA: Frog in the Well Press, 1982.

Lootens, Tricia, 'Ann Bannon: A lesbian audience discovers its lost literature'. *Off Our Backs*, **13**, 11, 1983.

Marchessault, Jovette, 'A lesbian chronicle', in *Lesbian Triptych*, transl. Yvonne M. Klein, Toronto: The Women's Press, 1985.

Marcus, Jane, *Virginia Woolf and the Languages of Patriarchy*. Bloomington: Indiana University Press, 1987.

Marcus, Jane, *Art and Anger: Reading like a woman*. Columbus: Ohio State University Press, 1988.

Marks, Elaine, 'Lesbian intertextuality', in G. Stambolian and E. Marks (eds) *Homosexualities and French Literature*.

Martin, Biddy, 'Lesbian identity and autobiographical difference[s]', in Brodzki and Schenck (eds) *Life/Lines*: 77–103.

Martin, Del and Phyllis Lyon, *Lesbian/Woman*. New York: Bantam Books, 1972.

McIntosh, Mary, 'The homosexual role'. *Social Problems*, **16**, 2, 1987: 2–9.

McNaron, Toni A. H., 'When Chloe likes Olivia: Lesbian literary theory', MLA Convention Session, New Orleans, 1988.

McNaron, Toni A. H., 'Mirrors and sameness: Lesbian theory through imagery', MLA Convention Session, New Orleans, 1988.

Meese, Elizabeth A., *Crossing the Double-Cross: The practice of feminist criticism*. Chapel Hill: University of North Carolina Press, 1986.

Meese, Elizabeth A. and Alice Parker (eds) *The Difference Within: Feminism and critical theory*. Amsterdam: Benjamins, 1988.

Merck, Mandy, '*Lianna* and the lesbians of art cinema', in Charlotte Brunsdon (ed.) *Films for Women*. London: BFI Publishing, 1986: 166–75.

Merck, Mandy, 'The train of thought in Freud's "Case of Homosexuality in a Woman"' *m/f*, **11/12**, 1986: 35–48.

Merck, Mandy, 'Difference and its discontents', *Screen*, **28**, 1, 1987: 2–9.

Millett, Kate, *Sexual Politics*. New York: Ballantine Books, 1970.

Moers, Ellen, *Literary Women: The great writers*. Oxford and New York: Oxford University Press, 1985.

Munt, Sally R., 'The inverstigators: Lesbian crime fiction', in Susannah Radstone (ed.) *Sweet Dreams: Sexuality, gender, and popular fiction*. London: Lawrence & Wishart, 1988: 91–120.

Munt, Sally R., 'Is there a feminist in this text? – Ten years of the lesbian novel 1979–1989'. *Women's Studies International Forum*, **15**, 2, 1992.

Myron, Nancy and Charlotte Bunch (eds) *Lesbianism and the Women's Movement*. Baltimore, MD: Diana Press, 1975.

Nestle, Joan, *A Restricted Country: Essays and short stories*. London: Sheba Feminist Press, 1988.

Newton, Esther, 'The mythic mannish lesbian: Radclyffe Hall and the New Woman', in Martin Bauml Duberman, Martha Vicinus and George Chauncey, Jr (eds) *Hidden from History: Reclaiming the Gay and Lesbian Past*. New York: New American Library, 1989, 281–93.

O'Brien, Sharon, '"The thing not named": Willa Cather as a lesbian writer'. *Signs*, **9**, 1984: 588–603.

Palmer, Paulina, *Contemporary Women's Fiction: Narrative practice and feminist theory*. Hemel Hempstead: Harvester Wheatsheaf, 1989.

Palmer, Paulina, 'Contemporary lesbian feminist fiction: Texts for everywoman', in Linda Anderson (ed.) *Plotting Change: Contemporary women's fiction*. Kent: Edward Arnold, 1990: 43–62.

Plummer, Kenneth (ed.) *The Making of the Modern Homosexual*. London: Hutchinson, 1981.

Radford, Jean, 'An inverted romance: *The Well of Loneliness* and sexual ideology', in Jean Radford (ed.) *The Progress of Romance: The politics of popular fiction*. London: Routledge & Kegan Paul, 1986: 97–111.

Raynaud, Claudine, 'A nutmeg nestled inside its covering of mace: Audre Lorde's *Zami*', in Brodzki and Schenck (eds) *Life/Lines*: 221–42.

Rich, Adrienne, *On Lies, Secrets and Silence: Selected prose 1966–1978*. New York: Norton, 1979.

Rich, Adrienne, 'Compulsory heterosexuality and lesbian existence'. *Signs*, **5**, 4, 1980: 631–60.

Rich, Adrienne, *Blood, Bread and Poetry: Selected prose 1979–1985*. New York: Norton, 1986.

Roberts, J. R. (ed.) *Black Lesbians: An annotated bibliography*. Tallahassee, FL: Naiad Press, 1981.

Rosenfeld, Marthe, 'The development of a lesbian sensibility in the work of Jovette Marchessault and Nicole Brossard,' in Paula Gilbert Lewis (ed.) *Traditionalism, Nationalism and Feminism: Women writers of Quebec*. Westport, CT: Greenwood Press, 1985: 227–39.

Rosenman, Ellen Bayuk, 'Sexual identity and *A Room of One's Own*'. *Signs*, **14**, 3, 1989: 634–50.

Ruehl, Sonja, 'Inverts and experts: Radclyffe Hall and the lesbian identity', in R. Brunt and C. Rowan (eds) *Feminism, Culture, and Politics*. London: Lawrence & Wishart, 1982: 15–36.

Rule, Jane, *Lesbian Images*. Freedom, CA: Crossing Press, 1975/London: Peter Davies, 1976.

Russ, Joanna, 'To write "Like a woman": Transformations of identity in the work of Willa Cather'. *Journal of Homosexuality*, **12**, 1986: 77–87. (Reprinted in Monike Kehoe [ed.] *Aspects of Lesbianism*. New York: Hawthorne, 1986.)

SAMOIS (eds) *Coming to Power: Writings and graphics on lesbian s/m*. Palo Alto, CA: Up Press, 1981.

Schneider, Susan R., *French Lesbian Theory*. Palo Alto, CA: Institute of Lesbian Studies, 1985.

Sedgwick, Eve Kosofsky, *Between Men: English literature and male homosocial desire*. New York: Columbia University Press, 1985.

Sedgwick, Eve Kosofsky, 'The beast in the closet: James and the writing of homosexual panic', in Ruth Bernard Yeazell (ed.) *Sex, Politics and Science in the Nineteenth-Century Novel*. English Institute Essays 1983–4. Baltimore, MD: Johns Hopkins University Press, 1986.

Sedgwick, Eve Kosofsky, 'The closet, the canon and Allan Bloom', *Gay Studies Newsletter*, November 1988: 8–10.

Sedgwick, Eve Kosofsky, *Epistemology of the Closet*. Hemel Hempstead: Harvester Wheatsheaf, 1990.

Segrest, Mab, *My Mama's Dead Squirrel: Lesbian essays on Southern culture*. Ithaca, NY: Firebrand, 1985.

Shabram, 'The women loving women', in D. Choong, O. Cole Wilson, B. Evaristo and G. Pearse (eds) *Black Women Talk Poetry*. London: Black Womantalk, 1987.

Shaktini, Namascar, 'Displacing the phallic subject: Wittig's lesbian writing'. *Signs*, **8**, 1982: 29–44.

Shockley, Ann Allen, 'The Black lesbian in American literature: A critical overview'. *Conditions: Five*, 1979: 133–42.

Shockley, Ann Allen, 'Black lesbian biography, "lifting the veil"'. *Other Black Women*, **1**, 1982: 1–13.

Smith, Barbara, 'Toward a Black feminist criticism' in *Conditions: Two*, **1**, 2, 1970: 25–44.

Smith, Barbara, 'The truth that never hurts: Black lesbians in fiction in the 1980s', in Joanne M. Braxton and Andrée Nicola McLaughlin (eds) *Wild Women in the Whirlwind: Afra-American culture and the contemporary literary renaissance*. New Brunswick: Rutgers University Press, 1990: 213–45.

Smith-Rosenberg, Caroll, 'The female world of love and ritual: Relations between women in nineteenth-century America'. *Signs*, **1**, 1, 1975: 1–29.

Snitow, Ann, Christine Stansell and Sharon Thompson (eds) *Powers of Desire: The politics of sexuality*. New York: New Feminist Library/Monthly Review Press, 1983.

Stacey, Jackie, 'The invisible difference: Lesbianism and sexual difference theory', in collection of papers for the *Homosexuality: Which Homosexuality?* Conference, Amsterdam, 1987.

Stacey, Jackie, 'Desperately seeking difference', in Lorraine Gamman and Margaret Marshment (eds) *The Female Gaze*. London: The Women's Press, 1988: 112–29.

Stambolian, George and Elaine Marks (eds) *Homosexualities and French Literature: Cultural contexts/critical texts*. Ithaca, NY: Cornell University Press, 1979.

Stanton, Domna, 'Difference on trial: A critique of the maternal metaphor in

Cixous, Irigaray, and Kristeva', in Nancy K. Miller (ed.) *The Poetics of Gender*. New York: Columbia University Press, 1986: 157–82.

Stein, Gertrude, *How to Write*. West Glover: Something Else, 1973.

Steven, Peter, 'Gay and lesbian cinema', in Peter Steven (ed.) *Jump Cut: Hollywood, politics and counter cinema*. New York: Praeger, 1985: 278–323.

Stimpson, Catharine R. 'The mind, the body, and Gertrude Stein'. *Critical Inquiry*, **3**, 1977: 499.

Stimpson, Catharine R. 'Zero degree deviancy: The lesbian novel in English', in Elizabeth Abel (ed.) *Writing and Sexual Difference*. Chicago: University of Chicago Press, 1982: 243–59.

Stimpson, Catharine R. 'Adrienne Rich and feminist-lesbian poetry', in Stimpson, *Where the Meanings Are: Feminism and cultural spaces*. London and New York: Routledge, 1988: 140–54.

Trebilcot, Joyce, 'Dyke methods of principles for the discovery/creation of the withstanding'. *Hypatia*, **3**, 2, 1988: 1–13.

Tribilcot, Joyce, *In Process: Lesbian radical essays*. Albany, NY: SUNY Press, 1989.

Vance, Carole S. (ed.) *Pleasure and Danger: Exploring female sexuality*. Boston, MA: Routledge, 1984.

Walker, Nancy, '"Wider than the sky": Public presence and the private self in Dickinson, James, and Woolf', in Shari Benstock (ed.) *The Private Self: Theory and practice of women's autobiographical writings*. University of North Carolina Press, 1988: 272–303.

Walters, Suzanna Danuta, 'As her hand crept slowly up her thigh: Ann Bannon and the politics of pulp'. *Social Text*, **23**, 1989.

Weeks, Jeffrey, *Coming Out: Homosexual politics in Britain from the nineteenth century to the present*. London: Quartet, 1977.

Weeks, Jeffrey, *Sexuality and its Discontents: Meanings, myths, and modern sexualities*. London: Routledge & Kegan Paul, 1985.

Weisen-Cook, Blanche, '"Women alone stir my imagination": Lesbianism and the cultural tradition'. *Signs*, **4**, 4, 1979: 718–39.

Whitlock, Gillian, '"A martyr reluctantly canonised": The lesbian literary tradition'. *Hecate*, **10**, 2, 1984: 19–39.

Whitlock, Gillian, '"Everything is out of place": Radclyffe Hall and the lesbian literary tradition'. *Feminist Studies*, **13**, 3, 1987: 555–82.

Wittig, Monique, *The Lesbian Body*, transl. David Le Vay. New York: Avon Books, 1975.

Wittig, Monique, 'The straight mind'. *Feminist Issues*, **1**, 1, 1980: 102–10.

Wittig, Monique, 'One is not born a woman'. *Feminist Issues*, **1**, 2, 1981: 47–54.

Wittig, Monique, 'The category of sex'. *Feminist Issues*, **2**, 2, 1982: 63–8.

Wittig, Monique, 'The point of view: Universal or particular?', *Feminist Issues*, **3**, 1, 1983: 63–9.

Wittig, Monique, The mark of gender'. *Feminist Issues*, **5**, 2, 1985: 3–12.

Wittig, Monique and Sande Zeig, *Lesbian Peoples: Material for a dictionary*. New York: Avon Books, 1979.

Woolf, Virginia, *A Room of One's Own*. New York: Harcourt, 1957.

Zimmerman, Bonnie, 'What has never been: An overview of lesbian feminist criticism'. *Feminist Studies*, **7**, 3, Maryland, USA, 1981. (Reprinted in Elaine Showalter [ed.] *The New Feminist Criticism*. London: Virago, 1986: 200–224.)

Zimmerman, Bonnie, 'Daughters of darkness: Lesbian vampires'. *Jump Cut*, **24–25**, 1981: 23–4.

Zimmerman, Bonnie, 'Exiting from patriarchy: The lesbian novel of development', in Elizabeth Abel (ed.) *The Voyage In: Fictions of female development*. Hanover: University Press of New England, 1983: 244–57.

Zimmerman, Bonnie, 'The politics of transliteration: Lesbian first-person narratives'. *Signs: Journal of Women in Culture and Society*, **9**, 4, 1984: 663–82.

Zimmerman, Bonnie, *The Safe Sea of Women: Lesbian fiction 1969–1989*. Boston, MA: Beacon Press/London: Onlywomen Press, 1991.

Notes on Contributors

Sonya Andermahr is a postgraduate student at Warwick University, doing research on contemporary lesbian fiction. She teaches English and Gender Studies, and is interested in all aspects of feminist theory.

Lisa Henderson is Assistant Professor of Communications at the Pennsylvania State University. She is also a lesbian activist, and writes about sexual politics, cultural theory, and the production and consumption of popular media.

Hilary Hinds teaches Literature and Cultural Studies at Fircroft College of Adult Education in Birmingham. She is co-editor, with Elspeth Graham, Elaine Hobby and Helen Wilcox, of *Her Own Life: Autobiographical writings by seventeenth-century Englishwomen* (London: Routledge, 1989), and is currently compiling another anthology of seventeenth-century women's writing with Elaine Hobby. This is her first public engagement with contemporary texts.

Katie King is Assistant Professor of Women's Studies at the University of Maryland, College Park. Her previous articles have been on gay studies, feminist theory and the apparatus of literary production. She is currently writing on what counts as feminist theory, and proselytising a field she calls 'Feminism and Writing Technologies', which examines the politics of distinctions between the 'oral' and the 'written'.

Reina Lewis is Part-time Lecturer in Cultural Studies and Art History at West Surrey College of Art and Design. She is completing a PhD on nineteenth-century women writers' and artists' relationship to colonialism, and in her spare time (!) writes on issues of contemporary lesbian culture. She lives in Brighton and contributes to local lesbian culture by compering women's cabarets.

Sally Munt is Lecturer in Cultural Studies and Feminism at Brighton Polytechnic. Before this she taught in Adult Education for the Workers' Educational Association and the University of Sussex. She is presently completing her PhD and a book on crime fiction and feminism for Routledge. She discovered first feminism and then lesbianism by reading novels. On the home front she is coming to terms with being thirty-something by watching a lot of television.

Gillian Spraggs was born in 1952 and brought up in Middlesex by Christian fundamentalist parents. In 1971 she escaped to the University of Cambridge, where she took a degree in English, and in 1980 was awarded a PhD for work on Elizabethan and early Stuart literature. A former teacher, she has been active in the campaign to raise awareness of lesbian and gay issues within the National Union of Teachers. Her essay 'Exiled to home: The poetry of Sylvia Townsend Warner and Valentine Ackland' appeared in *Lesbian and Gay Writing*, edited by Mark Lilly (London: Macmillan, 1990), and 'Divine visitations: Sappho's poetry of love' is published in *What Lesbians Do In Books*, edited by Elaine Hobby and Chris White (London: The Women's Press, 1991).

Angela Weir and **Elizabeth Wilson** first met in Gay Liberation. Angela Weir works in the legal department of the London Borough of Camden. She has for many years been active in the women's movement, was a member of the Rights of Women group, and co-authored *The Cohabitation Handbook* (London: Pluto Press, 1987). She has written articles on women and social policy, and co-authored 'The British Women's Movement' with Elizabeth Wilson for the *New Left Review*. Recently she was involved in the Campaign for Access to Donor Insemination. She and Elizabeth Wilson are bringing up her daughter.

Elizabeth Wilson is the author of a number of books, including *Adorned in Dreams: Fashion and modernity* (London: Virago, 1985), *Hallucinations* (London: Radius, 1988) and *The Sphinx in the City*, with Juliet Ash (London: Virago, 1991). She has edited a collection of articles on fashion, *Chic Thrills* (London: Unwin Hyman, 1992). She is Professor of Policy Studies at the Polytechnic of North London.

Anna Wilson is the author of three novels: *Cactus*, *Altogether Elsewhere* and *Hatching Stones*, and co-editor, with Lilian Mohin, of *Past Participants*, a lesbian history diary. She was in the past active in the London women's liberation movement but has since been consumed by academia. She is currently completing a dissertation at Boston University on feminist fiction as a means to social change.

Bonnie Zimmerman is Professor of Women's Studies at San Diego State University. She is the author, most recently, of *The Safe Sea of Women: Lesbian fiction 1969–1989* (Boston, MA: Beacon Press, 1990; London: Onlywomen Press, 1991).